The Divorce Sourcebook

Other books by Dawn Bradley Berry:

Equal Compensation for Women (Lowell House, 1994)
The Domestic Violence Sourcebook (Lowell House, 1995)
50 Most Influential Women in American Law (Lowell House, 1997)
Divorce Recovery (Lowell House, 1998)

THE DIVORCE SOURCEBOOK

Everything You Need To Know
2nd Edition

by
Dawn Bradley Berry

LOWELL HOUSE

LOS ANGELES

NTC/Contemporary Publishing Group

Library of Congress Cataloging–in–Publication Data

Berry, Dawn Bradley.
    The divorce sourcebook / by Dawn Bradley Berry.
        p.   cm.
    Includes bibliographical references and index.
    0–7373–0023–X (paperback)
        1. Divorce—Law and legislation—United States—Popular works.
    I. Title.
    KF535.Z9B379   1995
    346.7301'66—dc20
    [347.306166]   95–34272
                                                                        CIP

Requests for such permissions should be addressed to:
Lowell House
2020 Avenue of the Stars, Suite 300
Los Angeles, CA 90067

Published by Lowell House, a division of NTC/Contemporary Publishing Group, Inc.
4255 West Touhy Avenue, Lincolnwood, Illinois 60646–1975 U.S.A.

Text design: Michele Lanci–Altomare

Printed and bound in the United States of America
International Standard Book Number: 0–7373–0023–X
    3456   DOC DOC   6543

ACKNOWLEDGMENTS

Special thanks to those who helped to turn the idea for this book into a reality: Roberta Beyer, Clarette Bradley, Judith Finfrock, David B. Riggert, Kathleen Robertson, Nicky Whelan, Anne Kass, Cynde Goyen, Steve Feher, Patricia Murphy, Kathryn Lang, Sharon Newell, Lynn Peters, Clayta Spear, John Kirby, and Laura Kirby; my unfailingly good-natured and supportive editors, Bud Sperry and Maria Magallanes, and the rest of the Lowell House crew; and especially to my able and warp-speed assistant, Jacque Moise (and to Lee Ann Fisher, who helped when even Jacque couldn't keep up with the paper blizzard!). Thanks also to my husband, Willy Berry, Cloyd Hinkle and the office staff, and other friends, family, and colleagues for their steadfast support.

The stories in this book are true; however, the names of several contributors have been changed at their request. My thanks to them for their willingness to share their experiences and insights.

TABLE OF CONTENTS

Introduction

In her memoir, *Fear of Fifty*, Erica Jong writes, "Divorce is my generation's coming of age ceremony—a ritual scarring that makes anything that happens afterward seem bearable." Most of those who have been through this "ceremony"—even one in which the participants tried to make the ordeal as civilized and painless as possible—would likely agree.

According to the most recent statistics, 50 percent of all American marriages will end in divorce. What the statistics don't reflect, however, is the human suffering behind each and every divorce, no matter how amicable. In the words of one man, "It takes too long and costs too much." A friend of mine, having endured a miserable divorce from her first husband, warned her second husband that *their* marriage had *better* work, because she would rather face a murder trial than another divorce!

Divorce poses many legal, financial, and emotional challenges. On the positive side, people divorcing today have more choices and sources of support than ever before. As the divorce rate has increased, social stigmas condemning the divorced have all but disappeared. Innumerable books, support groups, legal aid clinics, classes, counselors, church programs, and products are at hand to ease the pain, expense, and aftermath of this difficult transition. Other services and goods are becoming increasingly available to those seeking to build new lives after divorce, whether as singles, solo parents, or stepfamilies. The law, too, continues to evolve toward making divorce easier, more economical, and less adversarial.

Yet despite all the developments, things can still go terribly wrong in a divorce. Children are taken away from loving mothers who have made their share of sacrifices and worked hard to support them, and are turned over to unemployed, deadbeat fathers simply because these fathers are at home. Good fathers who have been devoted, attentive parents are denied not only custody of their children but visitation rights as well when a vindictive mother makes false accusations of abuse. Couples who can't agree to a division of property appear before an impatient judge who orders everything—even the family home—sold at a loss and the money divided. Wives who have been battered in body and spirit are bullied by their abusive husbands into signing away everything. Parents blinded by hate lose sight of their children's terror and agony as they go to war over custody.

Fortunately, such events in divorce are becoming more rare. Because they still do occur, however, it is essential for anyone dissolving a marriage to know his or her rights and responsibilities, as well as what to expect and how to plan for problems that may arise.

Everyone feels crazy and out of control during a divorce. Knowing that this is normal can help make the ordeal more bearable—but doesn't make it go away. Children and adults both may feel frightened, bewildered, and angry and may often behave in ways that don't seem to make sense. The small details alone can be overwhelming, let alone the daunting task of restructuring new homes, habits, and relationships with children, friends, and relatives. Divorce has been described again and again as an emotional roller coaster. And most people say the upheaval lasts at least two years.

Yet people can now gain greater control of the legal process, as well as protect themselves and their children from much of the emotional upheaval. Divorce is a much different experience today than it was twenty years ago. No-fault divorce laws have helped simplify the procedure but have also had an adverse economic impact, especially on women. Changes in the law surrounding child custody and support have been a similarly mixed blessing for many families. Child custody choices are always heartrending and delicate. If hostility between the parents is added to the equation, the stakes rise sharply. Parents torn between the desire to spare their children the trauma of a court battle and the need to guard their children's welfare find themselves in a truly excruciating dilemma. The process of dismantling one family and building a new one has never been easy. People today have more choices but must also make more difficult decisions.

Property issues are more complex than ever before. In many cases, identifying what property is can be a vexing task in itself. Pensions, future earning capabilities, and business goodwill all require careful, expert handling. Add the complications of age, infirmity, abuse, or a spouse who is dishonest, and the difficulties may seem insurmountable. Yet, as millions know, they are not.

The Divorce Sourcebook is full of dos and don'ts, things the experts preach you must always do or warn you must never do. I've included only the advice I believe to be good, sound, and sensible. I've also endeavored to provide not only the what but the how, gleaned from professionals in various fields. At the back of this book you'll find an extensive list of sources of help, from books to therapy groups, from hotlines to public agencies.

But it's equally important to remember that we are all fallible human beings. None of us behaves ideally or does everything right, even when life is running at its smoothest. In the midst of a divorce, you can't expect yourself to do everything perfectly. Divorce brings out the worst in people. You will make mistakes, do things you're not proud of, and act in ways you ordinarily would not. Don't beat yourself up over your goofs. Take note of what you learn and move on. Skipping a day of work to wallow in bed, get sloppy drunk, and sob all afternoon doesn't mean you're irresponsible or ready for rehab. One tactical error in financial planning is unlikely to doom you to a life of destitution. One nasty exchange with your spouse in front of the kids won't scar them for life. Do the best you can and then let it be.

Millions of people have survived the tempest of divorce at least once. Some of their stories are told in the pages that follow. Most have gone on to build better lives, knowing in retrospect that they are stronger and wiser for having lived through it. So will you.

Divorce is not failure. It is a transition that happens to a large number of people at least once in their lives. It is about endings, but it is also about beginnings. Today, people have an ever increasing set of options to help them cope with the difficulties inherent in any divorce. This book provides an outline of these options and a road map of sorts to help those facing a divorce navigate their way through the process as smoothly as possible.

THE DEVELOPMENT OF FAMILY LAW AND SOCIAL ATTITUDES

A Brief History and a Look at Where We Are Today

In many ways, divorce is a complex, confusing, and difficult process. As a result, many people harbor misconceptions about what to expect when facing a divorce. A large part of this confusion can be attributed to the history of family law. Today's divorce experience has been shaped by legal, religious, psychological, and social forces. Theories and procedures have changed dramatically over the past hundred years and continue to evolve more rapidly than ever before. Understanding how we got to this point can provide a perspective on both the negative aspects of divorcing today—the expense, the uncertainty, the complexity—and the positive aspects—more choices, fair laws, and alternatives like mediation.

DIVORCE BEFORE 1900

The first divorce in recorded American history occurred in a Massachusetts Puritan court in 1639. Surprisingly, the divorce decree was awarded to a woman who had learned that her husband was a bigamist and already had a wife. The husband was fined, imprisoned, and finally banished to England. Four years later, a woman was again granted the next recorded divorce, because her husband had deserted her and was living with another woman. These circumstances fit the strict requirements at that time, when adultery was the only grounds for divorce. A man could divorce on grounds of adultery alone. A woman divorced for committing adultery could be banished, put to death, or at the very least be publicly shamed. Adultery alone was not enough for a woman to divorce a man, however; additional grounds such as bigamy or desertion also had to be proven. Partial divorces were established for cruelty or desertion. These partial divorces often caused great hardship on women, who remained economically tied to absent husbands. A husband who deserted his family could show up later and claim control of all the wife's earnings, even the money she had made after he abandoned her.

From the late 1700s until the mid–1800s, in many states, a divorce could be obtained only by petitioning the state legislature to pass a private legislative act ending the marriage. Not surprisingly, this process was often lengthy and difficult. It was far more available to men, with the most common grounds for divorce being an "immoral wife."

Yet by the late 1700s, divorce was common enough that scholars were criticizing the "high divorce rates." At that time, a study in Connecticut revealed that one in every hundred marriages ended in divorce. Andrew Jackson married a divorced woman, which created great scandal when he ran for president but didn't prevent his election in 1828.

Legal changes began in the early nineteenth century. Social reformers such as Elizabeth Cady Stanton, an early advocate of equality for women, had begun to speak out in favor of more liberal and egalitarian divorce laws. By the 1830s, women who were deserted by their husbands could get a divorce or at least regain the right to control their property and establish limited economic independence. During the 1840s, the process was simplified, and more women began petitioning for divorce. Historical reports indicate that then, as now, the most acrimonious battles were over child custody.

By the mid-nineteenth century, the courts had been given the authority to order divorces, including the power to award alimony to women whose husbands engaged in adultery or cruelty. However, many women did not seek a divorce until after a husband had deserted, so alimony was often impossible to collect. Divorce carried a heavy stigma at this time, too. Women were viewed as the guardians of decency and morality in the family and were often castigated for having "failed in the moral education" of a spouse who engaged in adultery or deserted the family.

During the mid-1800s, progress in divorce laws tended to be restricted to the northern states, whereas the southern states remained loyal to the stricter English tradition. An especially ugly bit of hypocrisy also retarded the evolution of fair divorce laws in the south. Many men resisted making adultery an equally applied ground for divorce because of the long acceptance of liaisons between white men and female slaves. Yet husbands often used a wife's interracial encounter as grounds for immediate divorce, accompanied by harsh legal and public condemnation and precluding an award of alimony.

Early divorce laws were more liberal in other countries, particularly those in Scandinavia. In the 1830s, Swedish couples could divorce on grounds of incompatibility, ill treatment, drunkenness, or hatred and bitterness between spouses. Two years of separation was grounds for divorce at the end of the eighteenth century in Denmark. A husband or wife, under old Irish law, could end a marriage simply by walking away from it on the first of February. "Deadly and notorious hostility" was sufficient to gain a divorce in Prussia in the 1750s, while in enlightened France, couples could get a no-fault divorce by mutual consent as early as the 1790s, although they did have to show that they had gone through an extended process of attempted reconciliation involving both families. When the French monarchy was restored in

1816, however, divorce was completely abolished. Divorce was unavailable or difficult to obtain in countries with Catholicism as the major religion, but most allowed divorce in some cases by the turn of the twentieth century, with the exception of Spain, Italy, and Ireland. Today, Ireland remains the only country in the Western world that still prohibits divorce.

When and how easily divorce should be granted has always been a subject of considerable debate in the United States. In the 1820s, Robert Owen, a journalist, congressman, and social reformer, campaigned publicly for laws providing easier release for those trapped in an unhappy marriage. Indiana was one of the first states to enact liberal divorce statutes. Anyone meeting the residency requirement could obtain a divorce even if the other spouse had disappeared and could not be located. This sparked controversy between those who believed that easier divorce laws encouraged immorality and those who felt that harsh restrictions were more likely to cause hypocrisy, adultery, and domestic violence. Vestiges of this debate still continue in modern society.

The Married Women's Property Acts of the mid-nineteenth century, first enacted in New York and Pennsylvania in 1848, protected the property rights of women who entered a marriage owning property of their own. However, they did not change the common-law rules that gave the husband full rights to all property acquired during the marriage, including the earnings of the wife. Perhaps the most important aspect of these acts was to recognize at least some rights of married women. At about the same time, organized groups began to work for greater rights and protection for working women, and for the right to vote. Such efforts were often made with the support and assistance of those working for the abolition of slavery. Writer, speaker, civil rights leader, and former slave Frederick Douglass was one of the early advocates of equal rights for women.

The first self-help book on divorce, entitled *How to Get a Divorce*, was published in New York in 1859. Yet the laws lagged behind changing social views. The slow development of divorce law in America can in large part be explained by the persistent moral, legal, and religious tradition mandating that marriage be a permanent bond.

After the Civil War, the divorce rate increased dramatically. Demographic changes occurred during the next twenty years that also impacted on divorce. The number of people who never married reached an all-time high in 1877. Everyday life began to take on more of the characteristics we now consider traditional, such as fewer children and closer emotional ties between parents and children. Women became less involved in farming or other family business and occupied the position of homemaker and keeper of peace and morality in the family. The law slowly began to change in response to the dominant social trends. For example, awards of alimony to homemakers rewarded a woman's devotion to her family and placed the burden of support on the husband.

State laws governing divorce fluctuated during the latter half of the nineteenth century, with some becoming more liberal and others becoming more restrictive or abolishing divorce altogether. Statistics from this period indicate that harsh divorce laws did little to preserve families. People simply went their separate ways and worked things out the best they could without the involvement of the legal system. Some of the family laws passed during this time were blatantly sexist or patently outrageous. For example, South Carolina laws set forth how much wealth a married man could bequeath in his will to his mistress at the expense of his wife. Not surprisingly, there was no comparable law for women.

The movement west during the late nineteenth century also affected divorce throughout America. Western states tended to have less restrictive grounds for divorce, shorter residency requirements, and laws that made the process easier. Some states, including Utah, North Dakota, South Dakota, and Indiana, viewed more liberal divorce laws as a business opportunity. Entire towns sprang up, often in areas where railroads or other forms of public transportation converged, just to cater to people seeking a "migratory divorce." Lawyers, judges, hoteliers, and restauranteurs all profited from the so-called divorce trade. Of course, there was public outcry over the alleged immorality of such enterprises, but the nation was also forced to recognize that divorce had become a facet of modern society and was not going to go away.

National statistics on divorce were compiled by Congress for the first time in 1887. At about the same time, the social stigma surrounding divorce began to lift somewhat. Many social scientists shifted the blame for divorce from the individuals to society and proceeded to work toward social reform. Educational programs on how to create a sound family life began to emerge, and books on how to have a good marriage grew in popularity.

The philosophy and purpose of divorce laws also changed around this time. Although the marital partnership was not considered a union of equals, it was assumed that marriage was a joint economic enterprise. Each person was considered responsible for contributing to the prosperity of the home and was fairly entitled to share in the fruits of their labor. In community property states, each spouse became entitled to one half of all the income and property the couple acquired during the marriage, based on the rationale that both spouses contributed equally to the economic assets of the home, whether by earning income or by maintaining the home and raising children.

DIVORCE IN THE TWENTIETH CENTURY

By 1900, most states had some system of divorce law in place, and while some significant variations remained, most shared similar elements. Virtually all were fault-based, according to the rationale that a lifelong union should not be dissolved unless one spouse committed a serious wrong against the other. This caused obvious problems for people who simply did not get along, especially in states such as New York, where for many years the only grounds for divorce was adultery. Individuals and their attorneys often went to ridiculous lengths to manufacture the evidence necessary to satisfy the legal requirements. Even in states that allowed divorce on grounds of mental cruelty, which eventually became the most commonly used ground, many courts required witnesses and evidence. People possessing dramatic abilities but few scruples actually made their livings as "professional witnesses." Proof-of-fault requirements often led to a tremendous waste of time, open perjury, and unnecessary hostility, especially since property awards were often based on fault. The cases were rampant with gender bias, too. Wives were frequently charged with "cruelty" for such things as inadequate housekeeping.

Changing Social Attitudes

Society has changed more during the twentieth century than it has in the past five hundred years. These rapid and extreme changes have had a direct impact on the nature of family life. Industry brought people off the farm and into the city. Job opportunities for women increased, and women enjoyed greater career independence as well as more diversions in their leisure time. The balance of knowledge and social awareness expanded with the advent of radio, movies, and television. Mechanization freed both men and women from time spent on household chores. Dance halls and nightclubs, previously open only to men, began welcoming women and couples. The expectations of the average person rose considerably. People began to see happiness and excitement in a marriage as a necessity rather than a luxury. As early as 1910, alarmists railed against the feminist movement as a leading cause of the breakdown of the family, and the debate raged on over whether divorce should be viewed as a religious sacrament or a legal contract.

Marriage counseling became available by the turn of the century, and "visiting marriage," similar to today's commuter marriage, was accepted as an alternative for some couples. Advances in psychology, such as the embrace of Freud's theory that unhappy marriage and divorce was a result of childhood events, began to turn the focus toward children from divorced homes.

Beginning in the 1920s, prevailing attitudes toward marriage and the family underwent drastic change. Couples began to experiment with new forms of marriage. "Trial marriages," the precursor of today's cohabitation sprung up. There is some evidence that cohabitation remained fairly common throughout the century, even in more conservative times. "We did the same things then that you do now," one woman, now in her seventies, told me. "We were just more discreet."

Popular acceptance of the idea that women could—and should—enjoy sex just as much as men sparked a sexual revolution in the 1920s. An increase in the number of pregnant brides followed, as did an increase in the divorce rate. This era also saw a rise in "collusion" between spouses who mutually agreed to dissolve their marriage yet were still required to prove a fault-based ground for divorce in court. By the 1930s, "mental cruelty" was a legal ground for divorce in many states and served as a catchall forerunner to today's no-fault statutes. Controversy over the issue of migratory divorce continued until 1942, when the U.S. Supreme Court ruled that Nevada's six-week residency requirement to obtain a divorce was valid.

By the mid-twentieth century, divorce was no longer an unusual event and a cause for whispering and gossip, yet a double standard remained. Although men who left their wives were often scorned as irresponsible gadabouts, women almost invariably received harsher condemnation after a divorce. When my mother divorced her first husband after World War II, she says she was labeled a "man hater." (She jokes that this had its advantages, though, because she had plenty of dates with men who thought they were "safe" with her.) By this time, however, divorce was becoming commonplace enough that it was viewed as a reasonable choice. My aunt told me that in 1935 she approached her marriage with some trepidation but realized that divorce was at least a realistic option if the marriage didn't work out. She said the judge who performed the marriage commented that none of the couples he had ever married had been divorced. This statement was not as astounding then as it would be today, but it does show that the subject could be discussed freely in the 1930s.

The Divorce Revolution

Author Lenore Weitzman, Ph.D., describes the changes that took place during the late twentieth century as a "divorce revolution." In her book of the same name, she explains the revolution's three components:

1. the soaring divorce rate;
2. the widespread adoption of no-fault divorce laws;
3. the changing social attitude toward divorce.

The divorce rate in the United States increased gradually but slowly between 1860 and the early 1960s, except for a brief period of substantial increase immediately after World War II. Between 1966 and 1976, the divorce rate doubled, and each year between 1975 and 1981 the rate soared rapidly. There were approximately 1.2 million divorces in 1981, with a minuscule drop by 1985. Statistics gathered since this time have shown that despite the trauma of divorce, the majority of divorced people do marry again. Approximately 50 percent of marriages in the United States in 1993 were remarriages involving couples in which one or both were previously divorced.

By 1973, more than 60 percent of divorcing couples had children. Not surprisingly, this led to changes in the law. "The best interest of the child" became the court's predominant concern when parents divorced. Controversy arose and continues to rage over such ideas as the "tender years" doctrine that advocates a preference that a child stay with the mother until at least the age of seven or eight. Debate also persists over how closely visitation and custody should be tied to child support, the rights of fathers to be equally involved in the upbringing of their children, and discrimination against working mothers in custody decisions.

Separate courts to deal with family issues became popular during the 1950s and are the norm today. Whether this separation has a positive effect is not clear. On the one hand, family courts may be more aware of related family services such as counseling and mediation, employ judges who specialize in family law, and provide a more centralized, specific forum for the resolution of family–based disputes. On the other hand, family courts in some areas suffer from such problems as inadequate funding, inefficient communication with other components of the local court system (such as when criminal charges are involved in an abusive marriage), duplication of efforts, and a lack of prestige, resulting in judges who are poorly paid and not as well qualified as those in other courts.

Married women were still considered subordinate in many ways by legal concepts that remained in place until the 1970s. Such laws included those permitting women to marry at a younger age without parental consent, requirements that the wife assume her husband's surname, power of the husband to determine the family domicile, the absolute right of the husband to his wife's sexual services without recognition of marital rape, and laws providing that only men may sue for loss of consortium (loss of love and sexual services) if a spouse was injured or killed.

Many other biases were subtle, and although the laws have changed, some still remain in practice today. The exercise of basic rights, such as registration to vote, obtaining a driver's license, and buying insurance, can still be more difficult for women who do not take their husband's name or share the same domicile. In 1994, a friend of mine who had kept her maiden name through eleven years of marriage was told by her husband's insurance company that it would not issue her an insurance card under his policy in her own name. She was forced to use his last name—which she had never legally taken!

As late as the 1960s and 1970s, despite the increasing divorce rate and resulting legal developments, subtle social messages hinted that single adults, especially the divorced, were somehow not a normal part of society. In the book *Divorcing*, psychologist Mel Krantzler writes of the difficulty of even buying single-serving portions of packaged food after his own divorce in 1970. At that time, there were also no support groups or social events to provide the acceptance and help available to divorced people now. Television and movies universally portrayed the content nuclear family that never grappled with divorce.

Fortunately, the 1970s and 1980s were times of tremendous change in this regard. In 1980, Ronald Reagan, a divorced man, was elected President of the United States. Divorce had become a part of so many lives that we no longer considered it abnormal. As the 1980s progressed, divorce became increasingly viewed as a common life transition, not an aberration or personal failure.

For the generation that came of age in the sixties and seventies—the baby boomers—two factors seem to play a major part in the frequency with which we divorce. First, we take our happiness seriously. We were perhaps the first generation to believe that we were entitled to fulfillment and satisfaction in our lives and were responsible for creating it. Happiness was more than a goal—it became a duty. We felt an obligation to work toward ending the misery in the world and in our own lives.

Second, the roles and options open to us were changing rapidly. Women learned that they could and should pursue careers outside the home. Men learned that they could and should be gentle, nurturing, involved fathers. Yet most of us grew up with traditional role models among our parents and other adults. We were uncertain how to make these new roles work, yet we were determined to try. We didn't know how to blend and balance what we expected of ourselves; we were torn and confused about what we wanted. Author Erica Jong has called it the "whiplash generation." Many tried to "have it all" and ended up with exhausting, fragmented lives. We tried so hard to be successful professionals *and* committed parents *and* responsible citizens *and* loving spouses that instead of fulfillment we wound up with lives in many parts that formed no coherent whole. Stress was no longer an affliction—it had become a way of life. No wonder marriages crumbled under the pressure.

Yet while the attitudes, legal process, and causes of divorce have changed a great deal over the centuries, the emotional issues have remained largely the same: problems of property division; how debts will be paid; child and spousal support; child custody and visitation; and the inevitable pain, upheaval, blaming, and sense of failure. The good news is that the social stigmas that made divorce more difficult have disappeared or at least lessened, and that far more sources of assistance and support are available for those facing divorce today.

Also, after centuries of going back and forth between more accessible and more restrictive divorce laws, the focus today is finally changing as the reality of frequent divorce has become an undeniable part of our society. Legal services are now geared toward how to better serve divorced families and improve the lives of all those who have been touched by divorce, including single individuals, blended families, grandparents, and the children of divorced parents.

NO-FAULT DIVORCE

One of the most important changes over the past twenty-five years has been the movement toward no-fault divorce.

The advent of no-fault divorce reflected a major change in both the law and social attitudes. When California adopted its no-fault divorce law in 1970, it was the first time in the modern history of the Western world that a requirement of fault as the basis for a divorce was abolished completely. Under the new law, one party could obtain a divorce by asserting that irreconcilable differences had caused the irremediable breakdown of the marriage. Other states, as well as other countries, were quick to jump on the no-fault bandwagon.

Everyone was anxious to eliminate the hostility, sham testimony, and abuses common under the fault-based system.

Undeniably, the no-fault system has eliminated many of the evils of fault-based divorce. Under the old system, alimony was often used as a threat or weapon by one or both parties. Support was generally awarded only to the "innocent" spouse, so a woman found "guilty" of adultery by the court was typically barred from receiving any alimony. A husband divorced for adultery or cruelty was frequently ordered to pay greater alimony than one divorced on other grounds. Property awards also followed this trend, and in some states judges were required to award more than half the property to the "innocent" spouse. Thus, vicious battles and exaggerated claims were not uncommon. Unfair settlements were sometimes leveraged under the threat of personal humiliation, professional damage, or the financial risk of bringing a case to court.

The new laws brought radical changes in several areas of the divorce process. One spouse could unilaterally divorce the other without his or her agreement. Financial awards were based on needs and resources rather than on good or bad behavior. Alimony and property awards sought to treat men and women equally, and a forum was established in which amicable divorces could be legally encouraged. The goal behind the change was to make the laws more modern, civilized, and realistic.

It is important to note that some things have not changed. The new laws did not entirely eliminate the concept of fault from divorce cases. Fault may be considered in awarding alimony, according to the law in some states. Also, behavior that directly damages the other spouse may still be punished. A spouse who has committed "waste" (harm to the couple's financial property, such as that done by gambling or buying elaborate gifts for a paramour), may be ordered to reimburse the estate. Likewise, virtually all states now allow one spouse to sue the other for torts (wrongful acts that cause injury), in the same way that strangers may sue one another. Domestic tort claims are often brought in cases in which one spouse has deliberately hurt the other by violence. Fault-based behavior also remains relevant in child custody cases where abuse or parental fitness is an issue.

Human nature will always be a part of divorce. Accusations and charges of wrongdoing can never be completely eliminated from the divorce proceedings. Hostility will always creep into an acrimonious divorce, no matter how hard the lawyers or judges may try to keep a hurt or angry client from using the court as a place to vent feelings or seek vengeance.

However, areas in which fault is very much an issue, as in cases of spousal or child abuse, are sometimes either glossed over in an attempt to remove all aspects of fault from the process, or occasionally exaggerated and misused, as when one partner falsely accuses the other of inappropriate behavior to try to gain leverage in unrelated matters, such as property division.

In addition to eliminating punishments, rewards, too, have been abolished under the no-fault system. People who faithfully invested in the partnership by being an ambitious breadwinner or devoted homemaker in spite of mistreatment by their spouse received no economic reward for their sacrifice.

Alimony awards were substantially restructured under the no-fault laws. The changes reflected the modern belief that women were or could become independent and self-sufficient after a divorce. In theory, exceptions were made for women with custody of young children, women in need of transitional or rehabilitative support for a period of education or job training, and older homemakers who could not be fairly expected to begin a new life or become completely self-supporting. Yet the general presumption against alimony has reduced the overall size, duration, and frequency of awards, sometimes with unfair results. For example, a woman is sometimes awarded an unrealistically short period of alimony, such as one year, in which she is expected to reconstruct her life, learn new work skills, and become self supporting after being out of the work force for ten or twenty years. Whereas most states leave the amount and timing of alimony awards up to the judge, a few states have a fixed time limit of one to three years. In Texas, alimony has been completely abolished.

Thus, despite the noble goals and truly positive reforms, the new no-fault laws were soon found to have the potential to create a variety of unfair consequences. In some cases, they merely removed the hostility to an even more inappropriate arena, that of child custody. Disputes over custody and support have become the new emotional dumping ground, one in which children are the real victims.

The Backlash Against No-Fault Divorce

Since the mid-1990s, there has been a growing nationwide movement to repeal or reform no-fault divorce laws, and various legislative attempts to return consideration of fault to the divorce process. By 1985, all fifty states had some form of no-fault divorce in place. But on Valentine's day, 1996, Michigan State Representative Jessie F. Dalman, led what has been termed "the divorce counter-revolution" when she introduced legislation designed to establish a two-tier divorce system. Under the proposed Michigan law, a childless couple could obtain a no-fault divorce upon mutual consent; but for those with minor children, or in which one spouse opposed the divorce, the filing spouse would have to prove marital fault of the other—proving violation of one of what Hofstra Law Professor J. Herbie DiFonzo calls "the unholy trinity": adultery, desertion, or extreme cruelty. By 1997, at least nine other states had introduced similar bills, and many states have now modified their laws to make divorce more difficult.

But many ask whether such laws actually achieve their laudable goal of strengthening marital commitment and family ties, or merely add to the expense and trauma of divorce for couples who have made up their mind to split. There is also growing concern about whether the laws may effectively trap women and children in violent homes. And what about the problems that led to the proliferation of no-fault laws in the first place—the deception, the collusion, the perjury; the invention of damaging and humiliating stories of grievous wrongdoing by one spouse, when in reality the couple simply did not get along and desired to end the marriage? During the 1960s, 90 percent of divorces on fault grounds were granted without contest, after brief, perfunctory hearings in which one party appeared to jump through the required hoops. The other 10 percent involved a dismal public airing of a couple's dirtiest laundry. Was this era of ugliness, dishonesty, and false blame really more positive for a couple's children? As Hofstra Law Professor J. Herbie DiFonzo wrote in the *Idaho Law Review*, "Bills to gut no-fault divorce and return to the scarlet-letter milieu of proving fault are nostalgic attempts to recapture what never was."

While few would disagree that marriage should not be viewed as a revolving door, especially by parents, it is also important to ask whether it is in the best interest of a child to grow up in a home in which one or both parents are miserably unhappy. Innumerable studies of the effect of divorce on children have concluded that children are damaged less by divorce than by exposure to intense conflict, whether their families are intact or divided. And one fact has been documented beyond question: Children who live in a home where one parent is brutally abusive to the other suffer horribly and face heightened risk for a whole host of problems, from academic failure to illness to suicide to the inability to form healthy family relationships of their own. Any laws that make it harder for women and children to escape abusive homes should be viewed with grave concern.

It is also essential to remember that no-fault laws were adopted not only to make divorce faster and easier, but also to preserve the integrity of the law and to preserve the dignity of the family enduring what was already a difficult and painful process. As stated by Professor DiFonzo in the *Idaho Law Review*, "In the face of overwhelming evidence presented of the farcical nature of American society's lengthy dalliance with fault-only divorce mechanisms, the conclusion that we should reinstall the unholy trinity of fault in our divorce pantheon in untenable. Conditioning a divorce upon one spouse's epitomizing the other as an adulterer, deserter, or beast provides not only a pathetic parody of the complex dynamic of intense psychological relationships, but also grossly overestimates the power of law over culture. The mightiest law is that of necessity: couples who desire to divorce will do so."

Experience bears out the truth of the professor's words. In reality, very few couples divorce impulsively, especially when children are involved. Even during the heyday of no-fault, most divorcing clients I encountered found the process emotionally taxing and particularly arduous. Of all the many, many people I spoke to in preparing this book, only one stated the opinion that her divorce happened too quickly. The overwhelming majority of people who seek a divorce have given the matter months or even years of serious reflection before putting the legal wheels in motion.

Family law attorney David B. Riggert comments, "There is no sense in making it harder to get divorced." Instead, Riggert believes that if one spouse is ambivalent about the divorce, the couple should seek counseling before filing. "If someone comes to me for consultation about a divorce, but makes a comment like 'This wasn't my idea,' I immediately ask if they have been to couples counseling. If they haven't, I suggest it would be to their advantage to try it before proceeding with the divorce—their money may be better spent on counseling instead of attorney's fees. Some couples I've sent to counseling have reconciled. I would much rather see them try this route first than invest a lot of effort and money—mine and theirs—on preparing for a divorce, then deciding they don't want to go through with it."

Legislative initiatives to keep families together are taking a variety of forms, many less drastic than the complete abolition of no-fault. Many states are seeking a middle ground between a return to fault-based divorce systems and pure no-fault schemes. Proposals to require mutual consent, separation periods, to allow courts to mandate counseling when one spouse opposes the divorce, or to require parents to participate in mediation represent less drastic efforts. Professor DiFonzo notes that divorce law can be structured to require that couples who divorce do so only after giving the matter serious reflection and after assuring that economically disadvantaged spouses and dependent children are treated fairly, without a step backward to fault-based systems.

However, while many of these legislative efforts seem positive, others may have unintended detrimental effects. For example, prohibiting divorce before a separation period of as long as two years gives rise to serious questions about what will happen during this interim period, especially with regard to child support, property division, and child custody issues.

Some states have addressed the issue of divorce by reforming their marriage laws, by requiring premarital counseling or other initiatives to make couples consider more carefully the commitment of marriage before they tie the knot. As of late 1997, at least eleven states had considered enacting legislation that would require or encourage such programs before marriage licenses are issued. These efforts have been widely praised as a more positive approach to preventing divorce than laws that make the process more difficult for a couple that has decided to split.

Yet some such reforms have a troubling side as well. In 1997, after heavy lobbying by conservative Christians, Louisiana adopted a new marriage law that allows couples to choose between two forms of marriage, "traditional" or "covenant." A couple wed in a traditional marriage may divorce after a six-month separation, while those in a covenant marriage cannot divorce unless they have been separated for two years or prove egregious wrongdoing by one spouse—adultery, abandonment, or mental or physical abuse. Couples who choose covenant marriage must also undergo counseling prior to marriage.

While supporters argue that the new law will force couples to consider more seriously about the lifelong commitment of consequences of divorce for children, opponents, including the American Civil Liberties Union, worry that the law could trap women and children in damaging marriages. As with divorce reform laws, while this new form of marriage has the noble goal of keeping families together, the reality remains that some families should not stay together, and it may make divorce difficult or even impossible in these unfortunate situations. Also, from a constitutional perspective, such laws are troubling in their religious underpinnings and regulation of matters recognized as highly private and personal. As more and more states consider such legislation, and more and more couples marry and divorce under the new schemes, the new laws will undoubtedly be tested in the courts on both pragmatic and constitutional grounds.

Changes in Child Custody Laws

As no-fault divorce became the norm throughout the United States, child custody laws changed in significant ways. First, in conjunction with the move toward equality between the sexes, the traditional idea that primary custody should automatically go to the mother was eliminated. All states now give men and women equal rights to custody based on what is in the best interest of the child.

As a corollary, most states now have adopted a legal principle allowing, or in some cases preferring, joint custody. Joint custody does not mean that the children will automatically spend 50 percent of their time with each parent. Instead, it means that both parents have the right to participate fully in the child's life and share important decisions, such as those affecting the child's health, schooling, and religious upbringing. Most children continue to live primarily with one parent—still the mother in the majority of cases—after the divorce. In practice, joint custody is often similar to the shared parenting commonly found under sole custody arrangements.

In addition, all states have now enacted laws such as the Uniform Child Custody Jurisdiction Act which are intended to discourage custody battles and parental kidnapping. Under federal and state laws, parental kidnapping or the abduction of a child across state lines is a crime, with exceptions made for cases in which abuse is involved or the abducting parent has cause to believe that the child is being endangered by the other parent. Other laws prevent international abduction and provide for the return of children illegally transported from one country to another. Stronger laws, along with the agencies that enforce them, have also been established for child support. These laws are discussed in detail later in this book.

Divorce and Demographics

Throughout history, political, economic, and religious factors have contributed to divorce rates. While the single most important factor in determining whether a particular marriage will end in divorce is the two people involved, certain social factors and individual characteristics do seem to make divorce more or less likely. Divorce rates tend to go down during times of economic hardship and rise in times of prosperity. The rates tend to be low during major wars and escalate when the wars have ended. Divorce rates usually increase in a socially progressive political atmosphere and decrease in a more conservative environment.

People of Catholic or Jewish faith have a lower divorce rate than do Protestants, although Catholics have seen an increase in their rate of divorce which parallels that of the general population. Religious practices are believed by some to tie in with racial differences in divorce rates. Hispanics, many of whom are traditionally Catholic, have a lower rate of divorce than other ethnic groups, for example.

Cultural factors may affect the entire divorce process. Attorney Judith Finfrock devoted a large part of her San Francisco practice to domestic relations law. Her firm was composed almost entirely of Asian attorneys, and about three-quarters of her divorce clients were members of an Asian ethnic group. "The Asian clients had different concerns than the Caucasians because of their culture," Finfrock explains. "Loss of face in the community was very big, especially for women. There were also cultural clashes to contend with. For example, it has long been acceptable for men to have concubines in the traditional Chinese culture. But wives in America wouldn't put up with it, since such behavior is not tolerated in our society. If a man's mistress became public knowledge, there would be a loss of face for the woman who accepted it. So in a divorce where there had been adultery, the wife wanted the husband's fault addressed in the court documents which became public records. California is strictly no-fault, and adultery can't be alleged as grounds, but many insisted it be stated somewhere in the documents."

In Finfrock's experience, property disputes also tended to be different among Asian couples. "There is more competition and discord over things that are viewed as status symbols in that cultural community, such as jewelry," she says. "At a traditional wedding, the bride wears and displays all the jewelry that she has received as gifts. Jewelry and gold are collected and valued, and it is always an important part of the property division."

Many of those who have studied divorce trends, including sociologist Constance Ahrons, Ph.D., have found that age at the time of marriage is one of the greatest predictors of divorce. Ahrons reports that couples who are twenty years old or younger when they marry have the highest likelihood of divorce. This parallels the fact that people with less education and lower incomes tend to divorce at a higher rate than those with higher earnings and education. However, well-educated women with high personal incomes divorce at a greater rate than women who are less educated and less economically advantaged. Also, the Western region of the United States has a higher divorce rate than the Northeastern region, due perhaps in part to the average lower age of citizens in the West and the higher concentration of Catholics in the East.

Social acceptance of cohabitation without marriage has also had an impact on divorce rates in both American and European countries. Since the 1970s, more couples have lived together and ended relationships without divorce, and this may have been a factor in the slightly declining divorce rates throughout the 1980s. Since then, divorce rates have stabilized, with approximately 50 percent of marriages today eventually ending in divorce.

The many factors involved in these personal choices make trends difficult to predict. Ahrons believes that as women become more independent, as life expectancies increase, and as divorce becomes a more accepted fact of modern family life, the rates are likely to either continue to stabilize or increase slightly. She points out that factors such as remarriage and re-divorce, which is becoming more common in today's society, must also be considered, as must declining birth rates and the increasing numbers of women who marry later in life or not at all. Longer life expectancies also make serial marriages more likely. Ahrons suggests that longevity may be the single most powerful reason why divorce rates are unlikely to decrease substantially in the future.

Today, marriage is generally viewed in the law as a civil contract, an emotional bond, and a financial partnership. The religious or spiritual nature of the marriage vows continues to be important to many people. We expect our marriages to be happy, to offer companionship, sexual satisfaction, and personal fulfillment. In short, both a realistic view of the multifaceted nature of the partnership, as well as high expectations for marriage, prevail.

ALTERNATIVES FOR PEOPLE DIVORCING TODAY

Divorce today not only is easier, but also offers more choices to families than ever before. As the legal costs associated with divorce have skyrocketed, more alternatives have become available for couples divorcing, especially for those with no children and relatively simple assets. Self-help books, do-it-yourself divorce kits, law school or court–annexed clinics, mediation, and other options have become more accessible to people seeking to avoid high legal fees.

As the divorce laws have gone through various stages of evolution, the role of legal profession has changed as well. Property disputes now require cerebral wrangling instead of the former battle to the lowest common denominator of marital behavior. Family law is no longer viewed as a poor cousin of more prestigious legal specialties. Divorce lawyers must be familiar not only with matrimonial law itself, but also with corollary issues of crucial importance, including business and property valuation, accounting techniques, child custody and support options, and tax law. As a result, respect for family law specialists has risen.

Science, too, has contributed to the change in our beliefs about divorce. Some scientists who have studied human behavior conclude that people are not biologically designed to be monogamous and stay with the same mate for a lifetime. People are beginning to understand that not every marriage that ends is a failure—some simply are not meant to last forever. Anthropologist Margaret Mead once responded to a question about her "failed marriages" with a statement that although she was married three times, none of the marriages was a failure. In today's world, other relationships such as jobs, friendships, and community ties are often temporary, and this is considered normal. Divorce and the new beginning that follows can be a healthy transition into a new phase of life, just as a change in career or a move across the country can be.

The media have also played a part in shaping our attitude toward divorce and the acceptance of family structures beyond the traditional nuclear group. During the 1970s, movies and television began to acknowledge the increasing numbers of divorced families. A few television programs, such as "One Day at a Time"—about a divorced mother and her two daughters— depicted the trials and triumphs of such families, and, most important, showed them as normal, healthy families, not "broken," not desperate, not failures. Films such as *Kramer vs. Kramer* and *War of the Roses* became more common throughout the eighties, showing the damage that can be done when divorce or child custody turns into war. In the nineties, abundant stories of the positive and negative aspects of divorce and single parenthood abound on television, in popular series like "Grace Under Fire," in movies like *Mrs. Doubtfire*, and in books like Terry McMillan's *Waiting to Exhale*.

Attorney Judith Finfrock is pleased to see the popular media beginning to reflect the reality of modern family life by presenting more families with divorced or single parents, custodial fathers, and other realistic circumstances. "The television show 'Cybill,' with Cybill Shepherd, is about a divorced mother with two children who have different fathers," she remarks. "Both fathers have ongoing involvement with the children and remain friendly with the mother, though they naturally have their conflicts. This is a good model for similar families—it shows that such families are normal, that parents can communicate and maintain good relationships through their ups and downs."

Divorce Magazine was conceived in 1994, when founder Dan Courvette, then an associate publisher of a Canadian wedding magazine, found his own marriage ending. Courvette realized that while there were scores of magazines dedicated to helping couples plan their wedding day, no periodicals existed to assist with the complexities of a divorce, arguably the most stressful and traumatic time in a person's life. So in 1996, he launched *Divorce Magazine*, billed as "help for generation 'ex'." The publication achieved rapid success, quickly expanding to produce four regional editions in North America. It offers user-friendly resources providing information, advice, and expert guidance in the areas of law, real estate, tax issues, relationships, mental and physical health, children, dating, blended families, and other issues to readers at various stages of the divorce process. Other publishers seem anxious to emulate the magazine's success. In early 1998, Japan launched its own divorce magazine, entitled *Liz* in honor of the much-divorced Elizabeth Taylor.

Given our great expectations for marriage, divorce is likely to remain a part of society. Therefore, the various tasks involved in restructuring families will have to remain dynamic. The future is hard to predict, but it seems safe to say that both the legal systems and social attitudes surrounding divorce will continue to evolve as long as human beings and their social institutions exist.

PREPARING FOR DIVORCE

How to Begin and What to Expect

Divorce usually takes longer than people think it should. As with any difficult transition, those embroiled in a divorce are naturally anxious to get it over with and move on. Unfortunately, people sometimes make unwise decisions or agree to property settlements or parenting plans that ultimately are not the best and most workable options. Unless the relationship is violent or there appears to be an imminent crisis, it may be better to take your time and make sure everything has been thought through carefully.

WHEN SHOULD I SEEK LEGAL ADVICE?

The decision to divorce may take several years to finalize. As soon as a couple decides to separate, the process of uncoupling begins, by mutual agreement or whatever arrangements fall into place. It is far better to seek legal assistance sooner than later. Speak with an attorney as soon as you are seriously contemplating a divorce. There are three main reasons why this is advisable. First, if you find an attorney with whom you feel comfortable, this will be one less matter to deal with later when things reach a critical state and you may be more emotionally upset. Second, patterns that you establish on your own after you separate can affect what happens later if certain issues have to be resolved by a judge. These patterns also affect the perception of the parties involved and may have an impact on mediation or settlement negotiations. For example, informal arrangements in regard to housing, child custody, and support set the stage for the final decree. Third, if your spouse initiates the legal process, you must be prepared to respond quickly. Whenever you receive a legal document, whether by personal service or by mail, you are usually obligated to respond within ten to thirty days. If you have an attorney, all correspondence and legal documents should go to him or her. The attorney should provide you with a copy of every motion, letter, settlement offer, or other significant document he or she receives. If you don't have a lawyer yet, or if you receive anything from your spouse or from his or her attorney, be sure that you speak with a legal adviser as soon as possible. Do not wait, even a few days. There may be work that needs to be done before the responding papers can be prepared, and action is often required within less than two weeks.

When possible, arrange issues such as child support, spousal support, and custody and visitation before you and your spouse move into separate residences. The agreements don't need to be formal, but they should be definite, put in writing, and shared with your attorneys. The date of separation may be significant. In some states, it can affect your financial responsibilities in major ways. This is another reason why it is essential to speak with a lawyer before the actual separation, if possible. This is especially important if you plan to move a great distance from your current residence, and absolutely crucial if children are involved.

If you have separated but are not certain about whether you will divorce or reconcile, it is wise to seek a decree of legal separation. Under this scenario, the couple remains legally married, but all the issues that would be addressed in a divorce (including division of property, support, and child custody) are outlined in a legally binding document. If you reconcile, the document becomes moot. If you divorce, it will form the basis for negotiating a final decree. Some couples simply incorporate the terms of the separation agreement into the decree unchanged, whereas others use it as a starting point to negotiate something different when the divorce becomes final.

EDUCATE YOURSELF

It can be tremendously helpful, from the standpoint of working effectively with lawyers and mediators and for building emotional strength and confidence, to familiarize yourself with the divorce laws in your state. This is usually easier than it sounds. In many areas, lawyers or professors in the family law field have put together handbooks, pamphlets, brochures, or other materials to help laypeople understand and use the laws of their state. If you live near a law school, visit their library and see what is available. Some public court or college libraries also have these materials.

Many law schools also have family law clinics in which trained law students working under the supervision of an attorney provide services to people involved in a divorce, from basic information to complete assistance through the divorce process. Bar associations often distribute pamphlets or consumer guides, conduct public seminars, offer live or recorded telephone information lines, and provide other services to the public. The telephone number of each state's bar association is listed in appendix B at the back of this book.

In many areas, local legal aid or court–sponsored clinics provide information and assistance, and divorce education classes are growing in number. These programs may be offered through colleges, local legal professional organizations, hospitals, churches, or other nonprofit groups. Most provide information, alternatives available in the area, advice on what to expect, and answers to questions.

These programs and services may be especially valuable to those who have not yet made the decision whether or not to divorce. Most offer guidance in compiling financial information, understanding the legal process, and locating different types of counseling and therapy. Many include input from various professionals, such as attorneys, counselors, and financial advisers.

PRO SE: SHOULD I HANDLE MY OWN DIVORCE?

In a word, no. Or at least, not entirely. The law surrounding divorce (and related matters such as pension rights, taxes, and creditor's rights) gets more complex by the minute. Even if you and your spouse can reach an absolute agreement as to how your property is to be divided, you may not be aware of how to structure your agreement to assure the results you want. In almost every case, it is important to have a qualified divorce attorney (or other specialized legal professional, such as a court clinic worker) at least review your papers before they are filed to make sure they are accurate and complete.

You can save a lot of time and money, however, by doing *most* of the work yourself. There are dozens of books, kits, and form packages available today, and new, innovative developments are springing up constantly. "We the People," a chain of fast-food-style legal clinics with stores in several states, provides low-cost assistance for people who wish to file their own divorces. The service is limited to divorces in which there are no children and no disputes over property. Customers pick up a workbook at the store—which even has a drive-up window—and return with the completed information. The company then prepares the required forms for the person to file *pro se* or after review by their lawyer, again, the wisest course to take. The entire process of completing the documents takes about thirty minutes. Since the stores are not staffed by attorneys, no legal advice is offered.

It can be both satisfying and financially smart to get the ball rolling on an uncontested divorce yourself. Many of the self-help materials and programs are excellent, especially those that are set up to conform with a state's particular law. However, be wary of any that claim to completely take the place of a lawyer.

Family law is uniquely fraught with pitfalls. Building a life with another person over a period of years is seldom an easy task; and neither is dismantling it. Even if you and your spouse have had a very simple life, the complexities of modern society— and, admittedly, the legal system—often conspire to make things more labyrinthine than is readily apparent. For example, consider a childless couple married two years, who are renting a cottage and owing on two credit cards and one car payment. They decide to part ways and agree to a division of their personal property. She gets the cottage and lease obligation, plus one credit card debt; he gets the car and the debt on it, plus the other credit card debt.

Sounds simple, doesn't it? But what about her retirement plan at work? And what if he loses his job and can't make the car payment? Although the divorce decree says the debt is his alone, a divorce order is only binding on the couple, not on their creditors. The lender can still come after her for the car payments if he doesn't make them, unless the loan is refinanced in his name alone. And what about his military benefits? How will next year's tax returns be prepared?

The point is that there is more to getting a clean, final, successful divorce than filing the papers with the right court. Often, others need to become involved, such as creditors, pension fund administrators, and government agencies. Even in what appears to be a simple situation, there may be property value concerns, tax consequences, and future risks to consider. For this reason, the best course of action is to do as much as you can on your own, which may range from nothing, when a couple is acrimonious and can't agree on anything, to getting all your papers in what you believe to be the final form for review by a lawyer.

Don't feel bad if you and your spouse can't agree on everything. Sometimes couples go into a siege and refuse to move forward because they're hung up on one or two points—who gets the coin collection, or whether Jimmy spends Thanksgiving with Mom or Dad. Get as close to an agreement as you can, then enlist the help of the lawyers. Attorneys are negotiators and counselors, too, not just gladiators. They can assist and advise couples in reaching their own settlement, or they can recommend going to mediation if appropriate. They can also spot inequities or mistakes in a proposed settlement and explain what the law requires (and what the court is likely to decide) in disputed matters. A good lawyer will always try to negotiate a fair settlement first, and consider litigation a last resort.

Thus, the books and kits can be extremely valuable tools for getting started. They can help you inventory your belongings, consider alternatives, chart the information you will need, and identify any bones of contention that will have to be ironed out. You will, however, need to get a qualified lawyer involved in the process at some point, because each individual case is different. Lawyers or mediators often provide their own checklists and "homework" assignments for organizing property, too.

The Internet

During the past few years, the Internet has emerged as a vast and comprehensive source of information on every imaginable topic, including divorce. Today, having an on-line computer is akin to having a desktop library. For those with access to cyberspace, websites devoted to divorce issues can provide information on local and national laws, sources of professional assistance, publications, videotapes, discussion and news groups, and other resources. If you are not on line through a computer at home or at work, check with your local public library. Many libraries now have computers that patrons may use to gain access to the Internet, as well as free classes on how to navigate your way through cyberspace (most people can learn the basics in an hour or two).

Various federal, state, and local government offices maintain excellent websites. For example, the Office of Child Support Enforcement has a site with links to very specific and detailed information on the laws and mechanics of child support in each state. The site is currently located at www.dhhs.gov/programs. Web locations change frequently, so if the URLs provided here are incorrect, a search using the name of the organization or government office will usually lead you to the correct site.

Do bear in mind that anyone can create a website, and some of the information you find may be inaccurate or inflammatory. I have seen many websites providing extremely helpful information, as well as a few with terrible advice to offer, such as encouraging people to play dirty to "win" a child custody battle at any cost or to try and handle a complex divorce without legal assistance. Weigh what you read on the web, or in print, against your own common sense, and always consider the source of the advice. Remember that your situation is unique, and you should consult a competent professional (counselor, lawyer, clergyperson, financial adviser) for specific recommendations. Check the appendix for a list of recommended websites.

CHOOSING A LAWYER

Choosing the right attorney to handle your divorce may be one of the most important decisions you will ever have to make. Remember, not only your money and property but your future security and the future of your children may be affected forever by the quality of the attorney you choose. For many people, divorce is the biggest legal, financial, and emotional undertaking of their entire life.

Recommendations for lawyers can come from many sources. Therapists and counselors who work with people going through a divorce are often able to recommend good lawyers, just as lawyers often recommend therapists. Friends who have been through a divorce and were satisfied with the legal representation they received are one of the best sources of recommendations. If you hired a lawyer in the past or are acquainted with lawyers socially, those individuals may be able to recommend colleagues who practice family law.

Most state bar associations have lawyer referral services. It's usually not a good idea to choose a lawyer on this basis alone, as most of the services are open to any licensed attorney who signs up and pays an administration fee. If an attorney is licensed as a specialist in family law in the state, however, this carries more weight, as all states that issue specialty licenses have stringent requirements to qualify for the designation. The American Academy of Matrimonial Lawyers is an elite group of fourteen hundred members with at least ten years of legal practice, at least 75 percent of which has been in matrimonial law. All members must also pass an examination. A list of these attorneys in your state may be obtained free of charge by calling (312) 263–6477.

Whatever you have been told about the stellar talents of a particular attorney, make sure you visit with the person to determine whether or not this is the right lawyer for you before making a final decision. A lawyer who is wonderful for one client may be disastrous for another. As in any close relationship, you have to be able to develop a comfortable rapport. Sometimes personalities and styles of doing business simply do not click. Remember, you will have to tell this person the most intimate details of your personal life. Choose someone with whom you feel comfortable sharing this information.

A lawyer who practices in a broad range of general fields may be well qualified to handle a divorce, if he or she has taken an interest in family law and kept abreast of current developments through continuing education programs or by regularly handling family law cases. However, when complex assets such as business enterprises, large amounts of money or stocks, or hotly contested custody issues arise, it is generally best to secure an attorney who concentrates most of his or her practice in the area of family law.

Attorney Judith Finfrock also urges clients to be sure the attorney they choose is familiar with the judges in the community. "Unfortunately, there are some judges who make one-sided decisions or enter totally inappropriate rulings. I've seen judges refuse to approve a perfectly fair settlement agreement the couple has reached, because they want to use their power or let their own biases come in. A few are completely crazy and out of control. Lawyers practicing divorce law should be well aware of the reputations of the judges who handle such cases in their community; and be willing to use their right to recuse [disqualify] a judge they don't feel will do right by their client."

The practice of law overall is becoming increasingly specialized. This is especially true in the area of family law as more and more subspecialties develop. There are divorce attorneys who focus specifically on such areas as corporations, family-owned businesses, separately owned businesses, international marriages, military marriages, elder divorces and retirement issues, and parenting issues. If a particular area in your marriage is of paramount importance to you or extremely complex, you may wish to seek referrals to one of these subspecialists through such an organization as the American Academy of Matrimonial Lawyers.

Feel free to make appointments with several lawyers and interview each one before deciding (the first consultation is usually free). Go prepared with an idea of the assets to be divided, whether property or custody issues are likely to be contested, and what essentials you want to get out of the divorce. Be sure you fully understand the fee arrangements and costs you will be required to pay before you enter into any agreement with a lawyer to represent you.

In the book *Divorcing*, renowned trial attorney Melvin Belli lists eight characteristics that should be possessed by a good divorce lawyer.

1. The lawyer will be both sensitive and objective. He or she will be willing to listen to and consider your feelings about your particular divorce, but also be able to help you channel your feelings into the most positive resolution of your situation in relation to your future happiness.

2. The lawyer will be straightforward about billing and charges, so there will be no surprises later.

3. The lawyer will not use intimidating legal jargon, but will explain in understandable terms what the legal terms mean and what the procedures are all about.

4. The lawyer will make you feel comfortable asking any question, and never make you feel naive or stupid.

5. The lawyer will not promise you the world, or give you unrealistic expectations. He or she will try to minimize your costs and avoid unnecessary adversity. Conversely, the lawyer will be willing to work hard to protect your rights and will not sacrifice your best interests.

6. The lawyer will communicate with you frequently, so that you don't feel your case is being neglected.

7. The lawyer will be familiar with the divorce laws of your state, and have experience in how the law is applied in the court in which your divorce will proceed.

8. The lawyer will seek to minimize your costs and serve your best interests by encouraging such procedures as mediation, negotiation between you and your spouse, and other efforts to resolve the issues which can be resolved outside of court.

Attorney's Fees

What a client may reasonably be expected to pay for a divorce varies tremendously, depending on a variety of factors. In Albuquerque, New Mexico, an area where living expenses are usually considered moderate in comparison with the rest of the nation, an uncontested divorce may run as low as $200 or as high as $3,000.

Divorce may cost anywhere from nothing to hundreds of thousands of dollars. The range of hourly fees among divorce lawyers of which I am personally aware spans from $50 an hour to $450 an hour. A client should be sure that he or she understands how fees are calculated, what other costs to expect, how payment schedules work, and all other matters relating to fees before any money is paid. Most lawyers will ask the client to sign a written contract, called a fee agreement or retainer agreement, which spells out the details about fees, including hourly rates for the various attorneys, paralegals, and others that might work on the case, whether such rates vary according to the type of work being done, when bills will be sent, and when the client will be expected to pay.

Your attorney should be willing to provide you with a summary of all hourly rates, anticipated costs, and other related information in writing. You should never be charged for secretarial time, unless the secretary is also a legal assistant or paralegal. In that case, you should be charged only for time spent actually doing legal work on your case, such as research or drafting documents, never for typing or straight secretarial work. Likewise, you should never be charged for the initial interview with the attorney unless you decide during the interview to go ahead and hire the attorney, and he or she actually begins to work with you to prepare your case.

Many lawyers charge a retainer, which is a sum of money that must be paid before work on the case will begin. Retainers serve as security deposits, and the lawyer will draw from the retainer to pay the fees as bills accumulate. Some refund any part of the retainer that is not used when the case is over; others keep any remainder as a bonus. Some require acceptance fees in the form of a lump-sum payment up front, with hourly fees additional. Still others charge a bonus, also called a result fee, or kicker, at the end of the case if they win a particularly good result for the client. Many find acceptance fees or kickers distasteful or even unethical, but they are becoming more common, especially for lawyers recognized as leaders in their field. Make sure you understand exactly what the money you are asked to provide will cover. Get a clear, detailed, written agreement and ask for an explanation of anything you don't understand.

Out-of-pocket expenses in a divorce case can also be considerable. These costs include court filing fees, mailing, photocopying, expert witness fees, travel costs, investigation fees, and miscellaneous other expenses that can add up to tremendous amounts. Expert witness fees are often particularly high, but these witnesses may be extremely important in a complex divorce case. Appraisers, accountants, psychologists, and vocational experts are often essential. If both parties can agree to have a single, neutral expert perform the required work, this will save money and the person's opinion will carry more weight if the case goes to court.

Many people find themselves in dire financial straits when facing a divorce, and the last thing they want to do is incur more debt. However, borrowing money to pay a qualified attorney and other experts to protect your rights during a divorce is one of the best investments you can make. More and more people have to take this option, and it is generally well worth it. Before you incur any debt, be sure you and your attorney have frankly discussed all anticipated costs of the divorce.

In many areas, public service lawyers are available to perform free legal services, including divorce representation, for people whose income falls below a certain level. Many lawyers occasionally do cases on a *pro bono* (free) basis to satisfy state licensing requirements, professional rules, or their own sense of ethics. Some local courts or law schools have divorce clinics staffed by students or paralegals who can help people draft their own divorce papers when they are able to reach a full or partial settlement with their spouse. These programs are usually supervised by lawyers who review the papers. A call to your local or state bar association can put you in touch with such groups.

Attorney Judith Finfrock advises those seeking a divorce lawyer to be aware that the size of the fee doesn't guarantee the quality of the results. "The best bet is to go to someone recommended by another who has been through the process. Interview more than one attorney. Look for someone who can mirror back what you tell them, so you are sure the lawyer heard and understood what you said."

Keep in mind that the more complex the divorce is, the higher the fees and expenses will be, and the more difficult it will be to estimate total costs. The level of disagreement between the spouses is the single most important factor in determining what a divorce will cost. Lawyers should never charge a penalty fee if the couple reconciles or put unreasonable pressure on the client to either settle or go forward. Ask the lawyers you interview to give you a reasonable estimate of what the divorce will cost, based on your honest opinion of how many issues are in dispute. Remember that in a hotly contested divorce, an attorney may not be able to predict a realistic total, because much will depend on your spouse, his or her attorney, and other outside factors.

A Word of Caution

Be aware that if you do not pay your legal fees, the attorney has the right to file a special type of lien at the end of the case or at any time either you or your attorney ends the relationship. You should receive an itemized bill for fees that have accrued at least every sixty days. If you have a question or problem with a bill, talk to your lawyer right away. Most states have some type of arbitration program for disputed attorney fees.

Watch for red flags when assessing potential attorneys. Be wary of a lawyer who promises to take care of everything you need, guarantees a particular result, or promises to gain a quick resolution of a complex matter for a small fee. Many people understandably would like to turn everything over to a lawyer and avoid the whole process, but this is a prescription for trouble.

You should be kept informed of everything that happens, and be present at all court hearings or conferences.

Also beware of the gladiator personality. Lawyers who go into battle looking for a glorious victory frequently cause far more trauma and expense to their clients than someone whose goal is to try and reach a fair and reasonable settlement with as little fanfare as possible. It is not uncommon to feel that the best lawyer will be one who takes the position of a warrior and does whatever is necessary to win the case exactly as the client wants it won, fighting to the death if necessary. This type of person may seem very appealing in the heat of the moment, when the hurt and anger are fresh. However, barracuda litigation is seldom the best tactic in any type of case, especially a divorce. This type of lawyer inevitably runs up large bills, causes unnecessary delays, and adds to the emotional turmoil inevitable in any divorce. Beware, too, of books and other self–help materials that encourage this type of behavior by either lawyer or client. In the 1989 film, *The War of the Roses*, Danny DeVito's character, a lawyer who had learned hard lessons, said it best: "There is no winning in this. There are only degrees of losing."

This does not mean it is wrong to take a strong stand on important issues, or to expect your lawyer to do the same. But there is often a fine line between fighting for fundamental rights and fighting for the sake of revenge or other inappropriate motives. At the other extreme, clients should also watch out for lawyers who are overly passive. The best lawyer will work hard to achieve a settlement that satisfies the client's most important needs and concerns, and remains ready to make a straightforward, dignified effort in court if necessary.

As fans of the TV show "L.A. Law" know, beware of the slimy Arnie Beckers out there. Although they are few and far between, there are a few sexual predators who will try to take unfair advantage of an emotionally vulnerable client. Some states even have begun to enact laws or rules of ethical conduct that prohibit any sexual relationship between attorney and client during the period of legal representation. Most ethical lawyers will not become personally involved with a client until the business between attorney and client has ended.

The Attorney-Client Relationship

By its very nature, divorce is one of the most emotionally charged fields of law. While it is important that a relationship between attorney and client be trusting and comfortable, it is equally important to set certain boundaries. Lawyers working in the family law arena are fully aware that they are dealing with people who are undergoing trauma. Most are sympathetic and compassionate and are accustomed to tears and outbursts. However, a lawyer cannot take the place of a confessor, psychologist, or best friend. Most family lawyers are as patient as they can be, but none can spend five hours a day offering emotional solace.

Lawyers are often faced with the difficult task of trying to steer a client toward a resolution that is in his or her best interest without offending or appearing to go against the client's wishes. Judith Finfrock emphasizes that the lawyer's first role is truly that of the client's "mouthpiece." "It's up to us to be able to put the client's own words into a concise, structured form that follows the legal requirements, so the judge will hear what the client wants to say," she says.

Yet she also points out that a lawyer must often explain to the client why some of their desires or ideas cannot be legally accomplished. "The position of attorney still carries authority, as it should—we do difficult work, and it gets more complex all the time, in the area of retirement benefits, for example. Most people do respect attorneys and are generally willing to follow what the law requires."

Finfrock has experienced little resistance from clients. She feels that few people really want to abuse the system or bring unnecessary hostility into the process. When a client does oppose her suggestions, other factors are usually involved. "With a lot of my male clients, especially, I had the impression they were being egged on by their friends. The guys at the bar after work would be urging them to fight for the kids, take the wife to the mat, put up a real battle. But most clients realize that there is nothing to be gained by fighting. They *want* their attorney to lay down the law and give them permission to do the right thing. As soon as you tell them they're not going to win anything by putting up a battle, they back down instantly. You have to give them permission to go back to their buddies and say, 'Hey, the lawyer told me I have no choice.' Then they can still hold up their heads on pool night."

David B. Riggert, a family law attorney in Bloomington, Illinois, finds that while nearly half the people who come to him seeking a divorce consultation believe they are ready to proceed with an uncontested divorce, in reality, many have not yet considered essential issues. The discovery that more work lies ahead may be frustrating for a client who wishes to proceed quickly and inexpensively, and may lead them to believe the attorney is churning higher fees. However, an attorney has a responsibility to protect the client's interests, including the duty to uncover issues the client may not have considered—such as whether the parent who will not have primary custody of the children will provide a life insurance policy naming the children as beneficiaries.

Try to be willing to listen to legal advice with an open mind. Consider whether what the lawyer is suggesting would truly be the right choice. For example, it is almost always best to compromise extensively to reach a settlement. Yet at the other extreme, some clients consider themselves to be at fault for causing the divorce and want to give away everything in order to assuage their guilt. A lawyer who advises against such a move is not being altruistic, but protecting the client's legal interests. A good lawyer–client relationship is one in which concerns can be discussed freely, various options weighed, and a course of action plotted that is both satisfying to the client and legally wise. It is often difficult to see things rationally and set goals during a period of severe emotional upheaval, and part of the lawyer's job is to bring the client back to a logical and rational perspective.

A lawyer can be reasonably expected to stay in regular communication with a client, answer questions patiently and honestly, keep the client informed of all significant events that occur in the case, and competently prepare as an advocate for the client's interests. A good lawyer should be willing to admit when he or she needs help from outside experts on things such as sophisticated business transactions and tax matters. The lawyer should explain to the client why an outside expert is being hired, how the lawyer came to choose that person, what the expert will do to help in the case, and how much it will cost.

On the matter of fees and costs, the lawyer should be willing, at any time, to tally the costs and fees that have accrued and to explain to the client how and why they were incurred. Regular, detailed billing statements should be provided at least every sixty days. However, the lawyer should not have to account for every paper clip that is used.

If there is not enough trust between lawyer and client to reach this balance, then perhaps the client should consider looking for another lawyer. It is not uncommon, especially in divorce cases, for more than one lawyer to be involved during the course of the proceedings. If you do not feel comfortable with your lawyer and do not feel that the situation can be worked out after making an honest effort to do so, do not hesitate to seek different legal counsel. Lawyers should not take such decisions personally. Also be aware that a lawyer has the right to terminate the attorney–client relationship if the client refuses to meet his or her responsibilities.

Remember that as the client, you are the ultimate boss for as long as the relationship lasts. In a divorce, the lawyer's first concern should be the goals of the client. A good matrimonial lawyer will also explain the limits of the law and will take his or her role as peacemaker, in addition to advocate, just as seriously. It is not the role of the lawyer to be a weapon for one spouse to use against the other.

In sum, a good lawyer–client relationship is a team effort, but the final balance of power always rests with the client. A client should choose a lawyer whose opinion and advice he or she can respect and value. If an impasse occurs, it is the client who will have the final say in all decisions, unless he or she is trying to trick or force the lawyer into unethical or legally improper behavior, which the lawyer must decline.

Should Both Parties Use the Same Lawyer?

From the standpoint of both professional ethics and the client's best interest, most lawyers will not handle a divorce for both parties. There are exceptions, however. Some lawyers feel that when the parties have been able to reach a fair, absolute agreement either on their own or with the help of mediators or other negotiators, one lawyer is sufficient to review the documents to be sure that they are in the proper legal form, if this is the only legal task that needs to be accomplished. This remains an area of considerable controversy. While some lawyers believe that one attorney should never represent both parties, Judith Finfrock sees no problem with representing both as long as the individuals are aware of their legal rights and have worked out a mutually agreeable settlement that covers all of the necessary issues.

AN OVERVIEW OF THE LEGAL PROCESS OF DIVORCE

Divorce law and most specific aspects of family law are governed almost entirely by the states. This means that the law varies a great deal from state to state, so it is difficult to give general guidelines on what a person can expect. The major principles of divorce, support, and custody laws are discussed in later chapters.

Furthermore, the steps a couple is required to take will vary depending on whether they are able to agree to some or all of the terms of the divorce, the complexity of the property and legal matters involved, and how well the opposing sides cooperate.

Naturally, the more disagreement and hostility there is, the more time and money will be spent in the steps that lead up to the actual divorce, such as pretrial discovery, formal settlement offers, interim hearings, and other legal maneuverings. Fortunately, 90 percent of divorce cases are settled without litigation in court. Many couples work out an amicable agreement and, depending on local requirements, may never appear before a judge. Others go through all the preparations for a full-scale trial, then settle on the courthouse steps. Many fall somewhere in between.

Getting Started

There are certain basic steps that are required to complete any divorce. To start, one party or the other files for divorce. This involves preparing a document that clearly, and usually briefly, sets forth the facts from that person's perspective. It requests the court to take certain legal steps, including dividing property, setting child or spousal support, and resolving custody. This document is usually called a petition for divorce, or petition for dissolution of marriage. In some states, it is called a complaint for divorce. The person who files this document to start the legal process is called the petitioner, or plaintiff.

The factual information in this document usually includes the date and place of marriage, names of the parties, names and ages of any minor children born of the marriage, a description of the property owned by the couple together (marital property), and property the spouse filing the petition claims as separate property. Peripheral issues such as a request to change the wife's name back to her maiden name may also be included. The petition also states the grounds for divorce, most often incompatibility, separation, or irreconcilable differences, according to the language of each state's no-fault statute. In some cases, fault-based grounds such as adultery are still stated.

The petition for divorce must also contain a statement showing that the court has jurisdiction to grant the divorce. Requirements for jurisdiction vary from state to state, as do residence laws. Some states or local jurisdictions require an affidavit listing property, debt, and other specifics to accompany the petition.

When the divorce petition is filed, a filing fee must be paid. These fees range from less than $50 to $200 or more. People with income below the poverty line may be able to fill out a form to be filed with the court, often called a certificate of indigency, which will result in a waiver of the filing fee.

Next, the other spouse files an answer, or response, to the petition. This document states whether the other party admits or denies what is stated in each paragraph of the petition. It may also contain that person's version of disputed facts, defenses, counterclaims, or requests to the court for other types of legal action. If the couple has reached a settlement agreement, this will be presented to the court for approval, along with a sample order or decree of divorce for the judge's signature. In many cases, this is the end of the process. However, if issues are contested, litigation proceeds.

Discovery

After the complaint and answer are filed, the parties usually begin the discovery process. *Discovery*, a legal process that is a part of every court case, means that each side may ask the other questions and request documents about any subject that may be relevant to the case. This involves disclosure of all assets, documents, and information essential to come to a fair resolution. It may be done formally according to the court's rules, so the judge can intervene if one party does not cooperate; or informally between cooperating spouses. Naturally, the process is easier and faster if people can willingly exchange essential facts and material. However, if one person is less than completely honest, formal discovery is essential.

The discovery process includes "paper" discovery, composed of interrogatories (questions to be answered in writing), requests for production of documents or other tangible items, and requests for admissions, which help sort out the facts that are not contested. Discovery may also include a request for inspection. This is a request to appraise or examine items and documents in possession of the other person which cannot be easily duplicated or provided. Examples include a home or condominium, a business, a boat, or real estate. A subpoena *duces tecum* can also be served on third parties, such as banks, to order that they provide documents at a specific time and place, such as a scheduled deposition or court hearing.

One universal requirement in all divorce cases is full and honest disclosure. Both people must lay their cards on the table and reveal all of their assets, earnings, and property. It is not uncommon for one spouse to try and conceal assets they do not want to share. Secrecy is not tolerated by the courts, however, and a judge will not hesitate to punish a person who tries to hide property or refuses to produce documents by making them pay the other side's attorney's fees, if a court order must be obtained to make him or her cooperate.

If you are trying to exchange informally and your spouse refuses to disclose information about property, earnings, and so forth, a written reminder that it will all have to come out eventually may be in order. Include the information that if you have to have your lawyer get a court order, your spouse may have to pay the fees and costs. Include a specific list of the information you request (funds in your savings account, the current value of your IRA, the location, number and amount in any other bank or other asset account). Keep a copy; if you do end up in court, this could be evidence that you made good faith efforts to get the information before involving the court, and that it was your spouse who refused to follow the rules.

Discovery also involves taking oral depositions, in which one party's lawyer questions the opposing party and his or her witnesses under oath. During a deposition, the attorney for the person being questioned is present to guard against inappropriate actions by the other attorney, such as overstepping the bounds of permissible questioning, deliberate intimidation, or straying too far afield from the matter at hand. The lawyer can raise an objection, which will go on the record for the judge to rule on later if necessary. Sometimes the objection process becomes abusive, when lawyers object to virtually every question and instruct the client not to answer, something that usually is not done in legitimate depositions. When this occurs, the deposition may have to be postponed to wait for a ruling from the judge. If the objections are legitimate, the questioning lawyers may be sanctioned. However, if the objections are perceived by the judge as merely an attempt to delay or hinder the proceedings, the objecting attorney may be punished and made to pay for the costs that his or her inappropriate actions caused.

The formal discovery process is often difficult, expensive, and seemingly endless, but it's where couples who are unable or unwilling to cooperate informally can finally get down to brass tacks and get a clear picture of each other's case. Discovery is governed by an elaborate set of court rules. Anyone who refuses to follow the rules may be brought to court in a pretrial hearing, and the party or attorney found at fault can be ordered to pay the fees and costs of the party who had to invoke the judge's assistance to get the discovery process completed. By the same token, if one person tries to use the discovery process inappropriately, such as by requesting voluminous materials that have nothing to do with the case or asking intimidating questions that are outside the accepted scope of the process, they too can be fined and reprimanded.

This is relatively unusual, though, as most ethical lawyers are well aware of both the boundaries and the importance of discovery. Cooperation is in the best interests of all concerned, though formal discovery may often be time-consuming, embarrassingly personal, and downright unpleasant. I once had a client in a fairly complex divorce action who, not entirely tongue-in-cheek, referred to interrogatories as "derogatories" and asked when we were going to "decompose" her husband. Like many cases, once discovery was complete and all the facts were on the table, that case was settled shortly before trial.

Discovery serves an important purpose if the case does go to trial. Even though the atmosphere at a deposition is fairly serious, with the presence of the attorneys and a court reporter taking down every word, it is less intimidating than being in a courtroom. Therefore, people often speak more freely and do not guard each word as they tend to do on the witness stand. Since the deposition (as well as the written discovery) is taken under oath, anything a person says may be used in court, as long as it fits within the requirements of admissible courtroom evidence. Therefore, if a party or witness tries to change his or her story later on the witness stand, an attorney may read the portion of the deposition that is contradictory. This is known as "impeaching" a witness. It virtually destroys the credibility of at least that part of the testimony, so it is a powerful tool.

The rules of discovery are far more liberal than the rules of evidence. Either party in a suit may request anything that is "reasonably calculated to lead to the discovery of relevant evidence," not just things guaranteed to be admissible in court. Judges are not amused when one person tries to hide information. It creates more work for the judge and damages the person's credibility. Therefore, in a divorce case, virtually everything involving property, salary, pensions, and all related matters must be disclosed.

Judges get impatient when people try to use the courts as a forum to vindicate their hurt or anger by bringing in matters that don't pertain to the business of ending the marriage. Discovery motions and other pretrial motions are sometimes overused and abused to hinder the process or annoy an opponent. The relevant issues in a no-fault divorce are the division of property and debt, child and/or spousal support, and child custody. The court does not want to hear about his affair, his bad temper, or her drinking problem unless it directly impacts on these issues—for example, if he spent all their savings on jewelry for his girlfriend, if he beat his wife and she has a separate claim for her injuries, or if her alcoholism has made her unable to care for the children.

Interim Order and Related Issues

Important matters must be considered while the divorce is pending. Child and spousal support, living arrangements, access to property, payment of debts, and child custody are often the subject of temporary or interim orders, which state how these things will be handled until a final agreement or order is filed. In some areas, they are required. As with the final decree, the couple can either work out their own agreement or let the judge decide.

Remember, any temporary agreements you reach informally with your spouse, especially those involving financial decisions, are best turned into a formal written interim order to be reviewed and filed with the court. Such agreements are often called stipulations. These are highly favored by courts because they demonstrate that the parties have agreed on certain things and the court won't be required to intervene. Generally, there is no court appearance required. You can state the matters you have agreed to informally, then ask your lawyer to put the document into the correct legal form, which is then signed by both attorneys and filed with the court.

During the interim period while the divorce is pending, avoid certain actions that can cause unnecessary risk or complication. Establish your own credit as soon as possible. Don't continue to mingle your assets with your spouse's in bank accounts. Don't start a new business or buy shares in a new venture until the divorce is final. This does not mean that you cannot get on with your life and take such steps as changing jobs or moving to a different residence. But it is best to discuss major changes with your attorney, because even things that don't seem to be related can have an impact on the outcome of your case. If you do make such transitions, consider whether an interim agreement should be changed or filed.

During the divorce, spouses have often been known to lock each other out of the house or dump the other person's belongings on the lawn. In Terry McMillan's novel *Waiting to Exhale*, a character involved in a bitter divorce has a garage sale in which she sells all of her husband's belongings for $1 each, including his antique automobile. A woman I know loaded all of her husband's clothing into garbage bags and set them on the curb, then called him to say that either he or the trash collectors could pick them up before garbage day. Such things are no doubt tempting if your spouse has behaved badly. However, you really don't have the legal right to prohibit your spouse from entering the house or to dispose of his or her belongings unless a court has said so.

If your spouse has abused you, you can obtain a protection order (also called a restraining order) that legally requires your spouse to stay away. This process is usually quick and easy. Check with your attorney, a local shelter or hotline, or the police to learn your options. If you get a restraining order, be sure that your local law enforcement precinct or station has a copy and knows that you are worried about your safety. Many law enforcement officers will help you by providing safety tips, patrolling your neighborhood more often, or checking with you on a regular basis. Call and find out what is available.

Settlement or Trial?

Once discovery is completed, the parties generally create a full or partial settlement agreement. If they can agree on all the issues in the divorce, both lawyers (or a mediator) will work together to draft a settlement agreement. This will be incorporated into a final decree or order that will be approved and signed by the judge. If there are still issues that are disputed, a partial or "bifurcated" decree may be entered, with the court reserving the right to decide on the issues still in dispute. Most lawyers believe it is better to hold off on the final decree until all issues are resolved.

If necessary, a full trial or hearing will be held. The parties present evidence, including the testimony of witnesses and experts, and then the parties await the decision of the court. In most disputed cases, a judge will decide the outcome of a divorce action, but jury trials are still available in some states. Again, only about 10 percent of divorce cases go to court on *any* of the issues involved, with child custody the most common bone of contention.

Nearly everyone who has been involved in litigation, whether as a party, a witness, or a legal professional, agrees that settlement is almost always preferable to going to trial. When the people involved are able to work out their own agreement, they are much more likely to abide by its terms and to resolve any difficulties that come up later. A trial is always an uncomfortable and expensive event and can severely increase the discord between the people involved.

Sometimes people believe that if a settlement is not reached early in the negotiations, the situation is hopeless and a trial is inevitable. This is actually the opposite of how things work. Very often cases settle the day before a trial is scheduled to begin, or, quite literally, on the courthouse steps the morning of trial. As one prominent family attorney has stated, an imminent trial brings everybody as close to reasonableness as they ever get. The only way to reach this point, however, is to keep preparing diligently for trial with the assumption that the case is absolutely, undoubtedly going to court. Also, be aware that property settlements can rarely be changed once they are approved by the court and made a part of the final decree. Last-minute glitches in settlement agreements seem almost as common as eleventh-hour resolutions.

Once the couple reaches an agreement, all the papers can be filed at once; or, if the petition and answer have been filed, the settlement agreement is filed and an order incorporating its terms is presented to the judge. In some areas, there is no waiting period, and if the judge has time to review and approve the papers and sign the order, a divorce can be granted in less than a day. Other areas have waiting periods that may range from thirty days to six months. In some states, a divorce is not considered final until the time to appeal the decision has passed (usually one to three months).

Divorce by Default

If one party has disappeared, does not want the divorce, or, as in one case I handled, simply refuses to be involved in the process, the divorce can still be accomplished. All states have provisions in their laws for "default" judgments against a party in a lawsuit who cannot be located or will not cooperate in the legal process. This usually involves proving that the person was properly served with process according to state requirements; showing that additional attempts were made to contact the person by the other party or his or her attorney; filing affidavits or other papers to show that the court record has been properly maintained and the person is not unreachable due to military service; and allowing a reasonable passage of time to show that the person had a fair opportunity under the law to enter an appearance had he or she wanted to do so. Any default judgment can be overturned later if the person comes to court within a specified period of time and proves that the case was not handled according to the rules. Once the time to challenge has passed, however, a carefully crafted default decree is every bit as binding as a decree in which both parties appeared in court.

Letting the Judge Decide

Often, if a couple cannot reach an agreement with respect to one or more issues, they will declare an impasse and leave it to the judge to decide how to resolve the dilemma. As a general rule, those who take this route should remember two things: First, judges do not like to be given this responsibility; and second, the decision of the judge may not make anyone happy.

Furthermore, even in a fault-based divorce, the courtroom is no longer considered a forum for vindication of wrongdoing. Judges have neither the desire nor the duty to take half a day of court time to hear about how Jane wants the condo in Aspen because little Joey was conceived there, or that John shouldn't have it because that was where he started his affair with Tiffany which led to this mess in the first place. This doesn't mean the judge does not care or is unsympathetic to the human feelings involved. But a judge is not a counselor, and his or her job is limited to making sure the property is divided fairly and legally and that support and custody issues are fairly resolved. In such cases, neither Jane nor John will get the condo—it will be ordered sold, and the proceeds divided between the couple. So it's far better to try, if at all possible, to work out an arrangement everyone can live with, whether on your own, through attorney negotiations, or with the help of a mediator.

If you find you must take your case to court, be sure you have discussed with your attorney in detail what to expect and what your role will be. In many cases, the judge will request a pretrial conference to narrow down which issues will go to trial. The lawyers will often prepare a pretrial report or a pretrial order. This is a written summary of what is at stake in the case, what has been resolved, and what factual and legal issues will be raised at trial. Informal hearings before the judge may be held on matters such as interim support at any stage of the proceedings.

If you actually do go to trial, the process is reasonably standard in most courts, although some procedures and the degree of formality may vary. Jury trials are rare in divorce cases. Generally, the attorneys will give opening statements, and the plaintiff will put on witnesses, introduce evidence, and present his or her case, followed by the defendant. The plaintiff may then present a rebuttal. The defendant may also present what is called a surrebuttal. Finally, the parties present their closing arguments. The judge may request memoranda or briefs to be filed before or after the trial on legal issues. It may take the judge some time, generally not more than a couple of months, to decide the outcome and enter an order that divides property, sets custody and support, and states any other rights and responsibilities of each party.

If your case must go to trial, remember that you are there to make a favorable impression on the judge and to sell both your case and yourself. Dress in a neat and reasonably businesslike manner. Avoid extremes in appearance or behavior. Force yourself to remain calm, speak clearly, and if you don't understand a question, say so rather than try to answer it. Testify truthfully and accurately, and don't offer information beyond the question asked. If you believe that something needs to be explained and you weren't given the opportunity to do so, ask to confer with your attorney.

Prepare and rehearse with your attorney before you take the witness stand. Get some idea of what to expect. Be sure to share all relevant information with your attorney, including things that could be embarrassing or damaging. Remember, your attorney has a duty to keep this information confidential. It can be devastating if the other side somehow learns of something detrimental and your attorney is not prepared to handle it. The court is not the place to seek vengeance against the ex. Keep your emotions in check, and don't refer to "that bastard" or "that slut." Strive to project an image of dignity at all times, and stay on the high road if the opposing attorney tries to shake you during cross-examination. Sometimes unethical attorneys will try to make a witness appear hysterical. Don't give them the satisfaction, and keep your cool at all times.

Divorce trials are never pleasant, but they need not be traumatic. Thorough preparation and practice with your attorney will give you the confidence and skills you need to present your case in the best manner possible.

GENERAL CAUTIONS REGARDING THE LEGAL SYSTEM

The legal process can be exceedingly treacherous. While it is safe to say that most judges, social workers, psychologists, and others involved in family law are honest, dedicated professionals, far too many abuses still happen. Stories of inequity, incompetence, and sexism abound. In short, the quality of justice varies greatly depending on the location and the people involved. Even judges who are trying to do their best by those who appear before them often issue orders that turn out to be detrimental to one or all of the parties involved, simply because they don't see any other option or are too weary to take the time to find a better way.

Also, divorce cases tend to have an inappropriate reputation, especially among new lawyers, as "easy." Even a divorce that seems to be perfectly simple, with no major disputes over property or custody at the outset, can escalate into a battle that may drag on for years and require substantial legal expertise before it can be resolved. I once took a case that was supposedly uncontested. Only one piece of property, an antique buffet, remained in dispute. Not only did the couple fail to reach any agreement as to who would get the buffet, they began questioning property they had already divided up. Then one person decided the child custody arrangement wasn't satisfactory after all. In the end, the whole thing blew up and spiraled out of control. The case dragged on for months and took several mediators, appraisers, lawyers, and judges to bring it to a final resolution.

The adversarial system often seems to get in the way of what could otherwise be a relatively painless divorce. "As amenable as you go in, it becomes adversarial," says one man who still recalls the pain of a divorce that turned into a bitter battle over property and child support.

His relationship with his ex-wife is still acrimonious some twelve years later. "In my case, the lawyers made it a lot worse," he explains. "My wife initiated the divorce, although I thought we still had a chance to save the marriage and wanted to try and work things out. She was making good money, but I still had to pay all of the legal fees. The fact is, good guys do get screwed. A lot of men really don't get a fair shake. I've always paid my child support, plus provided my daughters with a lot of extras on my own. I've also paid half of their college tuition. Yet she kept taking me back to court and trying to get more and more even though her career was successful and her income kept going up, and she remarried a man who makes good money, too. The legal system helped her greed and exploitation."

By its very nature, the legal system is subject to manipulation and misuse by those who wish to use it as a weapon against their spouse. And unfortunately, some unscrupulous lawyers deliberately prolong the process to run up fees. As a lawyer, I shudder to think of some of the abuses I have seen. I have met some of the finest human beings I have ever known in this profession, as well as some of the most loathsome and contemptible rats. While I am happy to say that the vast, vast majority of the lawyers I know are good, decent people, there still are a few sleazeballs out there waiting to exploit any available target.

A client facing divorce is emotionally vulnerable and must necessarily lay bare to the lawyer the details of his or her private life and finances. For this reason, people facing divorce make easy prey for crooked lawyers. This does not mean that a client seeking a lawyer to handle a divorce should be overly paranoid. As in any profession, there are a few bad apples, but just how many may be exaggerated. The tabloids, as well as the more respected media, tend to jump on any story full of lurid details of cheating, conniving, and love gone wrong. Stories of abuses by divorce lawyers make juicy copy and hit the headlines far more often than any mention of the vast majority of good lawyers who are working hard to get their clients a fair shake.

Yet women are especially at risk when an unethical attorney is involved. The expense and trauma of litigation may be used to pressure a woman to accept a settlement that is blatantly unfair. Some studies indicate that women, on the average, receive between 25 and 40 percent of the joint assets in most divorces, as opposed to the 50 percent that is presumed to be equitable.

Also, many of the principles that are supposed to be followed under the law in fact are not, when the case comes before a judge who does not choose to do so. For example, women are supposed to be compensated for the value of homemaking skills and nonmonetary contributions to the family, or the time and effort put forth in supporting the family while the husband earned a professional degree. In some cases, these matters get pushed aside and glossed over. In others, truly evil practices exist. For example, unethical litigators may attempt to portray an opposing party who seeks therapy to recover from the effects of the divorce as "crazy." Others allow or even encourage perjury by a client.

Of course, penalties exist for these behaviors if they can be proven, but this is relatively rare. Judges are often reluctant to draw the line between "zealous advocacy" and violations of court and professional rules. Judges often express frustration when the classic "swearing match" goes on in the courtroom. It is often difficult to tell, in an emotionally charged arena, which person is lying and which is telling the truth. And there still are a few judges out there who simply don't give a damn. Unbelievably, some judges still buy into sexist stereotypes and believe that women need less money than men. For example, some reason that women will eventually remarry a man who will support them. Others feel that a man will need to eat out and hire housekeeping help, whereas a woman will not. Sexism is especially ugly in child custody cases—discussed in chapter 6—and it works both ways.

Does this mean that nothing can be done, that everyone involved in a divorce is simply at the mercy of the legal system and the courts? Absolutely not. Every state has a lawyer disciplinary board and a judicial review board, which can hear complaints against unscrupulous lawyers and judges. More and more states are amending their codes of conduct for lawyers and judges to prohibit sexist behavior and provide more effective penalties for those who violate the codes of conduct. Some courts, overburdened by frivolous and unnecessary litigation, are starting to crack down on those who abuse the process for purposes of harassment or delay. A growing number of private organizations are sprouting up to assist those who are victimized by the legal process. People who band together with others who were treated unfairly can and do get results.

APPEALS

A person who believes the court decided a case in a way that was legally impermissible may appeal that case for review by a higher court. In cases based on state law, this generally means the state Court of Appeals or the state Supreme Court. It is the job of the appellate court to review the decision of the lower court and determine whether the decision was made on the basis of a legal error, whether the decision was not supported by adequate evidence, or whether the judge went outside the boundaries of his or her discretion. Different standards are applied depending on the type of case and the nature of the challenge.

In matrimonial cases, an appeal is often brought not so much because a party genuinely believes that the wrong decision was made, but to try to leverage a settlement with better terms than those set out by the lower court. Appeals are costly and time consuming, so a person who received a generous award by the lower court may be willing to give some of it up in order to bring the matter to an end and avoid what may be greater expense and frustration in the long run. If an appeal is truly frivolous and obviously brought for improper reasons, sanctions can be imposed.

A legitimate appeal is well worth the effort when the lower court made a mistake or a bad decision. In addition to righting a wrong in an individual case, an appeal may result in a reported decision from the higher court, which sets a precedent—a binding legal rule that must be followed by lower courts in the jurisdiction. This is how much of the development, clarification, and evolution in the law takes place.

MEDIATION
AND LITIGATION

How They Work

MEDIATION

Mediation has become a popular alternative for divorcing couples who can't reach a complete agreement on their own yet want to avoid the time, trauma, and cost of a court battle. Here, the couple meets with one or two mediators, who serve as a neutral third party or team to guide and assist settlement negotiations. Mediators point out available alternatives and work with a couple to forge an amicable solution to their remaining problems. Many believe this team approach, which usually combines an attorney and a therapist, provides the most balanced method.

One main goal of mediation is to turn a couple who are at odds with each other into a team capable of working together to solve a mutual problem. In addition to helping couples resolve the immediate problems of the divorce, mediation teaches cooperative skills that can remain useful in subsequent years if new issues arise.

Some view mediators and lawyers as an "either/or" choice. In many cases, it is best to involve both. However, if the couple sincerely wishes to resolve their differences on an egalitarian basis, and the balance of power between them is reasonably equal so that neither requires a personal advocate, a final settlement can be achieved through mediation alone. Just as lawyers may refer couples to mediation, mediators may also suggest lawyers get involved when necessary. Many recommend that the couple's lawyers review the final documents before they are filed.

Most lawyers favor mediation in appropriate cases. Attorney Judith Finfrock is a strong supporter of mediation for numerous reasons. "Sometimes the party who is at fault, especially when it is the man, feels that no one is listening to his side. In mediation, everyone gets to be heard, and this is what these people need. Once they've had their say, they can get down to the business of settling things."

Choosing a good mediator can be tricky. Most states do not have well defined requirements for mediator training and qualification, so almost anyone can call himself or herself a mediator and set up a business. As with lawyers, some mediators specialize in family issues, while others handle a wide range of disputes. Even within the area of family mediation, there are subspecialties: Some mediators focus on custody issues, some deal with property and support, and others specialize in long-term financial planning.

Mediator and attorney Roberta Beyer recommends finding a mediator through referrals from attorneys, counselors, clergy, and friends, or simply starting with the telephone directory. She urges potential clients to ask mediators specific questions before making a final choice. "Ask about educational background, work experience, and training. Since there is no certification or licensing procedure, a forty-hour course is the only formal training required to join the professional organizations, and one crash course is not enough to make someone qualified without an appropriate professional background," she says.

If you are considering one mediator rather than a team, and that person is a mental health professional, ask how the legal issues will be reviewed. Does the mediator have special training, or refer those matters to a lawyer? Also, ask the mediator if he or she is a member of any professional organization, how many years of experience or cases he or she has mediated, and whether his or her practice is primarily devoted to mediation or an adjunct to another profession. Finally, be sure to ask about cost, payment arrangements, scheduling, and other nuts–and–bolts information.

One essential component of a successful mediation, or any successful negotiation for that matter, is a willingness by both parties to compromise. Realize, too, that a settlement of all issues seldom happens overnight. It may take extensive and continued negotiation, whether the process is handled by the spouses themselves, lawyers, mediators, or some combination. Perseverance pays off, though. Ninety percent of divorces today eventually result in negotiated settlements.

Roberta Beyer practiced family law for more than ten years before devoting her efforts to mediation. "Early on, I realized that the adversarial way of trying to resolve family disputes was also the worst way," she says. "It was centered on blame and fault. Plus, it was oriented toward the past. Even after the no-fault grounds became the most common basis for divorce, there was still an emphasis on fault, for example, in custody disputes. People focused on the worst in the other partner to their own advantage. Fault always managed to creep back in."

In 1987, Beyer attended a seminar on mediation. "That was it—I decided that this was what I wanted to do. There were only three or four mediators in Albuquerque then, so when I got my training and started out, mediation was still fairly unusual."

Beyer loved her work from the start. "I felt that I was finally using my law degree in a productive way. It is so gratifying to me to help people work things out rather than take sides in a battle. There are tremendous differences in what the two systems involve."

When Beyer began mediating, she worked alone. Now, she teams with a psychologist. "As a team, we can address all of the issues that need immediate attention," she explains. "When counselors or psychologists mediate alone, they are usually good with the parenting issues but have trouble with the legal aspects of the property, tax, and debt issues.

"I have reviewed mediation agreements prepared by psychologists for their legal accuracy, and I've seen some that are a real mess," she continues. "I have had to undo what the mediator did, and sometimes that would ruin the agreement. I began to wonder why attorneys weren't doing more mediation. But when attorneys mediate by themselves, we aren't able to deal with all of the underlying issues besides the legal problems. I've been working with a great psychologist in a team approach for four or five years now. I help the couple with the legal matters, while my partner helps them deal with communication and the emotion issues."

Psychologist and mediator Stephen Feher, Ph.D., has worked both with a lawyer partner and alone, in which case he refers clients to family attorneys if they are not yet legally represented. He has also worked in court–annexed programs as a settlement facilitator in partnership with a lawyer or judge. Feher prefers to team with a female attorney in mediation. "A gender-balanced team has certain advantages. Sometimes with two men or two women, the partner of the opposite sex feels they have three men or three women ganging up on them," he explains.

Beyer believes full–service mediation is important. She has found that the inability to address all the issues to be resolved has been a problem in many of the court–annexed mediation programs. "In our community, the court clinic deals with child custody and visitation issues only. Yet everything spills over so much. Property, custody, and support are tied together," she remarks. "The mediators should be able to help the partners resolve all of their conflicts, because this is so important for the children. Studies on children in families going through a divorce show that one of the most important concerns for the children is that the parents not remain in conflict. That's one main reason it was important to me to be able to offer a full–service, therapeutic style of mediation. When people divorce, they remain parents, and they have to be able to parent together. We help them work on restructuring their relationship so communication between them will be positive after the divorce."

Like many professionals working in various areas of the

divorce field, Beyer emphasizes the importance of teaching communication skills. "Some couples who come in for mediation wouldn't be divorcing now if they had learned to communicate earlier. Ironically, some reconcile and build a better relationship through their attempt to mediate a divorce. But for the most part, they are here because one or both have decided that divorce is the appropriate action. We help them learn a positive way to interact in the type of relationship they have now, and prepare them for better communication in subsequent relationships with others."

Communication is an important part of forging a sound legal agreement as well. As Beyer emphasizes, "If we don't help the couple deal with the underlying issues, the agreement is likely to fall apart later on. If they can't communicate, problems are inevitable, especially when child custody is involved. The mediation process itself tends to make for stronger agreements that are more likely to stand the test of time than court-ordered settlements. People are happier when they make their own agreements. Compliance rates in mediation agreements are much higher statistically. When you get the emotional issues aired, it keeps the settlement in perspective."

Mediation is not limited to divorcing couples. It may also be used to help both straight and gay couples who have lived together in a long-term cohabitation come to an agreeable settlement at the end of a relationship. Mediation is also helpful during the years after a divorce, especially when disputes over children occur or the necessity to change a custody or support order arises.

"We did one that was really exciting, really different," says Beyer. "A couple had been divorced for twelve years, and their sixteen-year-old child was falling apart. The mother and father, along with their new spouses, came to the mediation along with the child. The first session was rough, with a lot of anger and raising of voices. But after four or five sessions everyone left hugging each other, and most important, the sixteen-year-old had turned around. It made such a difference that they could finally come out with the resentment and anger that had been sitting there for twelve years."

One key to Beyer's successful mediation practice is the approach of her partner, Beth Erickson, Ph.D., a marital and family therapist. "Beth practices systems therapy, in which the couple and the family is viewed as a system, and she studies the dynamics between the individuals."

Although she finds the team approach preferable in her own practice, Beyer notes that there are some very good mediators who do it alone. "Many mediators do a great job on their own, as long as they are able to deal with all of the issues. Therapeutic mediation is good in any case. We have to realize that when a couple is stuck over Grandma's piano, the piano is not what's at issue. Property often becomes a symbol of emotional issues."

Beyer believes this attention to emotional matters is crucial to the overall mediation endeavor. "The process of divorcing is tough and scary for the people involved. Our goal is to move them into a good, civil, positive business relationship."

Beyer also points out some important controversies in the mediation field. "There is a mistaken notion that mediation can only work when a couple is already in a civil relationship with an equal balance of power. In fact, the people in high conflict are the ones who really need our help. True, if there is a power imbalance along with an unskilled mediator, bad results can occur. A good mediation team's job is to balance the power. Mediation itself is empowering. If a person with no power in a relationship goes to an attorney and simply hands over her problem, this doesn't help her at all. With good mediation there is learning, and the person becomes a part of the decision-making process. We work very carefully when the balance of power is unequal. If we see one person being rolled over, we try to urge the other to be more fair. However, if they can't reach a fair agreement, and we see that one partner is trying to bully the other, we have the right to terminate the mediation and send them to attorneys. We have a moral and ethical obligation to see that any agreement we help a couple reach is fair to both partners and fair to the children."

There is a raging controversy as to whether mediation can ever work when a relationship has been violent. Beyer remarks, "It can work with highly skilled mediators *if* there is no current physical abuse, if clear boundaries can be set, *and* if both partners are in counseling. First and foremost, the process must be safe. Unless both people are seeing therapists and willing to set trustworthy limits, such as having no contact with each other outside the mediation, then mediation is not appropriate."

She adds that there are other instances in which mediation should not be recommended. "Successful mediation requires honesty," she states. "If one person is hiding assets or lying, it won't work. The couple needs to go into court and use the formal discovery process."

Likewise, mediation is inappropriate if one spouse has been involved in any criminal financial transactions. "That makes it too complicated—the attorneys need to handle all the issues involved," she says.

Beyer and her partner can generally tell if one of the partners is not being honest. "We can usually ferret out what is being hidden or explain why it will come back to haunt them later if they are dishonest. This is seldom a problem. Most of the people who come here want an amicable, civilized divorce. We really have few cases in which the people are violent or dishonest."

Mediation may also be inappropriate, according to Beyer, when the mediator has had a prior relationship with either spouse. "If an attorney has represented one, or a therapist has counseled one, there may be a lack of impartiality. Also, a mediator wears a different hat than a lawyer or counselor, even though many professionals do both types of work. The client may want to see the person again in the other capacity, and it can get very confusing."

She also emphasizes that people often look at things from a different viewpoint after the divorce. "If there is any possibility of partiality by the mediator, a client may not view it as a problem during the process, but could look back six months later and feel troubled. If the mediator has worked only with both parties in the other capacity, it might be okay. But it's still risky."

Mediation is generally far less expensive than trying to reach a settlement through litigation. "Mediation usually costs about one-third of what it costs to go to two attorneys, even if the relationship is not adversarial and no court action will be required. If the case does go to trial, the figure would be closer to one-tenth," Beyer explains. "I've done over 200 mediations, and I've rarely seen the process exceed $3,000 for both people. We charge $155 an hour for a couple to work with our team of two mediators, and we usually get things settled much more quickly than in the traditional legal process. The sessions run two hours each, and we only charge for the time actually used, so if a couple only stays for an hour, that's what they are billed for. Most finish in four to six sessions. A divorce can be a financial nightmare, and nobody plans for that cost in their budget."

Like most mediators, Beyer believes that attorneys should retain some involvement in a mediated divorce. "As mediators, we try to take care of everything and get the parties to draft a complete settlement agreement. But we advise them to get separate attorneys to do the final draft on the documents, or at least eyeball what was drafted here. Also, a mediator is not an advocate. It's important to have an attorney who represents each person take a look at the documents and advise the individuals on anything they have questions about so they feel secure with the agreement. We recommend couples not to consider the agreement final until an attorney has reviewed it and they have taken time to mull it over on their own. Typically, one person is in great haste to get the divorce completed, while the other is not," she observes.

"Divorce law has become so complex, in many ways it's like medicine. When there are complicated assets, we advise a couple to see an attorney specialist to review the agreement and make sure everything is sound, such as when there are complex pension issues," Beyer adds. "As a family law attorney, I'm capable of dealing with most of the matters that come up. But I wear a different hat as a mediator. In a typical case, 90 percent of the work to complete the divorce documents will be done here, and the rest will be executed by an attorney for a relatively small amount of money, generally $500 to $1,000, depending on the complexity of the case."

The mediation process varies according to the people involved and the nature of the matters to be settled, but a fairly standard process is followed in most cases. "The appointments are scheduled for two hours, which is generally just about right," Beyer explains. "We try to meet every week to keep the momentum going, but may have to wait longer between meetings if the couple needs appraisals of property or must deal with other matters. Most couples come to as many sessions as it takes to agree. Some come to one session and then work out an agreement on their own. We are always happy to work ourselves out of a job. We're successful in getting an agreement on all or most issues in 80 to 90 percent of our cases."

Although the mediation process is informally structured, special techniques are available to address specific problems. "Sometimes we use caucusing, in which we spend time with each person alone," Beyer says. "Sometimes we have to cajole people, sometimes we have to threaten to end the mediation. We use a particular technique when an impasse is threatened. We tell the people that the mediation isn't working, that they need to just give it up and go see their attorneys. Sometimes this gets them going, and they start working harder to try and settle their differences. We put the responsibility back on them.

"We do a lot of different things. The bottom line is that it has to be a process that works for both parties and culminates in a fair agreement. If one party insists on an agreement we do not feel is fair, we will terminate the mediation. Sometimes both will want an agreement that we think is one-sided or won't stand up to the test of time. In that case, we may indicate in writing that the mediators are not in concurrence with the couple's agreement; for example, when they decide to split up siblings and have one child live in the mother's home and one in the father's home, without getting any professional opinion that this is best for the children. Our note on the agreement sends up a red flag for the attorneys or the judge."

Beyer is pleased to report that such occurrences are rare. "We have a pretty good success rate in talking everything out. There are many ways to deal with the controversies that come up, and people do tend to make agreements out of fear. Working with Beth makes all the difference. She can get to the root of it and show the individual making the decision that he or she is agreeing to something inadvisable because he or she is afraid. It's like informed consent."

As mediation has become more common, Beyer's clients come from many sources. "We have a brochure we distribute, and we get a lot of referrals from attorneys, therapists, and especially from satisfied former clients. We work closely with the other professionals. Sometimes I tell people to talk to an attorney before we start mediation, when they have a fundamental misunderstanding of the law or no clue as to what their rights are. This happens most often in the alimony arena. There is a lot of bad information out there." Beyer also recommends certain books to her clients and is considering starting a second business: publishing a catalog of divorce-related books. She has also developed and published a coloring calendar for kids called "My Two Homes." The calendar includes stickers to mark special days, so children can keep track of time-sharing schedules in an upbeat and positive way.

Mediation is steadily gaining in popularity, and it does have many advantages in addition to saving money. People tend to be more creative and open-minded in the context of a mediation than in court. Both partners participate in building the agreement and develop better communication as part of the process. It tends to be less traumatic for adults and children alike and greatly increases the ability to carry out the terms of the voluntary settlement and to resolve any problems that come up in the future.

SUCCESSFUL LITIGATION

Kathleen Robertson has practiced exclusively in the area of domestic relations law, first at a large law firm and more recently as a sole practitioner. She urges those facing a divorce to work with an attorney who is a specialist in the family law field. "There are a lot of lawyers who just dabble in domestic relations work, and they are at a disadvantage," she explains. "Historically, the area of family law has been looked down upon. Male attorneys especially didn't like to practice in that area because you don't get a lot of glory or big money, and it's a very emotional environment. But family law has become extremely complicated. Today, people are beginning to recognize it as a more highly specialized and respected field of practice."

Like many professionals, Robertson suggests that those seeking a divorce attorney should ask friends for recommendations. She also suggests using bar association referral services, and checking to learn which attorneys are registered specialists in the field—although she quickly adds that many good family attorneys are not registered as specialists. She also urges people contemplating a divorce to educate themselves on the process. "Here in New Mexico there is a program put on by the bar association called 'Today's Law School,' which conducts classes to provide the public with information on different legal problems they face. People who are divorcing need to learn about community property issues, how to be a good consumer, and how to stay on top of things during the process." Similar programs are offered throughout the country, and are becoming more available.

In working with an attorney, Robertson advises clients to ask a lot of questions. "Be sure you get a representation letter that is detailed, that outlines what you can expect in the way of fees and other matters. Contingency fees are not allowed in divorce actions; in New Mexico there is a statute prohibiting them. I always talk to the client about the fees and other information as soon as we have agreed I will take his or her case. I also give an information questionnaire to every client, then I set up a consultation, in which we discuss all of the issues involved in their case in detail. I give them an overview of what issues are black and white, what issues fall into gray areas that don't have a predictable outcome, and the steps we will go through in the divorce process. It's important that the client and attorney work with each other and that both have realistic expectations. Some clients are looking for a 'mad dog' attorney to punish their spouse. I have to explain to them that this approach is bad for them, their kids, and the system."

Robertson counsels her clients on what to expect on a practical basis after divorce. "People often envision that they can maintain the same lifestyle after the divorce. I have to explain to them that this is not likely to happen. I don't have a magic wand to make it happen. All I can do is try to get them the best possible result under the law. I can't make the other side be reasonable or responsible if they won't do so."

Psychological counseling can benefit those going through a divorce. "I recommend therapy for almost all of my clients, if they're not already seeing someone," notes Robertson. "Nearly everyone divorcing has what I call 'situational schizophrenia.' There are some therapists who I know and respect, and I will personally recommend them."

She adds that it is often hard to draw the line between being supportive and meeting her professional obligations. "As a domestic relations attorney, I have to maintain a certain amount of objectivity and distance and not become too buddy–buddy with my clients. I can't let them start seeing me as Glinda, the Good Witch. If the attorney becomes too enmeshed in the client's personal life, he or she can't do a good job. We're not rescuers, we're advocates. Therefore, a client seeing a therapist is often better able to work with the attorney on legal issues, because the client doesn't expect the attorney to fill the role of therapist as well. Family lawyers still inevitably become more involved in their client's emotional lives than attorneys representing clients in other legal matters. Of course, you have to be empathetic with a client, because everyone is out of control during a divorce. Many clients seem to prefer female attorneys because women are seen as being more comfortable with emotional extremes."

Robertson believes that while boundaries must be drawn, the role of legal counselor remains an important part of the lawyer's job. "Especially in today's legal climate, it's important to have an attorney who will listen to the emotional reasons for the decisions being made by the client. For example, a person often has strong emotional ties to their home. An attorney must realize that while keeping the home may not be the most advisable financial decision for the person, it is his or her choice. I tell clients, 'This is *your* divorce.' I make sure they know any bad news up front and explain to them what their options are. But I make sure they understand that they have to be the one to make the decisions."

When a client does insist on making a decision that Robertson doesn't feel is in his or her best interest, she sends them a long letter documenting all the problems the person is likely to face as a result, with a reminder that he or she can't go back and change the decision later. "I tell them both directly and in a letter that the course of action is inadvisable, but they are entitled to make what I feel is a bad decision," she says.

Like most family attorneys, Robertson believes a settlement reached by the parties is always preferable to going to court. "It's best to limit the controversy, both in terms of dollars and emotions. Divorce is expensive, but there is a plus side to that, because the financial ceiling allows the battle to end at some point. The more economically sound decisions are usually the wiser ones anyway. For example, where people agree to split the cost of one expert witness, this not only saves their money, but the opinion of this person will have so much more weight with the court than two hired guns doing battle. A settlement may be reached after the neutral expert has made a report to both parties."

Robertson explains that the practical process of getting the divorce accomplished is the same in most cases. "First, I give clients the information questionnaire, which requires them to do some homework and get the necessary information and documents together. Then I have them bring in the information I need to draft the petition to get the divorce going. I then prepare a temporary domestic order, which is a document that must be filed under our local rules. It is a standard form that lists property and debts and requires that documents be exchanged between parties. Each party must file an affidavit, including proof of their income, rent or mortgage, fixed expenses, and full disclosure of assets so the court knows that nothing is being hidden. Next, I take care of any other interim relief that needs to be established, such as interim spousal or child support. Many clients don't realize that this interim relief is available. The interim order from the court outlines how fixed debts will be paid and who will pay what, so that the community's credit won't be hurt. Voluntary contributions, such as payments made into a 401K plan, usually stop during the interim period until the divorce is final."

The information questionnaire she provides her client covers issues not specifically dealt with in the interim order. "It also covers the client's personal history, work, education, and so on—everything I will need to put the case together. We look at the children's special needs and the emotional issues—who wants the divorce, why the client thinks it's happening, what he or she believes are likely to be sticky areas in reaching a settlement. If there are domestic violence issues, we must make these first priority and deal with them right away. I obtain a broad restraining order if there is any danger to the client or the children. The order may prohibit any contact at the children's school or preschool, the mother's work, and anywhere else they spend time. I also ask for a court-appointed psychological expert to assess the family immediately, and request that the abuser have only supervised visitation with the children until the expert has made an evaluation. We are fortunate in this community to have places where parents can bring children for supervised visitation without compromising one party's safety. In short, the first step is to get things stabilized," Robertson explains. "Violence and money are two big issues that have to be dealt with in interim matters. Then I can get to the nuts and bolts of the case. Whenever possible, I try to complete discovery informally. There are pros and cons to this, since informal discovery is not conducted under oath. But it costs a lot less, and the client usually knows whether the other party will be honest or not. It's a cost–benefit analysis."

Robertson favors a settlement in which assets can be traded off rather than liquidated, as long as the value can be accurately assessed and a fair settlement reached. "It's usually better to trade assets. For most couples, the two biggest assets are their house and their retirement plans. We have to look at the present–day value of each and also be sure we are trading apples for apples. I always try to retain one actuary to perform valuations on all retirement benefits requiring valuation, so that the same set of assumptions is used in appraising each asset. Again, it's best if one expert can be agreed upon by both sides."

An experienced family law attorney will also be familiar with ways to cut corners in cost without compromising a client's rights. "For real estate, I start with a market–value analysis, which a real estate agent will perform for free. If the couple can agree that the value is accurate, there may be no need to pay for a formal appraisal. Equity in the house can be determined by subtracting the mortgage balance from the agreed–upon value. Cost of sale and tax issues can be a problem if a house must be sold, and this must be analyzed on a case–by–case basis. I make sure the client knows what he or she will be facing in the way of direct costs, as well as indirect costs such as capital gains tax in the future. I work with CPAs in almost all cases."

It is far better for both the couple and their children if a couple can agree to a settlement on custody and support issues. As Robertson points out, "People must realize that what is in the best interest of the child is not necessarily what seems to be in the best interest of one of the parents. In this jurisdiction, we have a court clinic that will mediate contested custody issues. Some clients who wish to mediate other areas of disagreement find that private mediation is the route to take so that the entire case can be settled and an attorney can then prepare the final document. Attorneys may need to be involved throughout the mediation process, though. In order to effectively use mediation, both partners must be roughly equal in knowledge and balanced in power. One of the two parties usually has less knowledge and power and may not be functioning emotionally. This person needs an advocate. This doesn't mean the couple can't have a healthy divorce. But an advocate can give each party the baseline knowledge they need to make wise decisions. I believe mediation without attorneys only works when there is an equal playing field, and in practice this doesn't happen very often. One client brought me an agreement for my review that had been drafted after mediation. It took me a five-page letter pointing out everything in the agreement that was unfair. It was obvious that she was completely under the control of her husband. I learned that every asset he controlled had been grossly misrepresented in the mediation. She refused to sign the agreement and ultimately received a better settlement."

Robertson, herself a divorced mother, points out that big changes are happening rapidly in many areas of family law, including child support, another reason clients need a qualified family lawyer. "Many states are changing their laws to be more in line with the federal child support guidelines, with one schedule that recognizes that each parent has a duty to support the child. Also, many states now have laws specifically dealing with college tuition. I talk with my clients about the rights and responsibilities of being a parent. I try to help clients maintain the status quo for kids. Parents need to reach a custody agreement in which they acknowledge that neither will change the major areas of a child's life, such as their school, religion, or medical providers without the consent of the other parent."

She also warns that the statutory child support guidelines do not take into account extracurricular activity expenses or medical costs not covered by insurance. "I raise all of these issues and deal with them in separate paragraphs of the final order," she explains.

On the issue of spousal support, Robertson notes that while support may not be available in many cases, she always discusses it with her clients. "It's important to remind anxious clients that they may have long-term needs that they don't know about yet. For example, when someone who's been married forty years divorces, they may be unable to support themselves. Social Security benefits, spousal support, and retirement benefits must be reviewed and considered as sources of income. In New Mexico, we used to have to put something like an award of $1 a year in the decree to keep the issue of spousal support open. That way, spousal support wasn't waived forever. Fortunately, we don't have to go through this charade anymore. Our statutes were recently amended so that if someone has been married twenty years or longer, the court retains continuing jurisdiction to award support, even if it isn't awarded in the original decree. I look at every case as a potential spousal support case until I see that there is either no need or no ability by the other party to pay. Many women clients want to waive spousal support to avoid fighting with their spouses; however, divorced women are worse off financially after a divorce than divorced men. No client likes it when you tell them they are going to have to pay spousal support. More and more women are beginning to be ordered to pay support because they are earning so much money."

A domestic relations attorney must also remain familiar with other areas of the law in order to do a thorough job. "Other litigation areas often overlap," she explains. "Intentional infliction of emotional distress or other spousal tort claims may need to be pursued. Bankruptcy issues may arise. A good, creative attorney has to recognize and raise these issues. It's really complicated; you have to have so many areas of expertise to do this right."

Robertson urges clients to be candid with their attorney about any mistreatment of themselves or their children during the marriage. "Sometimes clients who are familiar with the no-fault system won't even bring up these issues. But they should.

For example, if there has been abuse, the attorney needs to know so that the client won't be sent to the court clinic for mediation with the abuser. Shuttle mediation, where the parties do not see each other and the mediator goes back and forth, is an alternative sometimes used in place of traditional mediation. Clients should be absolutely honest with their attorney about any emotional or physical abuse, intimidation, or threats. The cycle of violence often escalates during the divorce process," she says.

Because attorney's fees can be awarded differently in a family law case than in most cases, so that the party with higher earnings may be ordered by the court to pay attorneys' fees for both parties, each client must pay their own attorney and then receive reimbursement from the other party. "In a family law case fees often keep a lid on a battle that can go on forever. I'd rather see people keep their money and reach a solution that is reasonable, realistic, and as simple as possible."

Robertson also points out that a client who engages in obstructive or inappropriate behavior, which results in escalated legal fees, can be ordered to pay the other party's fees. She generally requires her clients to pay an advance to begin representation. Robertson cautions that it is often impossible to tell how much a divorce will cost. "It all depends on the other attorney, and whether the parties are going to be reasonable or unreasonable."

Robertson is often frustrated by divorcing parents whose views of the future are not realistic. "This is a big problem," she explains. "Clients sometimes fail to accept that they still have to be parents with their divorced spouses. They will have to communicate with each other. They get into this mind-set of 'my way or no way,' and emotions run rampant. It's sad, and it's way off the mark. Children need predictability and stability, and to be protected from the bad feelings between parents. Parents need to at least be neutral with one another when the children are present. When I draw up a parenting plan as part of the settlement agreement, I urge people to include a mediation clause. It generally states that if there is a problem involving the children, one parent will make a request to the other in writing. Then the other responds. If they can't reach an agreement, they will go to mediation. Going to court again should be the last resort."

Sometimes, Robertson finds that she must explain to a client that the law cannot fulfill his or her wishes. "Occasionally, I get a client who wants to prevent his or her ex from being around the kids—for example, because he has a girlfriend." She urges parents to remember that their divorce is from their spouse, not from their children. "You should be a role model for your children and show them how people treat and care for each other."

While Robertson believes that clients can do a lot of the preparation for divorce on their own, she feels that even divorce attorneys should not try to handle their own divorce. "I was divorced last year, and I could not have done it well on my own. I had no objectivity. I wasn't sure I could make my own decisions well, and I didn't want to negotiate with my husband's attorney. It helped me to see firsthand the emotional impact of a divorce: the fear, anxiety, loss of control. Now, when I talk to my clients, I have a better understanding of what they're going through."

She also draws on her personal experience to remind clients that divorce can have a positive outcome. "I was divorced from my first husband when I was very young and had a young child. The fear factor was much higher then. With hindsight, I can see it was a very positive step in my life. I experienced a lot of personal growth afterward. I learned who I was and who I wasn't, I went to college and graduate school, had a career in genetic engineering, then went on to law school. I found out that I could get emotional support from my own resources, and that I could live frugally. Years later, when I realized my second marriage was ending, I had a much different perspective, both as a divorce attorney and from my own life experience. I didn't want it to be a battle or emotionally devastating for either of us. It was also a very weighty decision that took a long time to make. We tried counseling, made a real effort to work it out. Yet once I saw we were going nowhere and made the decision to leave the marriage, I was anxious to get it done. I realized that this limbo period is very difficult for anyone going through a divorce."

SPECIAL
COMPLICATIONS

For one reason or another, many divorces cannot be concluded quickly and simply. When one or more complicating issues are involved, people need to be aware of the options and challenges they face, as well as potential pitfalls and sources of help.

THE VIOLENT MARRIAGE

It is estimated that as many as 25 percent of all women who initiate a divorce action are the victims of domestic violence. Ending an abusive marriage requires special handling and caution.

By "violent or abusive marriage," I am referring to a marriage in which one person routinely abuses the other physically, emotionally, sexually, or in a combination of ways. Violent marriages are almost always one-sided, based on one partner's attempt to establish complete control over the other. The dynamics are totally different from the mutually combative situation, in which the partners often "fight." Such marriages are characterized by constant arguments, but rarely deteriorate into physical brawls. If they do, they usually end quickly or improve rather than continue on a violent path. Relationships characterized by ongoing domestic violence are different, and the ending, while always desirable, must be handled in a different way than the conclusion of a healthy marriage.

When one spouse has abused the other, the rules of the game are inherently changed, because the people involved do not have equal bargaining power. The longer the marriage has lasted, the worse the problem will be. People who have suffered abuse over a period of years may have a severely distorted perspective of choices and reality. Many suffer from posttraumatic stress disorder and require professional help to rebuild a healthy, stable life. It is important to emphasize, however, that it is the abuser who is responsible for vicious, criminal behavior. The abuser is to blame—never the abused.

Of the victims of domestic violence, 95 percent are women. When one partner in a marriage abuses the other, his primary goal is to control her, and his secondary goal is to keep her from leaving him. When a marriage has been abusive, the most dangerous point in the relationship is often, ironically, the point at which it ends. More women are murdered by a husband or boyfriend when they try to leave the relationship than at any other time. For this reason, those divorcing an abusive partner should take special precautions from the day the decision to leave is made until the divorce is final, and even afterward. Many abusers keep trying to terrorize, cajole, or manipulate the other into returning, even after the divorce is final. Studies by the National Council on Stalking show that 50 to 75 percent of the women who leave men who have abused them are stalked afterward. Not surprisingly, children may also be in great danger at this time.

The abused wife should take special precautions for her physical safety, and be certain that those who know her whereabouts or other confidential information will not reveal it. Also, she may need the assistance of an advocate or other professional to use the legal remedies and social services available. Many court systems, shelters, and other agencies now employ advocates. A call to the local shelter, court, or state domestic violence coalition (all states now have one) can provide information on services in the area. These organizations can also help victims formulate a safety plan to help insure her security before, during, and after her separation from an abusive spouse. Family law attorneys should also be aware of the special services for abused spouses.

If a person has suffered injuries because of abuse, she may have a tort claim for personal injury that can be brought in conjunction with the divorce action. Any attorney representing a victim of domestic violence should be familiar with this option and how to use it. In addition, a permanent injunction or specifically tailored order should be made a part of the final decree, either prohibiting the abusive spouse from contacting the victim in any manner, or setting strict limits if child visitation is involved.

As discussed in chapter 3, mediation is generally inappropriate in cases where the marriage has been abusive, especially if the threat of violence remains. Successful mediation depends on two people with equal bargaining power who can reasonably consider their alternatives and reach a fair agreement. Where one partner has been consistently bullied and controlled by the other, this is usually not possible. The victim often agrees to unsatisfactory terms out of fear, intimidation, or a desire to get away from the abuser. Also, it is unfair to force her to spend the hours it takes to mediate an agreement in the presence of her batterer. In an abusive situation, it is usually far better—and often essential for the victim's safety—to restrict all offers and negotiations to communications between attorneys or other advocates. Some courts have mandatory mediation programs, but many make exceptions if the marriage was abusive. For those that don't automatically exclude people from violent marriages, an attorney, court advocate, or social service worker can intervene and convince the court that mediation is not appropriate.

Child custody and visitation must also be given special attention when a violent marriage ends. Most courts today place substantial weight on evidence of any abuse in the home in determining custody, although some are still stuck in the Dark

Ages and blame the victim for "allowing" the children to remain in a home where one parent beat the other. Incredibly, courts have been known to rule that even fathers who had murdered the mothers of their children were not necessarily unfit parents! For this reason, it is essential that the abused parent have sensitive, competent legal representation.

Most experts who work with children agree that growing up in an abusive home is one of the worst things that can happen to a child, whether they are abused directly or not. And it is estimated that almost all children in homes where one parent batters another are aware, at least on some level, of what is going on, and they suffer terribly for it. As stated by top divorce attorney Raoul Felder in Emily Couric's *The Divorce Lawyers* (see Resources), "When you hit a kid's mother, you are hitting a kid, you are doing damage to that kid. You can't really separate the two . . . the household is crazy by definition at that point. The law is not adequate to deal with crazy situations."

Felder says, and many agree, that spousal abuse alone should affect that parent's rights as a custodian of children. Many advocacy groups are now arguing that joint custody should never be awarded in cases where one parent was violent toward another. This makes sense, because those who abuse a child's parent have already demonstrated a lack of regard for the welfare of the child; and studies show that those who abuse a spouse often abuse children in the home as well.

In 1990, the U.S. Congress passed a resolution recommending that custody not be given to a parent who has abused his or her spouse, because doing so would be detrimental to the child. The resolution is persuasive, but it does not have the force of law. Judges still have broad discretion to make their own determinations about what is in the best interest of the children. Therefore, victims of domestic violence should be certain to inform their attorneys about the full history of abuse in the marriage, and request that a court-appointed or privately hired mental health professional be involved in custody decisions.

If the abusive spouse does get custodial or visitation rights, the option of supervised visitation and/or special provisions for the exchange of the child should be considered carefully. Some communities have come up with innovative solutions to these problems, such as centers where the parents can exchange the child without any contact, or locations such as the YMCA or YWCA that provide facilities for comfortable, subtly supervised visitation and recreation. Also, custody orders may be modified for good cause and can be changed later if the abuser convinces the court that he has stopped his criminal behavior, has sought treatment, and is committed to building a healthy relationship with the child.

An attorney handling the end of a violent marriage must be prepared to perform all the tasks essential for the client's safety. Attorney Judith Finfrock estimates that about 30 percent of the divorces she has handled involved domestic violence between the couple at some point. "In these cases, I also had to see that restraining orders were in place, and arrange for a mutual exchange of the children for visitation at a safe place so that the parents would not have to see each other. I will not hesitate to advise a mother to withhold visitation if she or her children are in danger," she says. "By doing so, I know I take a risk, because while most judges will agree that this is the right course of action if past violence can be proven, others hold visitation rights sacrosanct, and a lawyer can get in trouble for advising a client to go against them. But consider what's at stake."

It is becoming easier for a woman to have an abusive husband removed from the house. Unfortunately, the quality of justice battered women receive often depends on geography. Some communities have excellent programs in which anyone beaten by a spouse will be provided with assistance in obtaining a protection order; the abuser will be immediately arrested (and often given the alternative of staying away from the victim and attending a treatment program or going to jail) and prosecuted for his crimes; and police will even escort an abuser to the home, stand by while he gathers his belongings, and see that he leaves with a warning not to return.

This is the exception rather than the rule, unfortunately. In other areas, services range from piecemeal to nonexistent. On a more positive note, more and more communities are waking up to the horrible toll taken by domestic violence and are starting to treat it as a potentially deadly crime. As a part of their planning to make the break, victims of domestic violence are well advised to find out what services are available and how such cases are treated in their community. On the one hand, once an abuser is removed from the home, especially if he spends a night in jail and gets a clear message that his behavior is criminal and will not be tolerated, he may be convinced that it's time to shape up, stay away, or both. On the other hand, he may only become more enraged. Therefore, anyone who has been a victim of domestic violence should not let down her guard when the abuser is finally out of the home.

Every state now has a coalition against domestic violence. Check the government pages of your local telephone directory. Many have toll-free numbers as well as emergency hotlines. Some cities now have local groups as well, and special help is available in nearly all areas. Hotlines can refer you to shelters, support groups, and social service agencies. The National Domestic Violence Hotline is staffed twenty-four hours a day by trained counselors who provide crisis assistance and information about shelters, legal assistance, health care, and counseling. Its number is 1-800-799-7233 (SAFE) or for TDD, 1-800-787-3224. Local police, prosecutors offices, emergency medical personnel, the United Way, YWCA, and similar organizations can provide help or referrals. There are numerous books available for domestic violence victims including my *Domestic Violence Sourcebook* (see the Resources section at the back of this book).

For many women who have been abused, taking that first step toward a divorce can be tremendously empowering. Remember, however, that it is essential to establish a personal safety plan that covers in detail the periods before, during, and after your departure.

Child Abuse

Direct child abuse, while sometimes related to spousal abuse, also occurs in homes in which only the children are victims. Staggering numbers of children are victims of physical and/or sexual abuse in America. This crime often goes undetected, despite the ongoing public pressure to stop it and the presence of child protective agencies in every state. Today, not only do the laws make child abuse a crime and provide for state intervention where child abuse is present or suspected, but there are also laws requiring those who have close contact with children, such as doctors and teachers, to report suspected abuse.

In a divorce action, a parent seeking sole custody of a child who has been abused by the other parent should be able to take advantage of the many sources available to help protect the child's interest, often free of charge. Such resources include publicly employed psychologists, social workers, and child welfare advocates. A call to your local family services or child welfare agency can put you in touch with help. There are also special hotlines that provide information and referrals, and organizations working to prevent and stop child abuse (see appendix A).

The first thing victims of violence or the parent of an abused child should do when seeking a divorce is to locate an attorney familiar with the dynamics and dangers of family violence and make it clear to him or her that immediate assistance is needed. Provide your lawyer with detailed information about the abuse, and ask for help in familiarizing yourself with the available services in the community. Documentation is important, and records of medical treatment, social service intervention, reports of suspected abuse, and police involvement all may be crucial to the case. Be sure to share both formal records and informal recollections with your attorney. If you can't locate an appropriate lawyer on your own, ask for assistance through a local shelter, state or local coalition against domestic violence or child abuse, or domestic violence or child abuse hotline. If you have problems coping with the stress of dealing with children during your divorce, or believe you may have treated your children abusively in the past, it is *absolutely essential* that you get professional assistance immediately—both for the sake of your children and to protect your rights to custody and/or visitation. The appendix lists many organizations that can provide advice, information, and referrals to professionals in your area who can help.

Sadly, one parent will sometimes make false accusations of abuse, particularly sexual abuse, against the other in an attempt to gain sole custody of the child. Attorneys are faced with delicate problems when representing either a parent accusing the other or one accused of abuse, often in cases where there is no clear-cut evidence to either prove or disprove the charges. Today, continuing legal education programs are available to train family lawyers in assessing the merit of sexual abuse charges.

THE NO-FAULT SYSTEM AND THE DISPLACED HOMEMAKER

No-fault divorce has simplified the legal process and has undoubtedly made divorce an easier and more straightforward procedure for the couple composed of two mature, reasonable people who have amicably decided to end their marriage. However, the no-fault system has created great difficulty for some individuals, particularly for women who have been abused by their husbands or have spent many years out of the workforce as homemakers and mothers.

In her book *The Divorce Revolution*, Lenore Weitzman, Ph.D., characterizes the advent of no-fault divorce as having transformed the entire landscape of American family law in a mere decade. She echoes what is perhaps the most common criticism of no-fault divorce: namely, that for women and their minor children, it often leads to a sharp decline in the standard of living after a divorce, while men nearly always experience substantial economic improvement. "Why," she asks, "would a legal reform designed to create more equitable settlements end up impoverishing divorced women and their children?"

Weitzman believes the rules that seek to achieve "equality" have in fact the opposite effect by depriving a woman of the financial support she needs. "When the legal system treats men and women 'equally' at divorce, it ignores the very real economic inequalities that marriage creates. It also ignores the economic inequalities between men and women in a larger society." Overall, alimony is awarded in only 16–20 percent of divorce cases today.

Other experts echo Weitzman's concern. "The implementation of no-fault divorce by most states in the 1970s and 1980s is arguably one of the most important changes in women's work lives in this century," says Patricia Murphy, Ph.D., a vocational rehabilitation counselor and author who frequently testifies as an expert witness in divorce cases. The involvement of a vocational expert—who may be appointed by the court—can be essential to determining the amount, type, and duration of support that is necessary.

Murphy generally favors the concept of rehabilitative alimony, as it gives recognition to the damage caused to many women as workers, whether the marriage was abusive or not, in terms of the vocational impairment that inevitably occurs when a person spends a period of years out of the paying work world. "For example, one category of divorced women is the displaced homemaker," Murphy explains. "The status of these women is roughly equivalent to displaced male workers who lose their jobs when a factory closes. Both are in need of rehabilitation, such as career counseling, vocational evaluation, training/retraining, résumé development, and assistance finding job leads." The problem arises when the courts fail to recognize the reality faced by a woman entering the world of paying work outside the home after being absent from it for a number of years, or for some, never having been in that world at all.

The importance of recognizing the value of homemaking and child care activities also needs to be addressed. As Murphy says, "The inclusion of an actual dollar valuation of these activities in the divorce process will go a long way in identifying the homemaker as a worker, and, perhaps, in establishing a better set of facts for decisions about spousal support and the rehabilitation needs of each woman in the divorce process."

Murphy provides an example from a case in which she was involved as a vocational expert. Her first task is always to identify a client as a worker. In this case, Liz, a Utah woman, had worked primarily as an unpaid homemaker and mother. Although she had a degree in nursing, she had only a few months' work experience and had been a homemaker for twenty-five years. Her nursing license had expired, and she would need at least one year of college to bring these skills up to date, plus other licensing and registration requirements. Furthermore, she no longer had a desire or the ability to be in the nursing profession. Liz had been severely abused by her husband and had lost the vision in her left eye as a result, which precluded her from certain jobs, including nursing work.

After Liz and her husband separated, she held several low-paying jobs without benefits. The divorce left her confused and frightened about her vocational goals and future as a worker. Liz also suffered from post-traumatic stress disorder (PTSD), which, though often not recognized as a disabling condition, gave rise to personality traits such as fear, depression, guilt, passivity, and low self-esteem, which impacted her ability to work. Battered women often suffer from a particular form of PTSD known as battered woman syndrome (BWS). The diagnosis of BWS allowed Murphy to understand why Liz had been unable to move up vocationally, though she had been employed at a battered women's shelter and felt strongly committed to continue to provide a service to formerly battered women. However, she could not make more than $8 per hour at this work.

Murphy worked with Liz to analyze the various jobs that could help her fulfill her goals, raise her income, and develop new skills that would be transferrable to other settings in the future. Together they settled on a plan through which Liz could establish a carpet cleaning business and hire formerly battered women as employees. The flexibility of the business would allow her to take community college courses to develop more skills in small business management and related areas. She could also enroll in courses that would assist her in overcoming her low self-esteem and other impairments related to BWS.

Testimony by vocational experts is now being allowed by most courts on an individual's inability to participate in an occupation for which she has prepared. Awards in domestic tort actions can include not only economic damages, but also noneconomic or "hedonic" awards to help compensate the person for the loss of enjoyment of their life and the loss of career choices.

Murphy came up with several alternative approaches to calculating the support and compensation Liz should receive, including those that could not be developed as vocational rehabilitation plans, such as a return to nursing, and what she had lost as a result. Other approaches took into consideration the value of her services to the family, her projected earning abilities now (based on U.S. Department of Labor statistics), the cost of rehabilitation and psychotherapy services, and the cost to purchase the franchised carpet cleaning business and set it up, plus the cost of the recommended two-year community college program.

In the final analysis, Murphy was able to demonstrate that the total cost of the vocational rehabilitation plan to get Liz started in her chosen business made the most sense both economically and in terms of quality-of-life concerns for Liz. The damages she could reasonably have claimed through a domestic tort action were far greater than the cost of the rehabilitation plan. "These analyses offer Liz's attorney a powerful tool in both the no-fault divorce process and the domestic tort process," Murphy explains. "What is disallowed in the no-fault divorce process may be allowed in the domestic tort process." However, she cautions, it remains unclear whether psychological and/or physical injuries of abused women can be used in straight no-fault divorce cases. Therefore, she advises vocational experts to prepare no-fault divorce cases as if a domestic tort case will be filed, even if it may not be practical due to difficulty, time constraints, or remaining barriers in state law.

SPECIAL CONCERNS FOR MILITARY FAMILIES

Divorcing couples with one or both partners in the military service face special issues. Military retirement pay and related benefits acquired during the marriage are generally considered marital property, subject to division between divorcing spouses depending on state law and individual circumstances. These need to be handled carefully by a qualified attorney, who must be sure the appropriate government offices are notified if benefits are to be divided. Military pensions are discussed in greater detail in chapter 5.

Child custody and visitation can be especially tricky for military families, since people in the service do not have the same choices and control over where they will live or be sent as the civilian population. Furthermore, some military bases do not provide housing for family members. Therefore, anytime a military parent has full or joint custody of a child, these contingencies should be addressed in the decree.

PRENUPTIAL AGREEMENTS

Contrary to what many people believe, prenuptial agreements are not new, though their use has become more common in the last twenty years or so. They have existed since the turn of the century and came into regular use during the 1920s, when wealthy men wishing to marry younger "trophy wives" were afraid the young women might claim their fortunes upon the man's death or divorce. For the next fifty or sixty years, courts frequently refused to enforce such agreements as being against public policy. However, most judges today are prone to abide by the agreements, *if* they meet certain requirements, which tend to vary from state to state. Approximately fifteen states have now adopted some version of the Uniform Premarital Agreement Act, which sets out specific standards. Other states continue to rely on their own common law.

Prenuptial agreements (also called premarital agreements) are becoming more and more common as people marry later, second and third marriages become more common, and women more often enter marriage with substantial property or lucrative careers of their own. Many people favor premarital agreements as a sensible and practical way to deal with a fifty–fifty risk factor. Some compare them to a property settlement created when a couple is still in love. But these contracts are controversial. Some of the country's leading matrimonial lawyers believe no marriage should begin without one; others see them as nothing but trouble to be avoided at all costs. My own opinion falls in between these two extremes but is closer to that of the latter group for several reasons.

First, a premarital agreement inevitably carries the subtle suggestion that the couple does not expect the marriage to last. Consequently, one or both partners may go through the marriage under the shadow of a little dark cloud suggesting that there is a lack of trust, an absence of faith in the union. One lawyer who practiced family law for many years told me he has never seen a marriage subject to a prenuptial agreement that did not eventually end in divorce. It seems, too, that the agreement is almost always pushed on one spouse by the other. As a client of mine once said, "I couldn't believe it when he brought me this thing to sign two days before our wedding. It made me feel less of a woman." No matter how fair or thoughtfully worded, all prenuptial agreements seem to contain an element of coercion and the implied expectation of divorce.

Second, any legitimate aim of a premarital agreement can be accomplished by more traditional legal tools, such as wills, deeds, trusts, and various types of contracts. These tools, in addition to being free of the stigma of mistrust inherent in a prenuptial agreement, tend to be more stable and more efficient in accomplishing their goals. Some judges find premarital agreements distasteful and will look for any way (and there are many) to avoid enforcing their terms. Most of the same judges, however, are perfectly comfortable enforcing a will or deed. Another advantage to using more traditional devices is that they often provide tax benefits not available under prenuptial agreements.

Third, premarital agreements tend to be unstable, legally flimsy documents for other reasons. Couples often face unexpected events over the course of a marriage, and changed circumstances can affect the meaning and effect of this type of agreement. For example, I once worked on a divorce case in which a wealthy oil baron had prepared a premarital agreement for his wife to sign. It essentially stated that each would own their currently held property and all proceeds from it as separate property; any gifts from one to the other would become the recipient's separate property. During the ten years the marriage endured, circumstances changed drastically as oil prices dropped, and the man, at one point, feared his company might go bankrupt. At that time he transferred a large amount of money to his wife by giving her several certificates of deposit (CDs) as gifts. When he decided to leave her, the CDs were still in her name. Under the terms of the premarital agreement, they had changed, or "transmuted," into her separate property, according to the couple's intentions at the time of the transfers. Certainly this was a result he did not foresee or intend at the time he convinced her to sign the agreement.

The purpose of a premarital agreement is to spell out exactly what will happen to a couple's money and property during the marriage, if the relationship does in fact end, or if one partner dies. The main concern of courts in deciding whether or not an agreement should be enforced is whether it is fair in its terms and was openly entered into between people operating on equal footing. Courts commonly look at such criteria as whether each person had separate, independent legal advice; whether there was "duress," or pressure, by one person on the other to force him or her to sign; and, above all, whether there was full disclosure by each party of all of his or her assets and debts.

A prenuptial agreement may also be held invalid and unenforceable by the court if it is the product of "undue influence"; that is, if either the husband or wife dominated the other, who was weaker, had greater needs, or was in distress at the time the agreement was signed. Agreements that are very one-sided are inherently suspect, for example, one in which one person is a millionaire and the other, who has nothing, would receive nothing upon divorce. Those that are signed a very short time before the wedding are likewise disfavored. Vast differences in age, education, or experience between the couple will also raise questions. Ironically, people often sign premarital agreements—documents which inherently suggest a lack of trust—without reading them closely or obtaining independent legal advice because they love, trust, and believe in the person they are about to marry.

Because the character of property as separate or marital property may change depending on how the parties treat it, lax record keeping may also provide a basis for challenging a prenuptial agreement. Generally, property acquired during the marriage is presumed to be marital property. This means that the court will start with this assumption, and it will be up to the person stating that a particular item of property is separate to produce the evidence to prove that this is so. More than a premarital agreement stating general intentions may be necessary, especially where property has been mixed, transformed by sale and purchase, or otherwise changed.

It is important to remember that no one factor alone will usually be sufficient to convince a court that a premarital agreement should be disregarded, unless it is something very extreme (such as lying about assets), or the judge simply dislikes premarital agreements and will look for any reason to refuse to enforce one (of course, this could be challenged on appeal).

Sometimes part of an agreement will be unenforceable, but the rest will be allowed to stand. For example, premarital agreements cannot legally set limits on the amount of child support to be paid in the event of divorce, because public policy requires current law and family circumstances to be considered in this area. However, a court might delete the section of an agreement purporting to set child support and enforce the rest of it rather than toss out the whole thing. This is a common practice with any type of contract.

Premarital agreements are subject to attack by an opposing spouse on a wide range of grounds. If you are leaving a marriage that was governed by such an agreement, discuss these matters carefully with your attorney whether you favor the terms of the agreement or not. If there is the slightest hint that there was coercion when the agreement was signed or unfairness in its terms, many judges will simply invalidate the agreement and make their own decisions on property division.

DIVORCE IN LATER YEARS

Although divorce rates overall are far lower among people over age fifty, those who do divorce in their later years face special challenges. Divorce is difficult at any time in life, but it creates unique burdens for senior citizens. Older women who divorce often face serious financial hardship, especially if they spent the bulk of their married lives as homemakers. Aside from the difficulty of adjusting to a vastly different and unfamiliar way of living, older women seeking employment after divorce often face tremendous difficulty in finding an appropriate job.

Older men who divorce face a different set of problems. Those who were in traditional relationships in which the wife handled all the domestic chores often face considerable problems when they must learn to perform these tasks for themselves. Also, some psychologists believe that men suffer more from lack of companionship and family support after a divorce, especially in later years.

For both men and women, a divorce late in life is likely to cause confusion, loneliness, and difficulty in adjusting, especially if the marriage was one of long duration. Studies have found that it is more difficult for divorced elders to maintain their morale and optimism about the future. Human beings naturally become less flexible and open to change in later life, and older people have different physical and emotional requirements than younger people. The support of family members, particularly the children and grandchildren, can be a lifeline for divorcing elders, though it may be difficult for them, as well.

Yet even for people with plenty of loving family support and financial security, the effects of a divorce in later life are often devastating. The intense stress of a divorce can also cause physical, mental, and emotional problems for older people. People with medical problems such as high blood pressure or heart conditions can be especially vulnerable to such difficulties.

Attorney Judith Finfrock has handled numerous divorces between elderly clients. "These divorces were the absolute worst. Most of the clients I had were women, and they suffered so much pain. They never expected to be in this position at this stage of life. They thought they were going to be able to live out the rest of their lives with someone, and suddenly they find themselves alone, losing their security and companionship. It's heartbreaking."

Elderly people going through divorce may experience more severe emotional trauma than younger people. Much of this relates to the aging process, with its accompanying loss of strength, mobility, opportunity, and increased chance for illness. When the companionship and day-to-day assistance a couple has provided each other ends, each person must replace these essential needs with new support systems. It is more difficult, too, for elderly people to change the identities that they have grown comfortable with over the years, and harder for them to make new social connections. The alternatives in employment, recreation, and other opportunities open to elderly people depend on the unique circumstances of each individual and the community in which he or she lives. Older people may also be more subject to manipulation by unscrupulous people.

Spousal support and health insurance coverage are especially important considerations in elderly divorces, as are pension benefits and similar assets. Those divorcing later in life should get a lawyer familiar with the special needs of older clients, or one who will associate with a specialist in elder law.

As demographics shift and the number of people of retirement age grows, more attention is being paid to the special issues faced by divorcing elders. Organizations such as the American Association of Retired Persons offer support and information (see appendix A).

VIOLENCE IN THE COURTROOM

A shocking trend in America's divorce courts is the increased incidence of violence—often deadly violence—in family courtrooms. Most incidents of court security violations or outright violence occur in criminal trials, but the second most likely place for violence to erupt is in the emotionally charged atmosphere of the divorce court. Although there is little statistical evidence on courtroom violence, news reports suggest that severe violence, which is often deadly to parties, judges, lawyers, and bystanders, is on the rise in the family courts.

Several factors have been cited as contributing to the increased carnage. Again, placing family law in the arena of the adversarial system may make the process of divorce more frustrating and aggravating than it needs to be. Furthermore, family courts often deal with domestic abusers, who are frequently irrational and dangerous, particularly when a spouse they have sought to control through force is finally breaking free of them.

Of course, nonviolent, healthy people are not driven to murder each other simply because of stress brought on by a divorce. But as stated in a recent article in the *ABA Journal*, "Divorce, separation, and child custody disputes all tend to bring out the worst in people." Endless delays, exorbitant costs, and the sense that people have no control over their case all contribute to the frustration and anger couples already feel, especially in a bitter child custody dispute. Some professionals who regularly work with divorcing people believe that just about everybody caught up in a divorce is skating on thin emotional ice. Even the most stable individuals can be expected to suffer from the effects of grief and frustration. For those already prone to violence or mental disorders, the process may push them to the breaking point.

Many believe that the system itself must take part of the blame. Judge Kevin Burke, quoted in a 1993 article in the *ABA Journal*, said, "The system of divorce in this country is way out of step with reality." He explained that family court was created in an era when couples were expected to stay married for life, and divorce was relatively rare. Today, divorce has become extremely common, enormously expensive, and increasingly adversarial, with everyone fighting to "get even." Burke believes that even some of the positive changes in the system, such as looking for the best custodial parent rather than giving custody automatically to the mother, can have a downside. "It has raised the stakes and causes more disappointment for people," he said.

Overzealous lawyers are often blamed for fueling the battles between divorcing couples. However, lawyers can also fall victim to the violence of unstable clients. Statistics published by the American Bar Association indicate that more divorce lawyers have been injured by their clients than any other type of attorney.

Several solutions have been offered to this problem. More and more courthouses are installing metal detectors and scanners. Specially trained security personnel can also make a difference. Older courthouses typically had common areas where everyone involved in a case could mingle, but newer courthouses are starting to use designs that reduce encounters between those who may be hostile toward one another. Other recommendations include panic buttons to summon help and bulletproof benches for judges. Additionally, many lawyers are now insisting that clients who show signs of instability get professional help as a condition of representation. Many lawyers routinely recommend therapy to any client going through a divorce.

In Hennepin County, Minnesota, which includes the Minneapolis metropolitan area, the court is taking a two-level approach: first, instituting better security in the courtroom, and second, trying to reduce the anxiety and stress associated with family litigation. Efforts have included beefed up security to make the building weapon-free, and regular dialogues between judges and lawyers from various practice areas to discuss ideas and concerns about courtroom violence, with particular attention to the family court system.

The county, for many years a leader in the area of domestic violence intervention, has also established a program called Divorce with Dignity. Features of the program include active case management by the judge, with meetings, rules, regulation of the use of experts, and less litigation. The program's goal is faster, cheaper, and less acrimonious divorce. Couples are required to use one neutral appraiser—appointed by the judge—to set the value of a house rather than having two appraisals from opposing parties.

Members of the judiciary have begun to take a leadership role in looking at what changes are needed in family law, especially in examining whether the traditional adversarial system is designed and equipped to resolve family disputes. Also, there is greater emphasis on taking only the portion of the case to court which truly needs to be litigated, rather than rehashing the entire case. "In my state, 98 percent of the cases are settled," said Judge Burke. "The problem is that the way to prevent litigation is to prepare for trial. We need instead to prepare for settlement."

Burke emphasized that full disclosure of assets should be routine, and inflammatory pretrial motions avoided. Speaking a sentiment echoed by many judges, he emphasized that people must understand that if children are involved, the parents can never completely separate from each other and will have to deal with each other for a long time after the divorce. Burke, who worked on both criminal and family law cases when he was a private attorney, summed up the problem surrounding violence in family court when he remarked, "I found it easier to represent someone who killed a spouse rather than someone who wanted to divorce one."

DIVORCE
AND PROPERTY

Under today's system of no-fault divorce, the major issues to be decided in a divorce include the classification, valuation, and distribution of property; spousal and/or child support; and child custody and visitation. Children's issues are discussed in chapter 6. In this chapter, I hope to provide an overview of common legal concerns and how the law works in relation to property and support issues.

LEGAL PROPERTY SYSTEMS TODAY

There are two systems of property ownership recognized for divorce purposes in the United States. Eight states follow the community property system, with its roots in Spanish law, whereas the others use a system known as common law, or marital property.

Although the two systems have important differences, the distinctions have lessened in recent years. To simplify the issue as much as possible, I will refer to "marital property" to identify the property considered to be owned jointly by both parties under either system. Bear in mind that such property is identified by different labels in different states. Likewise, "separate property" refers to property solely owned by either spouse that does not need to be divided upon divorce because ownership is already established.

Formerly, some states divided property according to title rules, which provided that any property held in the name of one spouse or the other was separate property and belonged to him or her alone, so it could not be divided by the court. All states except Mississippi have now abolished these title rules.

While community property states start with the assumption that marital property (called community property in these states) will be divided fifty–fifty between the couple, in practice the division is seldom precisely equal. In common law states, courts are supposed to apply equitable distribution standards to divide property "equitably," or as "justice requires." These rules give judges more latitude, and property awards tend to vary greatly. There are some important differences between the two legal schemes; however, the goal is essentially the same: fairly dividing property the couple owns together. The difficulty arises first in trying to identify what property should be divided, and second in deciding just what *equal* or *equitable* means.

As discussed in chapter 1, the new divorce and property laws favoring no–fault and more flexible distribution have both their detractors and their champions. Most view the changes as essentially positive but not without negative components. It is indisputable that a man's career and income generally leave him better able to adapt to his situation during the years immediately following a divorce, while the woman often has limited earning potential because her career development took a backseat to the marriage and children, and because the fact remains that women, on the average, still earn less than men in nearly all professions. In the words of Emily Couric, author of *The Divorce Lawyers*, "Equitable distribution and community property will work only once women have equal opportunity and experience in the workplace with accommodations for child care that do not jeopardize their career development."

Classifying, Valuing, and Dividing Assets

The simplest way to approach property division is to begin by separating out property that is clearly owned by each person separately or would automatically go to that person, such as clothing. Next, figure out what is jointly owned, including intangibles, and see what you can and cannot agree to divide. Many couples are able to reach an agreement on their own fairly quickly. For others, negotiation through lawyers or with the assistance of a mediator can lead to a fair solution on the sticking points. Charts and checklists in books such as Violet Woodhouse and Victoria Felton-Collins's *Divorce and Money* (see the Resources and Suggested Reading section) can be very helpful in streamlining this process.

When substantial marital assets are to be divided, three tasks must be accomplished:

1. classification of each asset as marital or non-marital property;
2. a valuation stating how much each marital asset is worth;
3. the division of these assets.

A fair division requires consideration of such factors as whether a large, indivisible asset should be awarded according to a percentage of ownership to the husband and wife, whether it should be sold and the money divided, or whether one party should get full ownership and be ordered to buy out the other party's interest in the property over a period of time. Such decisions may have a tremendous impact on the value of the property.

When preparing to value, classify, and divide marital property, although the law varies from state to state, remember that courts generally consider specific factors, including:

1. each spouse's contribution to the marriage, including homemaking and child rearing;

CHAPTER 5

2. the economic circumstances of each party;

3. how long the marriage lasted;

4. whether either partner interrupted his or her career or education, and whether one contributed to the career or education of the other;

5. whether it might be more desirable to allow one or the other to retain any asset as separate property (for example, to keep a business concern going rather than sell it off piecemeal); and

6. what each partner contributed to producing income or incurring debt.

The idea is to start with the presumption of a fifty–fifty split, then apply these factors to see whether adjustment should be made. For example, a wife who takes the primary responsibility for managing the home and raising the children, but also makes valuable contributions to a family business, may be found to be entitled to more than 50 percent of the marital assets. Today, this type of award is generally preferred to alimony when sufficient assets are available. However, a substantial property settlement does not exclude the possibility of alimony. For example, an older wife who had been a homemaker for the duration of the marriage and would face a substantial drop in the quality of life she had enjoyed while married is often awarded alimony.

INCOME

All income earned by either spouse during the marriage is generally considered marital property. But some states distinguish between two types of income earned during a marriage. Passive income is that which accumulates as a result of property owned before the marriage, such as interest, appreciation, and rent. Earned income refers to money earned through a job or other activity that goes on during the marriage. Generally, passive income remains separate, while earned income becomes part of the marital property estate. As in most areas of matrimonial property law, however, these classifications are subject to confusion and frequent change. If passive assets are reinvested or otherwise actively used, they are often considered earned income.

THE FAMILY HOME

The home a couple has shared is a special piece of property that must be handled carefully for several reasons. First, the home often has deep emotional meaning. Children may benefit from staying in a place that is familiar and stable. The home is also the biggest asset many couples own, and one that is subject to fluctuating value. Some states, reacting to problems that arose with the advent of no-fault divorce, will not allow couples all the options that might otherwise be available in dealing with the family home. In a few states, the parent who gets custody of children must stay in the home and either trade out other property or buy out the other spouse's portion. This can be difficult on the parent if the relationship is acrimonious, if he or she is not able to afford a buyout, or if there is not sufficient property to trade. Most states allow a couple to reach their own agreement on what to do with the home.

A real estate agent will estimate the fair market value of a house for free. This is a good starting point and may be all you need in some circumstances. However, if you are going to be refinancing a mortgage or getting a new one in one spouse's name, a professional appraisal by a certified appraiser may be required. This can cost $200 to $500. Be sure that you assess this and related refinancing costs in figuring out your settlement. In considering the value of a home, remember too that maintaining a home can be a financial drain. Consider the total cost of the home, including upkeep, utilities, mortgages, taxes, appliances, and likely repairs.

Many married couples hold real estate in what is called

joint tenancy. This is essentially a form of ownership in which each person owns all of a piece of property jointly with another person. It includes the right of survivorship: If one person dies, the other gets full ownership automatically without the requirement of any will or other estate planning tool. This can be a problem during a divorce. It is generally simple to transfer joint tenancy into a form of ownership known as tenancy in common, in which people share ownership of a piece of property, but there is no right of survivorship. Tenancy by the entireties is similar to joint tenancy, but it can't be turned into tenancy in common unless both people agree. If you own any real estate together, be sure to talk to your lawyer about this as soon as you have decided to divorce.

If the home is likely to be sold at any time, it is important to consider possible liability for capital gains tax. This tax must be paid on profit accrued on real estate. It is assessed at variable rates, depending upon an individual or couple's tax bracket and other factors. While capital gains tax generally runs about 20 percent, this is subject to many exceptions and adjustments. For example, if a couple buys a home for $60,000, lives there five years, divorces, and the spouse who receives the house in the property settlement sells it the following year for $80,000, he or she will have to pay tax on the $20,000 gain, adjusted for improvements. Payments made for improvements (as opposed to general upkeep or necessary repairs), built-on additions, or outdoor additions such as pools, garages, and gazebos affect the amount of tax to be paid.

There are ways to avoid this liability. If the home being sold is the primary residence (meaning it has been used as the main residence for at least two years), and the money from the sale of that home is invested in a new home, which will serve as the primary residence and has an equal or greater value; and if it is purchased within eighteen months of selling the first house, then the capital gain is rolled over. This option may be available several times, as long as the money from the home that is sold is again reinvested in another home of equal or greater value. If this continues until the seller is over the age of fifty-five, a once-in-a-lifetime option to avoid the capital gains tax (a profit of up to $250,000 for an individual or $500,000 for a couple) may then be used, and it will never have to be paid. However, if the home is sold before the owner reaches fifty-five, and the money is not reinvested in another primary residence, the tax on all of the amounts that have been rolled over must be paid. For example, if the first home was purchased for only $25,000, and the last home sells for $200,000, this will mean a very hefty tax bill.

This liability should be addressed in the divorce decree. It may be assigned to one person, or apportioned between them. This can require detailed maneuvering and should be handled by an attorney or financial adviser familiar with the liabilities. Furthermore, federal tax laws are predicted to change substantially during the latter half of the 1990s. Be sure you get up-to-date information.

If this is the route you decide to take, consider the cost of selling a house, beyond the tax consequences. Real estate agents generally charge a commission of about 6 percent of the selling price. There are also closing costs, escrow fees, recording fees, and other incidental expenses that can add up to several thousand dollars. Some areas require inspections and things such as termite treatment, which can also be expensive. Make sure you have achieved a clear picture of all these costs before you agree to any final settlement agreement.

BUSINESS AND CAREER-RELATED ASSETS

As life in general has become more complex, so has our property. Future earning capacity, business holdings, or other career-related assets may be among the most valuable property a couple owns. These may include pension and retirement benefits, professional licenses, insurance, business goodwill, and other miscellaneous assets such as discounts and perks.

Lenore Weitzman brings up an important point in her book *The Divorce Revolution*. Whereas many couples used to invest in a family farm, today most invest in themselves and their careers. The real wealth often lies in their future earning capacities. These assets may be much more valuable than the tangible pieces of property a couple owns. Weitzman states that future earning ability is one of the most important new forms of property and constitutes a major asset, which should be included in marital property that the courts are empowered to divide upon divorce.

Most jurisdictions now recognize that this property is highly valuable and believe that if it was acquired during a marriage, it should be included in the pool of marital property to be divided. Obviously, it can be difficult to place a dollar value on many of these assets, especially where future benefits are involved.

Consider the value of all intangible property, or things you may not initially view as having much value. For example, if you live in a rent-controlled apartment or co-op, or your apartment has an option to convert to condominium or co-op space, this may be highly significant. Also, look at the potential value of such things as artwork, collections, and hobby equipment.

THE FAMILY-OWNED BUSINESS

One of the most difficult property division problems that could be faced by the couple, attorneys, and financial advisers in a divorce is that of the family-owned business. It is very difficult to value and divide such companies accurately and fairly for several reasons. In addition to the difficulty of placing a value on a family business, its classification as marital or separate property may be equally vexing. Some of the first questions to ask in determining whether a business enterprise or professional practice should be considered marital property, in whole or in part, include:

1. Was it established before the marriage or after the marriage?
2. Did it grow substantially during the marriage?
3. Was such growth due to any support of the spouse not working full time in the business?
4. Was the separate property of either invested in the business?
5. Was it a joint enterprise run by both partners?

If any part of the business is to be considered marital property, a value must be placed on it. In general, calculating the monetary worth of the hard assets such as buildings, inventory, and supplies will not be too difficult. However, the most valuable component of many businesses is their goodwill, which refers to the value of the business above and beyond the worth of the tangible assets. For example, a store that has just opened its doors is far less valuable than an identical store that has been in business for twenty years, because the new store has not built up a customer base or a reputation for quality, or demonstrated the staying power of the older store.

These determinations are always complicated and the outcome depends on many factors, including the unique nature of the business. For example, a medical practice may be worth little in terms of its value in the marketplace. Because its worth is so closely tied to the individual doctor, it would have little worth above its equipment and supplies if the doctor left the practice and sold the business. This is especially true for a highly specialized professional. It is often impossible to determine the actual, "real" value of an ongoing business until a sales contract has been negotiated between a willing buyer and a willing seller. Even then, there is no guarantee that the agreed price reflects the true market value of the business.

Labor is also a valuable commodity. One partner in a marriage is often primarily responsible for running a family business, ranch, or farm. Many times, though, the other partner contributes a great deal to the growth and value of the enterprise, either by working for it directly with or without regular compensation, or by rendering work support, such as random errands, seasonal assistance, and filling in for absent workers. When personal and professional lives are so closely intertwined, it may be difficult to place a dollar value on this type of work. However, it is essential to consider the contributions of a spouse who works either without compensation or as a salaried employee in terms of the contribution to building a successful business enterprise. If you worked in a family-owned business—whether you were paid or not—retrieve any records, schedules, or diaries that you may have kept of your daily activities. If you didn't keep such documents, try to write out in as much detail as possible the work you did for the business or any work you did to help improve property, such as maintenance or repairs. This information is important regardless of whether the business is jointly owned or the separate property of one.

In placing a value on the assets of the business, it is important to have them appraised at the present market value. It is also essential to consider whether it is a high-risk or low-risk business. Different businesses require different approaches in valuation. When a business has limited assets but constant cash flow, such as a professional practice, capitalized earnings is the favored method to use. On the other hand, when a business such as manufacturing or retail has a great deal of capital tied up in assets but a more limited cash flow, the focus should be on the market value of the assets. Other types of businesses have a fair balance between both assets and cash flow, and in such a case, calculation of value should be by an excess earnings method. IRS ruling 59/60 deals with methods of valuing closely held corporations such as a professional practice.

Confused? So are most people. This is why it is essential to involve professionals well versed in business valuation anytime this will be an issue in a divorce. If there is a family-owned business, get it assessed by a certified business appraiser. See appendix A for sources of referrals to these professionals. Be sure you understand the fee that will be charged and exactly what you will get in return for that payment. This does not mean that you should blindly hand over all your books and records to someone and simply ask him or her to figure it out. Qualified professionals should be able to explain their recommendations and assessments in terms you can understand. They should be willing to explain the alternatives available, why certain decisions are recommended, and the risks involved, and they should answer your questions fully. If you are uncertain, get another opinion.

Tracing Assets for Classification as Separate or Marital Property

Most couples in a marriage combine all or at least part of their assets into a joint pool. Frequently, this involves the pooling of clearly marital assets, such as depositing two paychecks into the same joint account for the use of both parties. However, couples often take separate property, such as funds received by a gift or an inheritance after marriage, or money saved before the marriage, and add these resources to marital property for a major purchase, such as a home. This is called commingling. Of course, this makes perfect sense during a marriage but can cause tremendous headaches if the marriage ends and the couple has to try and sort out separate property that has been commingled with marital property.

Tracing involves following the property that is claimed as separate back to the original source of ownership. This is easy with some types of property. For example, an antique table that was given to one person by his or her grandmother may become a part of the total furnishings of the home, but the table stays as it is—one piece of property—easy to separate from the rest of the furnishings.

Such property as money, stocks, or even land may be difficult to separate out, especially if it has been sold and the money reinvested. As long as the property can be traced back to its origin without gaps in time, separation will be fairly easy. If one link in this chain is missing, the property will often be considered too commingled to divide and will be treated as marital property. For example, inherited stocks may have been traded, sold, new stocks purchased using additional money from one person's salary, sold again, and then the money combined with marital income to buy a home.

The burden of proof in tracing separate property is on the spouse who is claiming that a portion of certain property is separate. States have different standards for tracing separate property, but the key is careful documentation. If the person can produce sound records showing what happened to the property at every step of the way, this is the best evidence available. States vary in how specific the evidence must be.

Proving separate property may be very difficult, as when money has been invested and reinvested, without a clear paper trail to show its every movement. But it can be done. The assistance of experts in the relevant field can be invaluable. Courts need concrete details, and such professionals can often assist in the preparation of flow charts and other visual exhibits to show how the property moved around and changed during the marriage. Even if the case does not go to court, such materials can be extremely valuable in demonstrating what can be proven and leveraging a fair settlement. Again, a good settlement is always preferable because it is a sure thing, while any courtroom procedure involves some risk and a sharp increase in expense.

HIDDEN ASSETS

Old movies often depict a detective crouched in the bushes outside the bedroom window of an adulterous spouse, waiting to snap the photograph that will provide proof of adultery in a divorce case. While such antics still go on, most of the detective work in today's divorces is financial.

Attempts by one spouse to hide assets from the other is something that occurs with appalling frequency in divorce actions. The types of assets typically involved include boats, motorcycles, and similar vehicles; real estate; stocks, bonds, and bank accounts; and phony debts. In a business, books, records, and accounts may be manipulated to obscure assets and make a successful business appear less lucrative by padding expenses, profit-sharing schemes, payments in cash, phony or temporary contracts with outsiders, and misuse of retirement plans.

The legal discovery process, which is a part of any litigated case, is designed to ferret out such hidden assets. If a party is dishonest, they may be subject to monetary sanctions levied by the court, a less favorable property division, and civil or criminal charges of perjury or fraud. If you suspect your spouse may have assets he or she is hiding, you will need to take special steps. It may be necessary to hire an investigator or other professional such as a forensic accountant.

There are many ways to hide assets. Some of the more common include collusion with an employer, manipulating a business by paying salaries to phantom employees or contractors for services never actually rendered, asking a parent, friend, or paramour to hold money, depositing funds into accounts in a child's name, cash skimming, delayed transactions, payments to phony debts, traveler's checks, and nonexistent securities or bonds. There are as many devious methods of hiding assets as there are dishonest people.

Pension and Retirement Benefits

There are two types of pensions or retirement plans recognized in the law. First, a vested pension is one that is guaranteed to be paid, whether an employee remains with a company for a set period of time, retires, or leaves earlier. For example, if a person worked for a company for ten years and then leaves, whatever is in the vested pension plan will be paid out at that time. A nonvested pension is not guaranteed; it will be forfeited if the employee does not meet certain requirements, for example, staying with the company for a set number of years. Most states today recognize both types of pensions as marital property if the pension was acquired through the efforts of one person during the marriage as part of his or her salary or compensation for work.

A federal law passed in 1984, the Retirement Equity Act, deals specifically with distribution of private pension benefits upon divorce. Under this act, private pension plans such as those provided by individual companies or unions must be handled in a very special way in a divorce. A qualified domestic relations order (often called a QDRO, pronounced "quadro") must be included as part of a divorce decree where such assets are to be divided. A QDRO tells the person in charge of distributing the funds that a specific proportion of the benefits must be distributed to an "alternate payee," the ex-spouse. This protects against plan administrators who, in the past, sometimes refused or were reluctant to pay benefits under the plan to anyone other than the individual named in the plan documents. When a QDRO is entered, the plan administrator can take up to eighteen months to approve the order. During this time, the court may order that the spousal shares be kept separate so that the pension holder can't withdraw any money that would dip into the other person's allotment. The pension holder can also be ordered not to borrow against the ex-spouse's share, or the court may order that the ex-spouse be designated to remain as the surviving spouse. The order may also specify the age at which each spouse can withdraw from the fund.

Retirement benefits do not necessarily have to be divided between the spouses. In many marriages, the couple will decide to allow the person who earned the benefits to keep them in exchange for the other getting full ownership of equivalent assets. For example, one person keeps the pension fund, the other keeps the house. In marriages where both have jobs that provide retirement plans, couples typically specify that each will keep his or her own benefits. A QDRO is not required where the plan will not be divided. In any case, however, an accurate value should be placed on the retirement benefits to ensure that whatever agreement is reached is equitable.

Different types of retirement plans must be dealt with in different ways to satisfy the legal requirements involved. This area of the law can become complex, and you may need the assistance of an actuary, a financial professional who specializes in pension and retirement planning. For example, QDROs can be used only to divide retirement plans subject to the Employee Retirement Income Security Act (ERISA). This act covers most plans but does not include government plans such as the U.S. Civil Service Retirement System, public employee pensions of state employees, or military pensions. Each of these requires a different, special type of order to divide the benefits. In any case, the procedure is similar. The appropriate order will assign a portion of the benefit earned by one spouse to the ex-spouse, the "alternate payee." Designing a QDRO or other appropriate order to divide these benefits is fairly simple for a qualified attorney, but it is essential to know how to deal with the specific type of plan.

Individual retirement accounts (IRAs) also require special attention. A QDRO is not necessary to divide an IRA, but the tax consequences may be significant. Again, your attorney should be well versed in such matters or able to obtain expert assistance from a tax attorney, actuary, or CPA. Consider, too, that a retirement plan owned by an employer or other entity may vanish if the company goes out of business, merges with another, or is otherwise changed over the years.

Anytime a pension plan or other retirement benefits are at issue, both spouses should become informed about the pros and cons of "opt out" options. Under such plans, a worker can choose a reduced pension to provide a survivor's benefit for the other spouse, or can elect to take full monthly checks after retirement during their lifetime. Under the Retirement Equity Act of 1984, workers may not opt out of survivor's benefits without the knowledge or agreement of the spouse. Thus, a worker must obtain the written consent of the spouse or ex-spouse, if a pension was split at divorce, before survivor's benefits may be effectively waived.

The question of how a pension should be divided at divorce may be sticky. Several approaches are possible. One option is for the spouse who earned the pension to provide the other with a lump sum or asset of equivalent value to buy out the value of the pension at the time of divorce. Sometimes pension payments are made to the ex-spouse before the one who earned them retires, according to the terms of a QDRO. Another alternative is to delay the division until the time the pension benefits are paid out, generally at retirement. Then the pension will be divided and payments made to each spouse according to the terms of the divorce decree. Which method is better depends on the individual circumstances, with the age of the parties being an important factor. Younger couples often favor the buyout or present payment method, whereas those closer to retirement age may prefer the second method. Those choosing the buyout method should make certain that the future value of the pension benefits is accurately calculated.

Get qualified advice on anything you don't completely understand. Employers, plan administrators, trustees, or actuaries can furnish information. Your attorney will probably know qualified people and may decide to hire them as experts in the negotiation process or at trial. Again, it is best if the spouses can agree on one expert. This will save money and give that person more credibility in the eyes of the court.

MILITARY PENSIONS

In 1981, a landmark U.S. Supreme Court decision called *McCarty v. McCarty* ruled that military pensions are not to be treated as marital or community property. This led to the organization of a nationwide lobby for federal legislation which would guarantee divorced wives of current or former servicemen an equitable share in the assets accrued during a marriage under a military pension. A group called Ex-Partners of Servicemen for Equality (EXPOSE) (see appendix A) was organized and made tremendous efforts for their cause, including the picketing of military facilities and garnering press attention to stories of wives who followed career military husbands around the world for twenty or thirty years only to be denied a share of their husbands' military pension later. The effort of EXPOSE and others outraged by the *McCarty* decision helped convince Congress to pass the Uniform Services Former Spouses Protection Act in 1982. This federal law overturned the *McCarty* decision and explicitly permitted state courts to treat military retirement pay as community or marital property if the court had jurisdiction over the service member. The law does not guarantee wives a definite share of these benefits, but leaves it up to the court of each state to award up to 50 percent of the disposable retirement pay and related benefits such as medical care and commissary privileges under some circumstances. Thus, the federal law is subject to the discretion of individual courts and the laws of the various states.

OTHER BENEFITS

Similar acts help protect spouses of other federal employees, such as foreign service officers, under the Foreign Service Act of 1980, and civil service workers, under the Civil Service Reform Act. Current Social Security law allows a divorced spouse to receive Social Security benefits drawn from the earnings of a working spouse if the marriage lasted more than ten years. This might be adjusted according to individual circumstances when both spouses have worked during the marriage. Your local Social Security office can help you determine the benefits to which you and your spouse are currently entitled. They can provide you with a form to fill out that will help you obtain your estimated future benefits.

INVESTMENTS

If you have investments such as stocks and bonds, try to review your portfolio before you get divorced. What is a wise investment for a married person may change with the financial transformations of a divorce. This is a good time to review all your investments and get rid of those that aren't performing well or don't suit your future needs. Be sure to get good advice on your investments and on the tax consequences of your options from your broker, attorney, or accountant.

If your spouse handled jointly owned investments, be sure you gain a complete understanding of the nature of the character, risks, obligations, tax consequences, dividends, transaction fees, and other incidents of owning each investment. In addition to stocks, the same type of analysis should be done for real estate investments, cash value insurance policies, limited partnerships, commodities, and any other valuable property that you own. All may have hidden pitfalls and require a thorough understanding of their true nature and value.

OTHER PROPERTY CONCERNS

Tax considerations must also be taken into account for other types of property or support, not just a home or business. Property division awards and child support are nontaxable, while alimony is considered income and taxed. For this reason, the label placed on a monetary property award can be very significant. It is easy to see why, in any case that involves substantial assets, the involvement of a good accountant (and sometimes other financial advisers) is essential. "It's far better for people to meet with an accountant before they sign the final agreement," says CPA Sandra Ricci. "People can cut their taxes so much by planning the timing of their divorce and the language of the decree."

Some accountants specialize in financial consulting on matrimonial cases. Any accountant or other financial adviser hired to work on a divorce should be familiar with the special demands of this type of case. Also, a professional hired as an expert in a divorce case should be acquainted with the nuances of courtroom procedure; for example, the need to protect his or her credibility as a witness by making a neutral assessment of the facts provided by the lawyer, who is an advocate for the client. Again, it is best if both people can agree to use the same expert.

The settlement agreement is like a snapshot. It can only resolve matters as they exist at the moment the agreement is signed and filed. It is not up to the court to plan your future for you, and it is very difficult to undo provisions in the decree that later prove unwise. Sit down with your attorney, tax accountant, and other advisers, crunch the numbers, and get a thorough, detailed explanation that you fully understand before you make any final decisions. Don't be afraid to ask plenty of questions—I believe that the only stupid question is the one that doesn't get asked. This is especially true when future consequences are at stake that could have serious effects on your financial well-being for years to come.

PRACTICAL MATTERS

It is best to get your financial changes resolved and finalized as soon as possible after you and your spouse reach an agreement, and certainly before the final decree is entered. This not only helps simplify and streamline the process, but it also helps you avoid an endless list of chores and details at the last minute, or worse, a decree that mandates a lot of behavior after the divorce that may or may not be followed by your ex.

As soon as a couple has decided to divorce and the initial decisions are made as to how some property will be divided, steps should be taken to start the process of establishing separate ownership of that property or debt. Joint accounts should be closed and assets put in individual's names. This is the time to begin working with creditors to refinance loans, mortgages, and other debts in the name of one partner, if possible. Any such matters that cannot be completed before the divorce is finalized should be put into a written agreement signed by both spouses and filed with the court, or stated clearly in the settlement agreement. For example, if the divorce will occur at a time when income taxes cannot yet be calculated, be sure to consult a tax professional to decide how you will file and how any refund or bill will be divided.

Most experts advise getting property settlements in the form of cash or specific property rather than any future promise. If payment must be delayed, be sure you are compensated for having to wait, in the form of interest or another type of increase in the payment.

Money is always a tough topic and is one of the most difficult areas to deal with, even in a very strong marriage. For most of us, money is a very emotional issue, one that can be highly volatile during divorce. People are sometimes tempted to exploit the emotional side of financial transactions to get revenge on a spouse or force a reconciliation. Others want to extricate themselves from what may have been a painful issue in the marriage as quickly as possible, without regard for the future. Yet such actions are as unwise as they are understandable.

Remember, you are making difficult decisions under tremendous emotional pressure, which may affect you and your children for the rest of your life. If you feel overwhelmed, take the steps you need to safeguard your sanity during this crucial time. Consider counseling, a stress management class, or a therapy group. The emotional roller coaster is an inevitable part of nearly every divorce. If you're having a bad day and feel that you are not at your best, don't pick this time to make big financial decisions or tackle difficult tasks. A slight delay is far better than a bad decision, which may have a detrimental impact for years to come. Take care of yourself: Enjoy some inexpensive treats such as renting a funny movie, or go on a hike through the woods or botanical gardens—something you know will lift your spirits. Do not hesitate to spend money on counselors or other mental health treatment if you feel the need. Money spent on your health and well-being is not a luxury, it's an absolute necessity, now more than ever.

Financial tasks can be overwhelming. It is often helpful to break down these chores into small steps. A huge amount may be accomplished a little at a time. There is an old cliché that goes, "Yard by yard it's hard, but inch by inch it's a cinch."

It can be especially difficult to make good decisions if your spouse was the one who made the decision to end the marriage. Yet even if you are hoping for reconciliation, it's important to protect your financial interest. Sometimes working on such matters, with the required cooperative effort, mediation, and/or counseling, can help a couple get back together. It's important to be an active participant in the divorce process, even if you hope and don't want it to happen to you.

Make sure any agreement you make with your spouse is in writing, and that the attorneys have copies. This may seem unnecessarily dismal, especially if the parting is amicable. But it's a good idea even if you trust your spouse completely. It avoids misunderstanding and confusion that can turn a friendly relationship unpleasant.

If you own a joint safe deposit box, be sure to take an inventory of its contents and remove any items, such as inherited jewelry, which are clearly yours as separate property. The bank officer can review and sign an inventory of a safe deposit box. The same type of inventory should be taken of all your valuable belongings. This does not mean that you have to write down a description of every piece of Tupperware in the house. But things such as coin collections, marbles, baseball cards, hobby equipment, and similar items may be more valuable than you know. It is smart to get such things appraised also. Remember too that children's property is their own. It stays with them wherever they go and is not divided in the settlement.

It is also important to consider what would happen to property if one spouse or the other were to die before the divorce is final. Be sure to review all property held in joint tenancy, wills, and life insurance policies. Your attorneys should be able to advise you or put you in touch with a different type of expert to help you deal with these matters.

If you have a large amount of money in a joint bank account, the terms of who has access to the account and how much of it should be spelled out in an interim agreement to be filed with the court. If you need funds immediately, you will usually be entitled to withdraw up to half of any jointly held account. But in reality, whoever gets there first can legally withdraw the entire amount. Although they may be ordered to reimburse the spouse's share later, by that time it could be long gone. Again, clarifying these matters not only avoids this type of risk but prevents argument and hostility.

Financial Planners

Financial planners are a specialized type of expert who can help people contemplating divorce identify potential risks in a settlement, understand tax consequences, get an accurate picture of assets and liabilities, plan for future needs, and determine what and how much support may be necessary. Some people who simply sell investments refer to themselves as financial planners, but a true financial planner is an analyst who is familiar with all types of assets and liabilities. The International Association for Financial Planning can provide a list of members who have met very specific and rigorous requirements. The association can be reached at (404) 395-1605. Get the right kind of expert who is qualified to handle your needs.

The same caution should be used in hiring a CPA. Like lawyers, there are various types of CPAs specializing in different areas of the accounting field. If you need a tax specialist, you may want to see if the person you are contemplating is an enrolled agent who is qualified to practice before the IRS. Call the National Association of Enrolled Agents at 1-800-424-4339. As you're planning your taxes, remember that some professional fees are deductible, such as attorney's fees to collect or secure alimony. Any fees for advice on tax consequences of your divorce from an attorney, accountant, broker, financial planner, or other professional may also be deductible if it is itemized and meets other requirements. Check with your professional advisers about this.

If you do not have copies of old tax returns, you may obtain them by calling the IRS at 1-800-829-1040. Ask for Form 4506. Be sure to give your current address, otherwise the form will be sent to the address on the latest tax return.

The Recalcitrant Spouse

It is perfectly natural for the people involved in a divorce to want to get it over with as soon as possible. For this reason, many final decrees contain orders to accomplish unfinished business, such as selling a home, refinancing a debt, or transferring title to property. It is generally better to accomplish as many of these matters as is humanly possible *before* the decree is signed, but both practical concerns and personal desires to get on with a new life can make a certain amount of unfinished business unavoidable.

This is not a problem if both parties are responsible, satisfied with the agreement, and anxious to get things squared away. But often, one will drag his or her feet for any number of reasons—a desire to make things difficult on the other, hope of reconciliation, lack of concern, or simple laziness.

Family attorney David B. Riggert cautions against the common inclination to agree to an unwise property settlement in order to expedite the divorce. "Clients often want the attorney to solve their problem immediately, they just want the divorce over and done with," he explains. "Husbands, especially, often don't care what the wife gets in the property settlement—they just want out. This is understandable, because people in the midst of a divorce are under tremendous stress. But later, when they're feeling better emotionally, they will be more concerned about financial matters. I have to remind them that if I do as they ask, two years from now, when the smoke clears, they may see things differently—and all too often, blame the lawyer. It's my job to do my best to satisfy both their current needs, as well as their future needs."

For those matters that may take time, such as the sale of major property, various methods can be used to ensure accountability, such as mandatory reports to the court on the efforts the person is making to accomplish the task. If the problem is simply laziness, recalcitrance, or a desire to be irritating, a gentle reminder, in writing, that if one person has to go to court to enforce the agreement, the costs and attorney's fees can be charged against the other, will often do the trick.

Throughout this book I have emphasized the importance of setting accurate values on property so that any division is fair to both parties. Often, however, people don't want to go through extensive analysis—each has personal priorities, both can agree on property division, and both are anxious to move on. This is an individual choice, and the emotional issues, plus the normal desire to bring a quick and clean resolution to a divorce, are every bit as important as the financial aspects. Just be sure you do enough analysis to know the consequences of your actions, especially with regard to matters that could be extremely important after the divorce, such as the tax consequences of taking the home. Certainly, nonfinancial considerations such as a strong sentimental attachment to a piece of property are equally important and should be given due consideration.

DEBT AND CREDIT ISSUES

Divorce is not only hard on the emotions, it's always a pain in the pocket as well. Discussions of property divisions and settlements are often somewhat deceptive when applied to reality. The fact is, the majority of divorcing couples do not have substantial assets to be divided; the more important issue is often who will be responsible for paying off the debts. This is a major component of the property settlement in most divorces.

Debts are classified in the same way as property: separate or community/marital. Any debt that a couple incurs during their marriage is presumed to be a marital debt, with both people responsible for payment. Debts that existed prior to the marriage are usually separate. In general, debts that are incurred after a couple separates but before the final divorce decree is entered are considered separate debts, except for items that are considered necessities, such as clothing, food, shelter, and maintenance of children. But this may vary according to the state and any agreements that have been made with creditors.

Keep in mind that a property settlement agreement covers only the relationship between the spouses. It is not binding on creditors. Thus, if a couple buys a car in both their names, and the lender who finances the loan relies on the income and credit history of both people, the fact that the divorce decree says the husband will get the car and be totally responsible for payment of the loan does not mean the creditor can collect only from the husband. If he refuses to pay, goes bankrupt, or disappears, the lender can legally look to the wife for payment, no matter what the divorce decree says. Therefore, it is best to try to negotiate new, separate loan contracts with creditors before signing the final papers. If this is not possible, the person no longer responsible for making payments on a debt under the terms of the decree should take other steps. He or she may wish to keep a security interest in the property until it is paid off, as many businesses do when selling merchandise on credit. For instance, if there is still quite a bit of money owed on the car that is going to the wife, and she is taking the car and assuming the debt, the husband may want to keep his name on the title and indicate in the decree that he will retain an interest in the car until it is paid off.

Other provisions to ensure compliance with the decree can also be added to its terms, such as an agreement to indemnify the other spouse for any money he or she has to pay a creditor if the other fails to follow the terms of the agreement. However, it's still best to get all obligations separated before the decree is final, in case the other spouse vanishes or goes broke.

One strategy for coping with debt is to sell jointly owned property before the divorce to pay off or at least reduce the debt load. Also, before or as soon as you and your spouse separate is the time to clarify exactly how your debts will be paid and how your credit options will be handled. Home equity lines of credit, margin accounts from stockbrokers, charge accounts, and other such accounts may be closed, frozen, or adjusted so that both spouses must sign for any advances or withdrawals.

Cash flow statements can be helpful in assessing where your money goes on a day-to-day basis. This will help you determine where you can cut costs and how much you will need in the future. Cash flow charts, personal financial statements, and other financial worksheets for people going through a divorce are available from various sources, such as banks, financial planners, and books on money management. One good book full of such worksheets is *Divorce and Money* by Violet Woodhouse and Victoria Felton-Collins (see the Resources list at the back of this book). Financial advisers, classes, credit counselors, and other sources of assistance are also available in most areas.

Many people experience a severe letdown when they see their financial life spread before them on paper. Remember, most people today do live beyond their means yet still maintain a fairly stable financial life. Focus on your monthly obligations, not the total amount you owe, and try to come up with a realistic analysis of what you are going to need to make ends meet.

Credit

Under a federal law called the Equal Credit Opportunity Act, every individual has the right to apply and be fairly considered for credit without discrimination on the basis of sex or marital status. But because divorce may affect your credit record and eligibility in various ways, it is best to negotiate new credit terms in a separate agreement with each of your creditors. Default by your ex-spouse on a marital debt that he or she was supposed to pay can leave a black mark on your credit record as well.

If your creditors won't agree to refinance a debt in your or your spouse's name alone, remember that your credit ratings are subject to change. Creditors who were unwilling to change a debt or account to the name of one person at the time of divorce may be willing to do so later, after each person has had an opportunity to establish a track record on their own. If you can't negotiate a change now, check again in a year or so. Also, it is important to keep all joint debts currently paid during the divorce proceedings, even if one party has to pay more than his or her fair share. Adjustments can be made as part of the final settlement, and if payments are missed, creditors are less likely to let go of joint liability and reestablish the account in one name. As soon as any accounts that remain in both names are paid off, they should be closed.

What if you have never had credit in your own name or have had credit problems during your marriage? The answer is to reestablish a good credit rating as soon as possible in your name alone. Start by setting up bank accounts and applying for credit cards that are easy to obtain, such as gasoline company and department store cards. If possible, consider taking out a bank loan for a reasonably small amount, such as $1,000, putting it in a savings account, and simply using the money from the loan to make timely payments on the debt. All these actions can help you build a solid credit rating and become eligible for additional forms of credit.

If you have never had credit in your own name, or have had credit problems in the past, be sure to get a clear picture of your situation and try to establish credit in your own name *before* the joint accounts are closed. TRW, one of the nation's largest credit reporting bureaus, will provide a free status report once a year or more often if a person has been denied credit. TRW's address and telephone number is listed in appendix A.

Before the divorce is final, get a copy of your current credit report. There are local credit reporting agencies in most cities, as well as national agencies (see appendix A). If you have been denied credit, you may obtain a copy of your credit rating for free. Otherwise, there may be a minimal charge, usually $10 or less. It might be helpful to get your spouse's credit report as well.

Creditors are often willing to make adjustments in their current payment plans for an individual who has been through a divorce or other change that affects his or her financial life. If you believe you may have trouble meeting your current credit obligations, call your creditors to discuss the possibilities. Most will be willing to work with you if you are up front and make your best effort to keep your payments current.

More options are becoming available each day for people with a problematic or nonexistent credit history. Talk to local banks, savings and loan companies, and credit unions. Do not fall for "no questions asked" or 900–number credit companies. Unfortunately, there are a lot of scams out there. Make sure you know the source and full terms of any credit agreement you enter, or you could end up with more problems rather than solutions.

Credit Counselors

The only person I know who hasn't experienced some sort of debt overload at least once is one very meticulous CPA. Virtually all people are at risk for getting in over their head in the deep waters of debt, particularly since the cost of living keeps going up and credit is easier to come by every day. Fortunately, there are many people who can help consumers get their financial lives back under control.

Many credit counselors are affiliated with nonprofit organizations such as the United Way, YMCA and YWCA, and even churches. The National Foundation for Consumer Credit sponsors consumer credit counseling services with offices nationwide (see appendix A). These people can help you deal with immediate crises, negotiate a more realistic payment plan with creditors, learn better ways to manage your finances to make your money go further, set up a budget, and avoid problems in the future. The service is sponsored by various creditors who realize that it is in their best interest to work with debtors in reworking payment plans, rather than having to go through the headaches of foreclosure or simply not getting paid.

The credit counseling service works only with clients who are able to pay their bills on some type of monthly plan. It does not assist those who need the protection of bankruptcy. The counselors charge only nominal fees, which usually come out of the monthly payment that is set up to deal with the client's debts. The counselor reviews the total debt owed by the client, works with the creditors to establish a payment plan, then collects direct payments from the client once or twice a month and in turn pays the creditors. The service can also help get late charges, wage garnishments, and other legal actions dropped. For more information, check your local telephone directory or call the national headquarters at 1-800-388-2227.

INSURANCE

American insurance laws and the types of plans currently available are changing very rapidly, so it is difficult to characterize how these assets should be handled upon divorce. What is clear is that insurance rights are important assets and must be handled carefully when a marriage ends.

If you are receiving alimony or child support, be sure that your spouse keeps you as the beneficiary on a life insurance policy sufficient to cover your needs if anything should happen to him or her. The person paying support can deduct insurance payments under certain circumstances. Your broker or agent should be able to advise on how this may be structured. Disability insurance is also essential and shouldn't be overlooked.

In reviewing your insurance, check all of your policies. Divorce may also affect auto, property, business, and other insurance in addition to life insurance.

Health Insurance

Under a federal law known as COBRA, a divorced person whose former spouse is employed by a company with twenty or more people and is a medical plan participant must be allowed to remain on the spouse's insurance plan for up to thirty-six months after the divorce. You are required to pay for your own coverage according to the terms of the plan. Contact the personnel department or plan administrator for specific information. Your lawyer should also advise you about this type of coverage. You can contact your local office of the U.S. Department of Labor for a booklet entitled *Continued Health Care Coverage,* which outlines the specifics of this law.

Some states also have laws providing for conversion of insurance policies to cover divorced spouses and children upon divorce. However, conversion policies may offer less coverage and lower benefits as well as higher costs than the original policy. A parent covered under a spouse's insurance policy will also need to provide insurance for children after a divorce and should pay careful attention and get qualified advice as to different options.

On a positive note, more insurance alternatives are now becoming available. Good coverage may be offered through sources other than one's own employment or a spouse's job. Professional organizations, private clubs, health maintenance organizations (HMOs), and other groups not traditionally considered as the type to provide group insurance are beginning to establish plans.

The type and cost of coverage may vary widely, so any person shopping for insurance needs to carefully consider all the different options for which they may qualify. The one that seems the logical choice at first may not be the best in the long run. For example, as a self-employed person, I could get health insurance coverage under my husband's group employment plan, a group plan established especially for the self-employed, or an HMO plan available through a writer's organization I belong to. Contrary to what might be expected, the plan offered by my husband's employer would be the least appropriate for me. It sets one fee to be paid by the employee for dependent coverage, whether the coverage is for one person (as it would be in our case) or an entire family including several children. Furthermore, coverage under that plan is limited to one group of hospitals and HMOs, which does not include my doctor. Therefore, the best plan for me was separate coverage through my writer's organization. Thus, what was once accepted as common wisdom in the insurance law is no longer always the case, given the rapid evolution taking place.

If you feel that you could benefit by mental health counseling or therapy, check your medical insurance coverage. A number of policies cover this type of health care. If not, call your local mental health association or family services agency. Many states or counties provide mental health assistance free, often through contracts with local clinics, centers, or providers. There are many different types of help available to those who need it, often free of charge. Make sure you get the type of help that is right for you. Many people going through a divorce do not need long-term psychoanalysis but only short-term counseling, stress management therapy, or support group involvement. Most agencies that provide mental health services will screen clients to determine the appropriate type of help. If you are unsure what type of assistance would be best for you, explore the available options and talk to a qualified professional who can help you determine what you need.

BANKRUPTCY

For a couple in a financially troubled marriage, divorce is often the last straw that pushes them over the brink into bankruptcy. A couple who is still married can file jointly for bankruptcy, and anyone, whether married or single, can file individually. When one spouse files individually, however, the effect on the other can be devastating if the couple is still married or if there is unresolved business, such as debts that have been divided by decree but not refinanced with creditors. If you are considering bankruptcy or fear that your spouse might file, talk to a qualified adviser. Remember, attorneys are often specialists in one field but not another. Have a frank talk with the attorney who is handling your divorce to determine whether he or she is well versed in bankruptcy law. If not, ask for a referral to an attorney who specializes in this area. There are also good books on the market that explain more about bankruptcy and alternatives for those with financial troubles.

Illinois attorney David B. Riggert maintains a bankruptcy practice as well as a family law practice, and finds that the two fields frequently overlap. "The big issue," he states, "is that people must realize early on that they will have higher household expenses and only one income to meet them." He cautions that women may be particularly vulnerable to unrealistic expectations of support. "They tend to presume that spousal support will be forthcoming, but if they are working or have the ability to work, the court may be unwilling to award them maintenance." Riggert emphasizes the importance of understanding that no matter how the divorce decree divides the couple's debt, both spouses will often remain liable to their creditors on joint debts unless they are refinanced through a separate agreement with each creditor. However, the language of the divorce decree may be vitally important if one spouse later declares bankruptcy. Most debts can be discharged by a bankruptcy action, but child or spousal support cannot. Therefore, it is essential that the language designating property division versus support is very clear and specific. Riggert advises, "Spell it out cleanly to make it stick."

Riggert believes it is essential to consider whether bankruptcy may be an option very early in the divorce process. "One of the first things I do is to analyze the ability of each spouse to maintain payment on the debts that are likely to be assigned to them. This is a vital consideration, and in most cases not too time-consuming or difficult. Unless it's a very complex case, I can generally make this assessment in thirty minutes or so, during the initial consultation. If I see that either party is likely to file, I immediately open discussions with the other attorney about his or her client's ability to handle the debt."

Riggert encourages all divorcing couples for whom bankruptcy may be an option to carefully consider filing a joint bankruptcy petition before they divorce. "For many, money problems led to the stress in the marriage that caused them to decide to divorce," he remarks. "Sometimes, when this is resolved they reunite. But at any rate, it is far better to consider bankruptcy sooner than later, for both emotional and pragmatic reasons. It's really hard on people when their ex declares bankruptcy, then they find that they can't meet the burden of the joint debt either, and they are forced into their own bankruptcy. Divorce should mean a fresh start, both emotionally and financially. It's better to go into your new life with a clean slate— you'll have enough emotional baggage anyway. Also, because the average cost for each bankruptcy filing is from $500 to $1,000, there is a built in incentive to file one joint bankruptcy rather than two single bankruptcies, to accomplish the same result."

While it is possible to challenge an ex-spouse's attempt to discharge a particular debt in bankruptcy, it is not easy to succeed. "In 1994, there were changes in the bankruptcy code designed to offer more protection to the non-debtor spouse," Riggert explains. "But the bankruptcy courts still feel that their primary duty is to protect the debtor. The petitioner's request to discharge joint debts can be challenged, but contesting a bankruptcy action is often difficult and expensive."

The looming threat of bankruptcy is another reason why you should make every effort to see that joint debts are transferred into the individual name of the party who agrees to take them over, as soon as possible. Unless a new agreement has been established between the creditor and the ex-spouse to provide that he or she is solely responsible for a debt, a statement in a divorce order making one person solely responsible will have no effect if he or she declares bankruptcy. When a person files for bankruptcy, all his or her debts are cancelled, with a few exceptions such as child support or spousal support.

Bankruptcy effectively cancels out the debt responsibility terms of a property settlement incorporated into a divorce decree. If you suspect your spouse is contemplating bankruptcy after the divorce, tell your attorney and discuss all the pertinent issues.

TYING UP LOOSE ENDS

All those who may be indirectly affected by the divorce should be notified as to the terms of the property settlement. These include insurance agents, stockbrokers, bankers, children's schools, accountants, pension fund administrators, and others involved in your financial affairs. Timing is essential. It's best to notify everyone who needs this information after the settlement is tentatively finalized, but before it is signed and filed with the court, if possible.

After you have taken the steps to divide and refinance your debts, change title documents, and review other records, check with the appropriate companies and agencies to make sure that the changes were made, and that they were made correctly. This can provide reassurance that your spouse kept up his or her end of the agreement, confirming that no mistakes were made. As we all know, errors are excruciatingly common in large companies and government bureaucracies. When I got married and changed my name, I wrote a simple letter to each of my eight credit card companies stating my former name and my new name and asking for a credit card with the corrected name. Of those eight, only *one* got it right. Since that time, I have double-checked everything, and the frequency of errors I have found is absolutely amazing. Be sure to check wills, trust documents, debts, credit cards, any documents of title, deeds, bank accounts, stock documents, and any other records you can think of. This will usually involve no more than a phone call, letter, or a quick stop at company headquarters, recorder of deeds' office, tax assessor's office, and title companies. The necessity of such errands can be aggravating and time consuming, but most people can accomplish it in a day or two. And it can be well worth it if a problem crops up somewhere along the line.

Financial Goal Setting

As you look to your personal or financial and personal future, it is important to consider certain matters that may have become overshadowed by the demands of simply getting through the day during a divorce. List some of your immediate, short-term, and long-term goals, such as where you would like to be in the next six months, five years, and ten years. At the same time, consider where you *don't* want to be. This helps sort out problems and pitfalls you want to anticipate and avoid.

Also, list major life events that are likely or inevitable in the coming years that may require specific financial and other consideration. Such events may include children who will be reaching college age, your retirement, or your own educational goals. This can give you a realistic picture of what income you will need in the future, and also help you make important decisions, such as whether you may want to request support to continue your education rather than getting a lower paying job immediately after the divorce.

SUPPORT

Spousal Support

Alimony is now called spousal support in most areas. Not only the name but also the purpose and character of this type of support has changed a good deal in the last half of this century, as social roles have evolved and states have adopted no-fault divorce laws. Today, the majority of women in America have employment other than (or in addition to) homemaker and mother. Also, in many families, the woman is the primary breadwinner, while the man makes less money or stays home with the children. It is generally expected by the court system that all adults, unless they are unable to work, should be self-supporting. Thus, instead of the "permanent" alimony that was once common, support awards today are designed to be temporary according to the individual circumstances of the people involved. For instance, a woman in her sixties who has never worked outside the home will not generally be expected to forge a new career and become entirely self-supporting at that stage in life. Likewise, a mother with several preschool children may be awarded spousal support sufficient to allow her to be a full-time mother until the children have reached school age. Texas is the only state that does not allow alimony. In Virginia, Georgia, and North Carolina, a wife's adultery or desertion can bar alimony. The husband's fault can be considered as a factor in the size of the award in fourteen other states.

According to Lester Wallman, a leading matrimonial attorney and co-author of *Cupid, Couples, and Contracts*, there are four important words to remember about alimony: Don't count on it. Yet Wallman advises that anyone who needs spousal support, especially older homemakers, should fight like hell to try to get it. Even if alimony is not awarded, it can be a valuable negotiating tool to get a more equitable property settlement.

Today alimony awards are generally based on the length and history of the marriage, the ability of the paying spouse to make the payments, the needs of the recipient, the age, health and standard of living of both partners, earning abilities of both, contributions of all types to the marriage, and the abilities of both parties to be self-supporting.

Evidence is emerging that indicates the courts are beginning to pay more attention to the value of a homemaker spouse who contributes to the success of a spouse with a demanding career. In 1995, General Electric executive Gary Wendt asked his wife Lorena Wendt for a divorce. During the course of the couple's thirty-year marriage, Lorena had taught to help put her husband through Harvard business school, then became a full-time homemaker, mother, and hostess (once serving a lavish business dinner eight days after delivering her first child). She argued that in light of her own contributions toward her husband's success, she was entitled to half the couple's estimated $90 million net worth. The court ultimately awarded Lorena assets worth over $21 million, two of the couple's five homes, plus lifetime alimony of $21,000 per month. She has since established a Foundation for Equality in Marriage, with the goal of advancing recognition of the contributions of stay-at-home spouses who make tremendous commitments to the success of both.

Alimony is a separate and distinct issue from the property settlement. It is also separate from child support, although sometimes when a spouse is paying both alimony and child support, it will be lumped together in one payment called family support. This can cause problems with tax classifications. The IRS may not agree with how the parties say they have divided this payment between child support and alimony.

The size, character, timing, and structure of alimony payments can have serious tax consequences. The assistance of a qualified tax accountant or attorney with specialized training in tax law is essential whenever you are contemplating any type of alimony. Also, alimony is sometimes characterized as part of the property settlement in order to manipulate the tax consequences. This is important to consider when contemplating a lump sum alimony award.

Alimony does not always end when the recipient remarries. In most states, it depends on whether the decree states that support ends on remarriage or cohabitation, or whether the payor goes back to court and asks for the decree to be modified due to this change in circumstances. Some states have statutes providing that alimony automatically ends on remarriage or cohabitation.

The current law and practice of spousal support is controversial. As discussed in chapter 4, temporary awards have been criticized for ignoring the very real circumstances faced by most working women. In general, women still earn only about

80 percent as much money as men, with the wage gap much higher in some fields. Furthermore, although the court may see a strong, intelligent forty-year-old woman who appears capable of doing many types of work, the same woman may in fact have been a homemaker and mother since she was twenty and is therefore entering the workforce in the same position as a much younger, inexperienced worker. Therefore, it is essential for a woman (or, in some cases, a man) who needs spousal support to present a detailed picture of her capabilities, plans, and needs to her attorney and, if necessary, the court.

This may involve the use of a vocational expert. These professionals may be hired privately or appointed by the court. As discussed earlier, vocational experts can assist people facing a change in circumstances to determine what type of work they want to pursue, what additional education or training they will need, their true capabilities and limitations, how long training will take, realistic expectations as to starting salaries, and in some cases, whether special help such as mental health counseling will be necessary before the person will be fully capable of self-support.

Vocational experts are being used more and more in this manner. In some cases, they may need to spend months working with a person to formulate a detailed plan spanning several years. In others, their task may be as simple as helping a nurse who has been out of the workforce to determine current salaries and locate refresher training to renew her license. In most cases involving spousal support, this type of professional involvement is crucial. Judges and lawyers work with vocational experts on a daily basis and can make appointments or recommendations.

Also, it is important to remember that support awards are never written in stone. They can always be modified when the circumstances of either party changes in some way so that the support is no longer necessary or fair. For example, if a woman expects to spend two years training for a job that will provide a modest salary, but unexpectedly gets a job after one year that pays much more, her ex-husband can ask the court to modify the award. In some states, however, spousal support is waived if it is not awarded in the original decree and cannot be requested later.

If the person paying the support suffers financial setback, he or she can ask the court to lower their payments. The support system is designed to be flexible according to the reality that people's plans and circumstances do change. However, the court has broad discretion in this area. If the paying spouse decides to change careers from surgeon to surf bum just to get out of support payments, or a former executive with an MBA protests she can't find any work at all, the judge will not be amused. Remember, modification is flexible, but it must be for good cause.

FAMILY LAW
AND CHILDREN

CHILD CUSTODY

Perhaps the best way to begin a discussion on child custody is by looking at some of the common misconceptions about custody law and how custody decisions are made. According to Anne Kass, a family court judge for many years in Albuquerque, New Mexico, three of the most common beliefs are that:

1. Courts favor mothers over fathers.
2. Children over a certain age can choose where they live.
3. Equal time between parents solves custody problems.

None of these notions is accurate.

Judge Kass stresses that the parents themselves make the decision on custody, often unknowingly and unintentionally, long before the divorce process begins. Parents begin when they establish patterns of looking after the child's basic needs, such as who gets up for 2 A.M. feedings, who stays home from work when the child is ill, who takes the child to the pediatrician. If only one parent takes care of these tasks, she explains, the other should not be surprised when the status quo is continued by a court that recognizes and affirms the decisions of the parents. This does not mean, of course, that the other parent is completely eliminated from the child's life.

Many states have laws requiring the court to consider the wishes of a child over a set age, usually twelve to fourteen. In fact, courts usually listen to the preferences of all children. However, Kass explains, judges do not automatically accept the children's wishes for numerous reasons. Children are sometimes influenced by inappropriate promises, such as a new car or no curfew. They may try to stay with the parent they feel needs them, they may have unrealistic expectations that a parent they hardly know will be better than the parent they have been living with, or they may take the materialistic route and choose the parent with more money. "In other words," she explains, "What a child wants is often not what a child needs." Judges hope the parents will come up with an agreement that will allow the child to spend time with both parents, and that the parents will abide by it.

Equal sharing of time is viewed by many, especially fathers, as a cure-all, yet psychological studies have shown that it is stressful for most children. It takes an enormous amount of energy for children to cope with both the practical aspects (such as having their things in the right place) and the emotional challenges (constantly shifting gears to adjust to the different rules and expectations) of an equal custody arrangement. They often feel a sense of divided loyalty and shoulder a heavy burden of inconvenience and confusion to avoid hurting either parent.

Judge Kass recalls the angry comments of an eighteen-year-old boy who had spent the past five years of his life shuttling between his parents' homes each week. "When my parents divorced, my mom got a new house and my dad got a new house. I got a suitcase," he remarks. "This fall I'm going to pack my suitcase and go off to college. I do not plan to visit either of those houses again anytime soon."

"Unfortunately, he had never told his parents how he felt and they were shocked at his reaction. Equal time is fair for parents, but it is rarely fair for children," says Kass.

When courts are called on to decide custody arrangements, they look at various factors. Courts do consider the preferences of the children and often utilize professionals such as psychologists and social workers to make recommendations. Courts are supposed to base all custody decisions on one bottom–line factor: the best interest of the child. Yet often the situation is inherently "no–win," because any decision will hurt someone.

It is always far better for parents to reach their own agreement rather than leaving it to the court. The agreement is sometimes called a parenting plan. It is usually made a part of the overall settlement agreement. No matter what the resolution, child custody suits are traumatic for parents and children, and they can cost tens of thousands of dollars. "Both the pain and the expense have a huge, negative effect on children," Kass remarks.

Erica Jong, writing of her daughter Molly and her current relationship with former husband Jon in her book *Fear of Fifty*, describes what can be achieved when parents put down their swords and work to become at least civil coparents: "I was always either flush or broke, but somehow I was able to pay the bills and raise my daughter. I even learned how to be a decent mother. Eventually Jon and I stopped suing each other and began to talk. Sometimes we even reminisce about old times and remember *why* we loved each other. And Molly's face lights up as if with a thousand candles."

Joint Custody

The most common type of child custody today is called joint legal custody. Joint custody means that both parents share responsibility for raising the child and actively participate in his or her life. It does not necessarily mean joint *physical* custody, or equal time custody, in which a child spends approximately half of the time living with each parent. Joint custody can encompass any type of time-share arrangement.

The label of *joint custody* may be quite significant in itself. Many psychologists criticize the term *visitation* as casting the noncustodial parent into the role of "visitor" in the child's life. According to the Joint Custody Association, a group based in Los Angeles, fathers in joint custody arrangements are late in their support payments far less than fathers who have visitation rights only.

The group, which advocates for joint custody rights, cites another study that showed that joint custody fathers contribute more voluntary extras beyond child support, such as paying for camp and music lessons 60 percent of the time, compared to 20 percent of visitation fathers. Furthermore, they return to court requesting custody changes or support adjustments only 16 percent of the time versus 31 percent for visiting fathers, according to the study.

Sole Custody

Sole custody refers to the situation in which one parent, still most often the mother, keeps the child in her home nearly all the time, with visitation rights by the other parent unless the court has found the other parent unfit or dangerous to the child, in which case there is no contact. Sometimes the court orders visitation to be supervised by a professional who can monitor what goes on between parent and child and assure the child's safety. In a sole custody arrangement, the primary parent has virtually all the decision-making authority as to how the child will be raised.

Divided or Split Custody

Divided or split custody refers to a situation in which two or more children are "split up" between the parents. For example, in a family with two sons, one parent may be primarily responsible for the older, and the other parent for the younger. This type of arrangement seems to work well for some families, especially if the two households are not far apart and the divorced parents get along well. However, it is controversial, because it divides siblings who may be close. Some judges require approval by a psychologist or other professional before agreeing to split custody.

What Type of Custody Is Best?

Any type of custody arrangement can be wonderful or disastrous, depending on the individuals involved and how they interact with one another. Also, custody arrangements may always be modified when circumstances change. The court that makes or approves the initial custody arrangement retains jurisdiction over the case, and it may be reopened in that court at any time that one or both of the parties request a change.

Psychologist Kathryn Lang feels that stability is a particularly important issue for children. "I have a personal bias in favor of one parent having primary physical custody, with visitation by the other. If parents are going to try to do a fifty-fifty split of the child's time, it should be large blocks of time such as one week, two weeks, or a month, rather than half a week with one and half a week with the other. This is very disruptive and hard on the child. It may meet the needs of the parents but usually isn't best for the children."

Like many professionals, Lang believes joint legal custody, in which both parents share decision making, is fine, *if* the parents can agree on major issues and each defer to the decisions of the other. "The success of joint custody depends on the maturity of the parents," Lang explains. "If there is any kindness in the marriage, then there can be kindness in the divorce. People who are inherently cooperative do better in divorce. There is a lot to be said for recognizing the fact that the other person is a good parent, has the best interest of the children at heart, and can be trusted not to do things that are detrimental to the kids."

Lang sees many parents get trapped in minor disputes. "People often get caught up in the petty stuff, start yelling and screaming, and proceed to work out their own issues with each other supposedly in defense of the kids. The best thing parents can do is to agree to try, agree and be pleasant to each other, and to recognize that they have a vested interest in the mental and emotional health of their children. This is essential if they care about the kids."

One study, conducted in the late 1980s, revealed that judges tend to believe that joint custody has not necessarily worked well in cases where custody is disputed, despite the fact that it is the preferred statutory plan in most states. Some of the reasons given by these judges were poor cooperation between parents, the instability for the child created by frequently shifting from home to home, distance between parents' homes, and acrimony or desire for revenge between the parents. Most of the judges preferred limited joint custody, in which one parent has primary physical custody while the other has liberal visitation and shares in decision making. Notably, the judges' reservations were limited to cases in which custody was disputed between the parents, not those custody decisions which were made amicably between the parents or with the assistance of mediators. Rather, joint custody, the study suggests, may not be the best arrangement where custody is strongly disputed and a history of emotional disagreement between the parents exists. "Joint custody sounds like a good idea, but in reality the person with physical custody calls the shots and the other has no say in how the children are raised," says one man whose family suffered continued conflict after the parents' divorce.

Although joint custody may be the best choice in many cases, it can be extremely detrimental when parents cannot agree on how the children should be raised or remain hostile for any reason. The factor most experts seem to agree is the most important in making any custody arrangement work is relative harmony between the parents. Australia was the first country to allow a judge to impose joint custody when parents could not come to an agreement on their own, but it later became the first to forbid it unless both parents agreed.

The more divorced parents are required to be in contact with one another, the more those in an acrimonious relationship find the opportunity to fight. Some of the states that jumped on the joint custody bandwagon early on have even modified their laws so that joint custody, while still available, does not get automatic preference over sole custody. Also, many fathers who fight hard for more time with their children find that they are later unwilling or unable to accept the responsibility that this type of arrangement entails. Courts are hearing more and more actions by mothers who ask the judge to order the father to spend the amount of time with the child that he requested and that the child expects.

Parents often perceive custody decisions by a court as punitive or unfair, and some certainly are. Yet it is essential to remember that a grant of primary custody to one parent is *not* tantamount to a finding that the other parent is unfit or in any way inadequate as a parent. Courts have to take all the evidence that is placed before them and weigh it against that impossibly subjective standard: the "best interest" of the child. It's easy to see what a difficult job this can be, how errors are sometimes made, and how painful the outcome will inevitably be for some or all of those involved in a custody dispute, especially the children. The trauma may be even greater if one parent pushes for a change of custody years after the divorce.

Working Mothers and a Catch-22

Judges are given broad discretion in the area of child custody decisions. While most do their best to apply appropriate criteria to reach a decision that is both fair to the parents and in the child's best interest, there still are judges out there who will let their own inappropriate biases creep into the process.

Divorcing mothers often find themselves in an impossible dilemma: Under today's no–fault law and rehabilitative alimony preference, women are expected to support themselves after a divorce and, in most cases, to provide the bulk of the support for their children as well. Women who work full-time though, especially those who place their children in day care in order to further their careers or education, may be vulnerable to change or even loss of custody for following the very course the law says they must. Author Erica Jong has described custody suits as "my generation's cruel and usual punishment for daring motherhood and a career at the same time."

Consider the highly publicized 1994 case of Jennifer Ireland, a Michigan mother who lost custody of her young daughter after she placed the child in day care while she attended university classes. The father worked, but his mother volunteered to look after the child during the day. The case is currently on appeal.

While men sometimes charge that courts automatically prefer the mother in custody disputes, legal scholars who have studied the process say that courts often hold mothers to higher standards of parenting and penalize them for working. A 1989 study conducted in the Massachusetts courts found that fathers who sued for custody were successful in getting sole or shared custody 70 percent of the time. A similar Los Angeles County study revealed a 63 percent success rate for fathers.

The Massachusetts study also found that women who temporarily separated from their children for any reason risked losing custody, whereas men who were absent for years without paying child support could return and gain custody. It also revealed that dating or remarriage worked favorably for fathers as a sign of stability, but mothers who dated were criticized.

The biggest area of prejudice against mothers, however, is work. In 1995, Los Angeles prosecutor Marcia Clark was slapped with a custody suit by her estranged husband for allegedly not spending enough time with her children during the O. J. Simpson murder trial, even though she had convinced Judge Lance Ito to recess early on Fridays so that she could spend more time with her family. Women are faced with both a catch-22 and a double standard based on a warped focus of parenting responsibilities. Fathers who take on such small tasks as making breakfast for their children before work are praised, while mothers who prepare three meals a day in spite of working full-time are criticized for not being there enough. In one New York case, custody of an eleven-year-old girl was transferred from her working mother to her unemployed father. The man had refused to pay child support for years and had been described by a court-appointed psychologist as "abrasive, antagonistic, and indifferent to the human race." Yet he was awarded custody of his daughter because he could stay home with the child.

Nicky Whelan was devastated when the court shifted primary custody of her son to her ex-husband because, she believes, she was single, working, and living in a small, two bedroom townhouse, while he was remarried and could offer the child a larger, two-parent home. "I was found guilty of committing single motherhood," she says. "Imagine what the courts would be telling me if I was on welfare. I didn't even receive child support when my son lived with me. I have a bachelor's degree, a full-time job, and volunteer in my community. I am, however, single and below average in pay. After nine years, the judge changed custody because my ex-husband lives at an address the judge considered preferable, and he is married. I call it the 'fungible mother theory'—the notion that one 'mother,' or stepmother, will do as well as another."

Whelan saw an ironic flip side to her situation, as well. "The psychologist that was brought into our custody battle let me know that if I were to find a man, she would reconsider her custody recommendations. Not only is this idea that I should `find a man, any man' in order to be a good mother outrageous, it ignores the reality of being a single parent. In our culture, the growing pressure on women to support themselves and their children leaves little time to build a real relationship. Yet when I did not take her suggestion and find a man, I paid the stiffest of penalties: A judge took away custody of my child. This judge had one leg firmly in the 1990s, and the other in the 1950s. He believes that he ruled in the best interest of the child. Instead, he may have ruled in the best memory of his childhood."

Given Whelan's experience, it is easy to see why she says, "If being single is a good reason for taking a child away, then single, educated, working mothers do indeed face an escalating risk from every direction."

Father's Rights

Although women are victimized by gender bias more often, men, too, suffer bigotry from ignorant judges. In one New York case, for example, a female judge refused to allow a father to keep his infant child overnight because she assumed he would not know how to take care of a baby.

Over the past fifteen to twenty years, the law has almost universally adopted the idea that fathers and mothers should have equal rights to custody of their children. Consequently, there has been a growing movement by fathers seeking better laws, more fair custody and visitation determinations in the courts, and public support for the rights and responsibilities of divorced fathers. Many organizations have been founded to assist divorced fathers (see appendix A).

Yet, while there has been increased lip service given to the rights of fathers, old attitudes die hard. For example, the controversial "tender years doctrine," a presumption that gave strong preference to mothers in custody disputes involving children of young age (generally under seven to ten years old), has been outmoded in theory, but many judges still accept the doctrine in practice.

Attorney Judith Finfrock feels men should get equal consideration in child custody cases, and she has represented a number of fathers on custody issues. She handled only one case in which the custody issue had to proceed through the entire court process, including psychological evaluations. But the father did receive primary custody. "To tell you the truth, I was somewhat surprised, because there is still a preference in the legal system for custody to go to the mother," she says. "I agree that this may make sense for a toddler or preschool child, but it's still hard for fathers with older children to get equal consideration."

She agrees with other professionals who feel that fathers who have exhibited abusive or criminal behavior toward the child or the other parent should not be allowed custody or unrestricted visitation. "The criminal system doesn't provide enough safeguards, and the well-being of the child has to be the top priority," she states. "But in other cases, fathers should have rights fully equal to those of the mother. Children need fathers as role models, and this is as important for daughters as it is for sons. Psychological studies show that daughters learn the level of respect and care they should expect in their relationships with men from observing the way their fathers treat their mothers. So it's essential that parents maintain a civil, respectful relationship after the divorce, and that fathers set a good example for their daughters to observe. For the same reason, fathers who are abusive to a child's mother should not be allowed to influence the child until they clean up their act."

Finfrock says she used to see greater efforts by fathers to gain custody or liberal visitation with sons rather than with daughters, but that seems to be changing. Her practice today includes a large percentage of Hispanic clients, and she sees an even greater effort by Hispanic fathers to maintain custody or close relationships with daughters than with sons. "Traditionally, Hispanic fathers take a more macho attitude with sons, expecting them to be strong, not to cry, that sort of thing. But daughters are seen as precious little jewels, special treasures. They're very protective of their girls and anxious to be a part of their lives. But sometimes the courts don't realize how important a father is to a child."

What does all this mean? It means that gender bias is still a serious problem in many courtrooms. Parents of both sexes who are unable to work out custody arrangements on their own should get expert legal representation if any custody dispute arises. The lawyer should be not only well versed in the nuts and bolts of the law, but also very familiar with all local judges who could be assigned to the case.

Hostile Parents and the Damage to Children

It's a sad yet undeniable fact that whenever custody is disputed or a shared custodial arrangement is volatile, the children suffer, even if the parents actively try to protect them. A good lawyer representing a client in a custody dispute will emphasize that their client must put the interest of the child first. The custody proceeding should be viewed as an opportunity to advocate in favor of the benefit to the child, not against the other parent.

Finfrock is surprised at how many of her clients with children have no concept of the relationship they will have to continue with the other parent after the divorce. "People come in, for example, with two children, ages nine and seven. When I tell them they will have to deal with their husband or wife for the next ten or eleven years, they are shocked. They thought they could just eliminate this person from their lives."

A parent seeking custody or increased visitation rights must be prepared to demonstrate, with concrete examples, why he or she is a good and devoted parent. As in all legal cases, information and evidence are powerful in a custody dispute. Parents will benefit by putting together a well-organized, detailed collection of information on their relationship with the child, the goals and responsibilities they are prepared to face in parenting, how they would encourage the child to have a good relationship with both parents, and as many related issues as possible. Unfair as it may seem, parents must also be certain that their own behavior is above reproach and willing to avoid actions that could be used against them by the other parent, such as living with a new mate during the custody proceeding. While judges are supposed to make decisions based on how the behavior actually affects the child, many judges can't help but be biased by their own personal opinions.

Record keeping can also be helpful in custody matters. Parents should keep detailed records of the time spent with the child, including the other partner's reactions, any problems that arise, and what activities are shared with the child. Records of child support payments and any extras purchased for the child can also be important. This does not mean that the parent must spend all the time with the child scribbling in a notebook. General records of the more important activities and expenditures are generally sufficient. Likewise, parents often overcompensate by trying to make every moment spent with the child as entertaining as a three-ring circus. Children sometimes complain that parents try to overentertain them when they are tired or simply in need of some quiet time with the parent.

Parents should also remember that judges are reluctant to bounce children around through frequent changes of custody and visitation arrangements. Therefore, the initial custody decisions should be as thorough, detailed, and carefully thought out as possible. While flexibility is a plus, it is not unusual for very specific matters to be addressed in custodial orders. I once read a custody decree that stated the father was to pick up his son from school several evenings a week, then return him to the mother's home at 8:00 P.M., but on Wednesday nights he could return the boy later, so he would not have to miss the end of his favorite television show. Such items may seem trivial but can be important to the child to help maintain some stability and continuity in his or her routine. Spelling them out in no uncertain terms prevents the kind of petty disputes between parents that can escalate into real problems.

You should also remember that although frequent changes in custody orders are disfavored, a child's life can change a lot in three or four years. It isn't unusual for custody or visitation arrangements to be modified as a child gets older and becomes involved in different activities. Again, such changes are far easier if the parents can communicate amicably and remain focused on the needs of the child.

Parents who have taken extraordinary steps to spend time with their children, such as moving or rearranging a work schedule, make a strong impression on judges and their professional advisers. A willingness to have a mental health professional monitor any change and periodically report to the court, especially in a potentially difficult situation such as a fifty–fifty living arrangement, can also be quite impressive to a judge.

Parents sharing custody of children must remember that demonstrations of anger or tension between them are always painful to a child. Continued, outright hostility over a period of years can be extremely destructive to a child's sense of well-being. Some enlightened parents who utterly hate each other but nevertheless love their children have used a unique type of couples counseling, which has proven effective in helping them to establish a civil, mature relationship. This type of assistance is becoming more common and is often available through marriage counselors, mediators, or family therapists. With help, most people can become effective coparents who can get along at least well enough to deal with the essential interactions without overt unpleasantness.

Above all, parents involved in custody disputes must remember two things. First, the child or children are the focus. The issue is not which parent will "win." Nor is the first concern the rights of the parents. The number–one issue to be decided is what arrangement will serve the best interest of the child, and how this can best be accomplished under the unique circumstances of the individuals involved.

Second, even the best team of lawyers, psychologists, and other experts cannot prepare a case alone. The parents must be willing to put in a lot of time and effort to prove that the child is the top priority and that the type of arrangement they request will serve this paramount interest. Even if a lawyer does not ask the client to do so, the parent must be willing to think for himself or herself and give careful consideration to whatever might help the case. Gather and organize as much information as possible, prepare lists of all potential witnesses, and think about strategy and testimony, then let the lawyer sort it out and decide how it may best be used. This can also save a great deal of money, as it can substantially reduce the amount of time the lawyer will have to spend working on parts of the case that can be handled by a willing client.

While a divorce is always traumatic, children bounce back and readjust in nearly all cases *if* the parents focus on their love for them and are willing to love them enough to put aside their animosity toward each other and behave in a civilized manner. Many believe that continued hostilities between parents is one of the most harmful things a child can face, second only to abuse.

Psychologist Constance Ahrons, author of *The Good Divorce,* stresses the importance of maintaining a "limited partnership" when couples with children divorce. This means parents must maintain an egalitarian relationship between themselves, set basic ground rules, and make a realistic list of the problems to be addressed.

Ahrons emphasizes the importance of parents keeping sight of the many good options available, with the assistance of professional help to establish a plan to minimize the family's loss and maximize its gains. She urges parents who have difficulty in communicating or cooperating after a divorce to look for common ground and to try to keep sight of mutual goals for the children. Sometimes this requires setting limits and stating boundaries in an explicit manner, especially when the balance of power between the parents is unequal or a subject of struggle. Counseling or mediation can help parents who have difficulty working together to establish a cooperative arrangement. As Ahrons states, "A good divorce does not require that parents share child care responsibilities equally. It means they share them clearly. Whatever living arrangements and division of responsibilities parents decide on, they cooperate within those limits."

Ahrons emphasizes that relationships between parents and children and between men and women are in a great state of flux at the present time, and that visions of family are changing rapidly. Parents who set a successful example for others are helping to change society and encourage growth in other families. When former spouses decide to put children first and their personal differences second, when they can see and face their problems and come up with realistic solutions subject to adjustment if necessary, and when they are willing to seek help from a third party when unable to reach their own solutions, then parents, children, and society all benefit.

How Are Custody Decisions Made?

There has been some limited scientific study of the inherently subjective processes used by judges in reaching child custody decisions. In general, judges tend to give great weight to each parent's sense of responsibility, overall mental stability, and maturity, as they perceive it. One study also found that while judges and the mental health professionals who advise them tend to agree on many factors, the two groups differed in their assessment of how much weight should be given to a child's wishes, to the preference of keeping a child with the mother, and to the preference for a two-parent home. A study that combined the efforts of legal and behavioral scientists found that judges attach greater significance to evidence which comes from the parents, from impartial sources not aligned with one parent or the other, and to the desires of older children. The opinions of psychologists hired by one party were given less weight than the findings of court-appointed psychologists.

Judges and mental health professionals generally agree that when considering joint custody versus single parent custody, the most important criteria to be considered include the age of the child, the willingness of the parents to cooperate in a joint custody situation, the quality of the child's relationship with each parent, the amount of anger and bitterness between the parents, and the psychological stability of the parents. The factors considered least relevant by both groups include the gender of the child, the wishes of a young child, the age of the parents, economic or physical similarities and differences, marital status of parents, differences in religious beliefs, whether the child would be in day care while a parent works, and the parents' economic stability.

One important criterion is whether the custodial parent refrains from displays of hostility toward the other. A parent who uses the child as a pawn, openly incites battle in front of the child, or poisons the child's mind against the other parent not only is hurting the child but may risk losing custody.

Unfortunately, false accusations of abuse to gain custody advantages are not uncommon. Family law attorney David B. Riggert reports that he is seeing an increasing number of false accusations of child or spousal abuse by parents trying to gain leverage in the divorce proceeding. "An often-used practice is to apply for an emergency order of protection charging the other spouse with domestic abuse in order to get immediate physical custody of a child," he explains. "I have clients who actually suggest this as a strategic move. I try to explain to them that there are legitimate ways to gain custody, and that not only are such false charges illegal and a waste of everyone's time and money, they could be terribly destructive to the child." Even worse, says Riggert, are the cases in which both parents wage a war by firing false and highly damaging accusations against one another. "People who do this fail to realize that if both manage to convince the judge that the other parent is unfit, the child may be placed in foster care and neither will get custody. Now, when a client appears to be ready to start a war, I ask, 'What is the worst thing that could happen?' Invariably, they acknowledge that it would be far worse for both to lose custody than for the other to be the primary custodian."

Two areas, inconsistency in decisions and the handful of judges who repeatedly base custody determinations on inappropriate considerations, seem to be among the major problems in judicial custody determinations today. While much of the unhappiness expressed by parents and children over custody decisions can be fairly attributed to the fact that any custody dispute is a no-win situation in which someone will be left unhappy, stories of outrageous bias, incompetence, and poorly reasoned decisions are still heard far too often.

Unfortunately, custody battles often rage on for years, whether the parties return to court or not. "You don't know them until you divorce them," says Cynde Goyen, whose divorce in 1986 included a bitter child custody battle. "He had his marriage his way and got his divorce his way. I feel that he used our kids to try to keep me. He demanded I move out of the house and then started immediately fighting for custody. It went on and on."

Goyen's experience is not uncommon. Parents often use their children as weapons and seldom realize how damaging this can be. "We thought we had settled the property issues, then he would use the custody battle to try to manipulate me into agreeing to a less favorable settlement," says Goyen. "It took over a year and a half until all the dust settled, and then he ended up with sole custody of our children. This was very unusual in the mid–1980s, and I felt the decision was a horrible judgment against me. It was devastating emotionally, personally, and socially."

Goyen said her husband was emotionally abusive during the marriage but grew much worse after it was over, because now the children had become involved. "After I had stayed home for nine years raising three children, I asked him for a divorce. He couldn't stand the idea of rejection, so he did all he could to try and hurt me back. He knew that taking the children away and denying me access to them would be the worst thing he could do to me," she explains.

Even after Goyen's husband "won" custody, he kept trying to poison the children's minds against their mother. "When I got an offer for a better job and had to move one hour away from the home, he made it really difficult for me to see them. He made the children believe that I was abandoning them and turned them against me. But I'm glad I made the move, because I needed the space to sort things out."

Goyen finds it difficult to shake her bitterness toward the legal system. "I believed in the justice system before, but I feel the court focused on petty issues and didn't really look at what was happening. The kids would have truly been better off with me for many reasons, but the court didn't see what was important or look at the whole picture."

Goyen is quick to add that she does not believe that primary custody should automatically go to the woman. The man to whom she is married today received sole custody of his three daughters after his own divorce. "What is interesting is comparing his situation and mine. There are similarities and differences," she says. "Brad is a good father and got custody for the right reasons. He actually raised his children, and he was the parent most involved with them during the marriage. He had far more cause to be upset with his ex-wife than my husband did with me, yet he never mistreated her. We have had some very interesting talks comparing our situations."

Cynde Goyen and her ex-husband still have unresolved differences, although he gradually stopped denying her visitation and has allowed the children to spend longer periods of time staying with her. Her oldest son has now come to live with her and her new family. Yet she still worries about her ex-husband's upbringing and influence on the children. "Their father has never really raised them at all. He is a selfish person, married to himself, really. He has gone through seven housekeepers in two years. This means complete strangers are raising my children. I can't believe that the courts feel that this is better, that this is in their best interest. It seems the only way he can show love to his children is through material things. Men who are good parents should absolutely have the equal right to get custody of their children, like Brad, my husband now. But some men are misusing their rights and seeking custody for the wrong reasons. This isn't fair to anyone, especially the children."

Custody and Relocation

One of the most difficult issues divorced parents may face, either at the time of divorce or years later, is how to manage joint custody and/or visitation when one parent wants or is required by their work to move a considerable distance away from the other. As Cynde Goyen's experience shows, even a short move can cause tremendous problems when parents have an ongoing conflict.

Yet it's not uncommon for one parent's need or desire to relocate to cause extreme upset or even hostility in what may have formerly been a friendly, civilized coparenting relationship. A mother with primary custody may be shocked to learn that a father who has refused to meet his obligations of child support or spent little time with his children can block her choice to relocate. Conversely, a father who has consistently paid all the required support and has taken an active part in raising his children may suddenly be faced with a situation in which he will be forced to travel great distances or pay transportation for his children if the custodial mother decides to move.

A parent's desire to relocate often brings conflicting legal rights into the picture. On the one hand, in America we recognize a strong right to travel and live where you like. On the other hand, parents also have a unique set of rights and responsibilities, and the right of reasonable visitation includes the right to see a child without having to undergo great expense or inconvenience. If you are contemplating a move, it is best to talk to a lawyer about your rights and obligations before you commit to a new job or home. Parents who are able to communicate well and maintain a good rapport in the interest of their child are usually able to work out a solution that both can live with, through changes in visitation schedules, sharing of transportation costs, and other compromises. If you must go to court for approval of the move, be prepared to show that it is in the best interest of the child; it is being done for a legitimate reason and not to make it more difficult on your former spouse; and if the children are in favor of the move, note this as well.

What *is* fair when one parent wants to relocate? There are no easy answers. The right of women to have equal opportunities to achieve a successful and fulfilling career and the expectation under modern law that they must do so to provide for their own support and a major part of the support of their children often makes relocation desirable or mandatory for career advancement. Custodial fathers face similar problems. Parents who remarry have a new spouse's career to consider in addition to their own. The issue of relocation has become such a headache that some states are changing their laws to be more specific about what is and is not allowed without court approval. For example, Illinois law currently allows the custodial parent to move anywhere within the state without specific approval by the court or the other parent. Under this system, a parent could move from Chicago to Cairo, a six-hour drive, but a parent living in the Quad Cities straddling the Illinois–Iowa border could not move across the river. Under a new law currently pending in the Illinois legislature, the geographic boundary would change to a 100-mile radius from the non-custodial parent.

Of course, parents may also specify restrictions on relocation in the parenting agreement encompassed in the final divorce decree. Family law attorney David B. Riggert recommends that the non–custodial parent formulate a reasonable restriction on relocation to be included in any such agreement.

In areas without definite legal guidelines, if the parties are unable to work out a compromise they can live with, the courts look at each situation on a case–by–case basis. Judges consider such criteria as the economic circumstances of each parent, the wishes of the child, the distance involved, and similar factors.

It is also important to remember that the court making the initial custody decision at the time of the divorce retains jurisdiction over the case to make any subsequent changes. Therefore, if one or both parents have moved since the divorce, it will be necessary to return to the court in which the original decree was granted to hash out any problems that come up later or take special steps to transfer the case. Parents who move without coming to a custody and visitation modification agreement, or without getting the court's permission to move when the other parent opposes it, can face the penalties that come from violating any court order. Furthermore, if the parent does not inform the other of his or her whereabouts, that parent may be subject to civil and criminal penalties for parental kidnapping.

PROFESSIONAL EVALUATION

When parents are unable to agree on custody issues or request an unusual arrangement, a judge, mediator, or the parents may decide to hire a mental health professional to conduct a custody evaluation.

The evaluator, usually a psychologist or social worker with a specific level of skill and training, usually begins by meeting with the children and parents. If the evaluation is to be a comprehensive evaluation, the evaluator will also speak with other important people in the child's life such as grandparents, potential stepparents, baby-sitters, teachers, and others. Another important group that should not be overlooked are close friends of the child, who often have insights into the child's feelings and thoughts that are not shared with adults. The evaluator may also visit the homes and workplaces of the parents and may conduct various psychological tests on the parents and on the child.

The findings of this person can be used in various ways. Sometimes, when a highly qualified professional conducts a comprehensive evaluation at the behest of the court, he or she will testify as an expert witness. Those who conduct more limited examinations are often made available as fact witnesses who offer information on their findings but do not state an expert opinion as to what custody arrangement would be best.

The recommendations of such experts may be helpful outside the court context, too, as in private settlement negotiations or mediation. In any case, the professional evaluation is usually far more valuable if the person conducting it is neutral; that is, appointed by the court or agreed on by both parents. A parent working with such professionals should keep in mind that while it may be tempting to outline a litany of the other parent's faults, this is not the focus of the professional's assessment and may be detrimental. Rather, the professional will pay the most attention to the relationship between that parent and the child, and to each individual's parenting contributions and skills. The parent seeking a favorable outcome should actively avoid hostility toward the other party, and concentrate on demonstrating an ability to provide a positive living environment, qualified alternative supervision for the child while the parent is not at home, nourishing food and adequate clothing, sensible discipline, and strong, genuine affection. Education is becoming increasingly important in custody determinations as well. Of course, if there has been abuse or other serious wrongdoing by the other parent, this should be brought to the professional's attention.

Unique Solutions to Custody Dilemmas

Although traditional patterns of custody still predominate, many parents are trying innovative arrangements. Parents who are able to establish a cooperative parenting relationship after the divorce are often able to come up with flexible, creative custody and visitation plans that provide a workable solution for everyone involved. Couples living a great distance apart have still managed to share joint custody of children through extended periods of time in each place, even alternating years. Others have taken the opposite route, in which the children stay in the family home, and each parent alternates between living in the home and in another residence nearby.

Such arrangements are often successful but can also cause tremendous upheaval for children, and not every arrangement will work for every family. Perhaps the most essential criteria are flexibility and communication. As circumstances change, children grow, or someone involved becomes uncomfortable with the situation, parents must be able to negotiate with each other to achieve a better solution.

CHILD SUPPORT

Unlike spousal support, child support is mandatory in nearly all cases, until the child reaches the age of majority, generally eighteen or twenty-one. A few states are changing their laws to require that child support be paid until graduation from college. The amount of support a court orders depends on state guidelines, how custody is arranged, and the earnings of both parents. Child support orders are always subject to later modification as the circumstances of the parents and children change.

State Support Guidelines

In 1988, Congress passed the Family Support Act, which required all states to adopt a uniform, statewide formula to set child support payments by October of 1989. All states now have guidelines written into their child support laws, which estimate the basic expense of raising a child and determine how much support will be paid by the parent who does not have primary physical custody. Most guidelines are based on the income of both parents and how much time the child spends in the custody and care of each. These guidelines are considered just that—guidelines—and not mandates written in stone. Courts will look at other factors such as the individual needs of the children involved, alternative plans proposed by the parents, and new children to be supported. Some states have several different formulas depending on custody arrangements or other factors.

In most jurisdictions, couples may depart from these standards if they mutually agree to do so. However, a judge has to review and approve all custody and support agreements to be sure that the child will be adequately supported, especially if the couple agrees to an amount below that recommended by the guidelines. Both parents have an obligation under the law to support the child; an agreement for zero child support will never be approved. While child support has no tax consequences in that it is neither deductible to the payor nor taxable to the recipient, custody arrangements generally state who gets to take the dependent deduction for the child.

Again, in most states, child support is required by law only until the children reach the age of majority and become legally responsible as adults for their own support. Obviously, many children are still in high school or college at majority. College tuition and other costs can be a real problem for divorced parents, because many states won't enforce a child support agreement which requires payment beyond the age of majority. However, savings for college may be considered as a part of the cost of supporting a child during their minority. Also, parents can enter into a contract apart from the child support agreement which will be enforceable as long as it meets the terms of any legal contract; namely, offer, acceptance, and the exchange of consideration. For example, the noncustodial parent may offer to pay the child's college tuition and housing costs if the other parent will pay for clothing, transportation, and other living expenses. This is something that should be discussed in detail with an attorney as early as possible, preferably when the original support agreement is negotiated.

The Family Support Act of 1988 made another extremely important change in the law. As of January 1, 1994, all child support orders must include an automatic wage withholding provision. If the employer of the noncustodial parent receives a copy of the court order, a portion of his or her pay will be withheld and sent directly to the custodial parent. Other income such as Social Security may also be withheld and sent directly to the custodial parent by using the court order. Under this new federal law, payments do not have to be late before wage withholding can begin. This law applies only to child support orders made after the effective date of the law. However, an employer must follow this method for any child support order if the payor is one month late.

States have various laws and methods to deal with child support enforcement when parents don't pay. Parents who are self-employed must sometimes pay a state's child support enforcement agency directly. The agency then pays the custodial parent. That way, the agency can monitor payments and take steps to enforce them if any are missed. In other states, or in individual cases, a court trustee or clerk collects payment from the noncustodial parent and pays the custodial parent. This allows the same court that issued the order to monitor payment.

Some studies estimate that approximately half of all parents ordered to pay child support under any type of plan or custody arrangement do not pay anything at all. Among the 50 percent who do pay, half of those do not pay the full amount. A number of communities are trying different ways to improve these sad statistics. The most successful seem to combine strict penalties for failure to pay child support with practical assistance to fathers. For example, in Racine, Wisconsin, an innovative project gives deadbeat parents two choices: go to the county jail, or get a job, keep it, and pay child support. The program assists the parents in finding work and developing the skills to keep the job. Child support payments are automatically deducted from paychecks.

It is important to remember that filing for bankruptcy will not get a person off the hook for alimony, child support, taxes, or mortgage payments. Even imprisonment may not end the obligation to make support payments. Sixteen-year-old fathers have been ordered to pay child support. In Massachusetts, a person who does not pay child support faces losing professional or business licenses and even their driver's license. States as well as the federal government are getting tough on people who do not accept their responsibility to support their children. Courts, too, are taking a harsher view of those that refuse to pay child support, especially repeat offenders. Courts are not hesitant to issue such tools as writs of seizure to impound and sell businesses or tools of trade.

The U.S. Dept. of Health and Human Services' Office of Child Support Enforcement is a federal agency serving all fifty states through regional offices (see appendix A). In addition, all states have agencies to help collect overdue child support, help locate parents, get child support orders established for those who do not have them, garnish wages and tax refunds, help parents set up automatic deductions from paychecks, get liens against property, and make reports on those who owe more than $1,000 to credit bureaus. State and federal parent locator services do computer searches to find parents who have disappeared and stopped paying support. This gets easier all the time as the information superhighway grows. Deadbeat parents are being located through driver's license records, the IRS, voter records, Social Security records, draft records, and many other kinds of data. State and local agencies often work in conjunction with the federal Office of Child Support Enforcement to locate missing parents.

It has been estimated that only 58 percent of single-parent households have child support orders in place, and that of these families, only half receive the support due. In response to this national crisis, both the states and the federal government have initiated various new efforts to make parents take financial responsibility for their children. In 1996, for example, the U.S. Postal Service announced that it would coordinate with states to assist in the identification and apprehension of deadbeat parents by displaying "Wanted Lists" in post offices of parents who had failed to pay child support.

The Clinton administration has declared child support enforcement a priority, and has worked with Congress to assist the states in developing more effective collection programs. Welfare reform legislation signed by President Clinton in 1996 included strong new measures against non-custodial parents who failed to pay the support they owed. The new law added tough penalties to those already available, including drivers' license revocation and seizure of many new types of assets. The legislation also recognized the importance to children of having access to their noncustodial parent.

To assist in this effort, the Child Support Enforcement program (CSE) is a federal/state partnership which promotes family self-sufficiency by securing regular and timely child support payments. State CSE programs locate missing parents, establish paternity, set and enforce support orders, and collect payments. CSE services are available automatically for families receiving assistance under the new Temporary Assistance for Needy Families (TANF) programs and to other families who apply for the services.

The CSE program has already begun to amass impressive results. During fiscal 1996, an estimated $12 billion in child support payments was collected, and paternity established for a million children. Almost 1.1 million new child support orders were established in fiscal 1995. Income tax refunds, lottery winnings, retirement benefits, real estate, and other property of non-paying parents may be seized or encumbered by lien to satisfy unpaid child support.

The "teeth" provided by this new law have proven sharply effective at the state level as well. In New Mexico, for example, child support payments collected by the Human Services Department increased by 27 percent in a single month after the state revoked the driver's licenses of nearly 11,000 people who had failed to pay child support and had not responded to a six-week amnesty program that gave parents an option to pay what they owed before the penalties were invoked. Other states have reported similar increases. The message is clear: parents must assume responsibility for the support of their children, or suffer serious consequences. State offices involved with this program are listed in the appendix.

Most states have a long statute of limitations so that parents may collect back support at any time, including after the child reaches majority. Most states will allow a suit for back support to be brought ten to twenty years after it became due. If this is required, interest may also be collected at the statutory rate, which is frequently higher than current market rates. Child support enforcement is discussed in greater detail in chapter 8.

Child Support Modification

Child support orders or agreements can always be modified by the court that entered or approved the original order. Parents who reach their own agreement simply file a written document reflecting the change with the court. When only one wants a modification, he or she must request that the court make the alteration and show "changed circumstances." The type of changed circumstances that may justify lowered child support by the noncustodial parent include a legitimate and substantial decrease in income, a reasonable increase in expenses such as a new child in the home, the fact that the custodial parent got a windfall, or that the child's needs changed (for example, both parents agreed to take the child out of private school). For a custodial parent, support may be increased if he or she can show a substantial decrease in income, increased expenses such as another child, that the noncustodial parent got a big raise or windfall, or that the child's needs have changed, warranting an increase—something not uncommon as children get older. Specific rules vary by state.

Most people agree that anyone who accepts the responsibility of parenting a child must be held accountable for the child's financial support. Yet this is an area with conflicting realities and no easy answers. With serial marriages and blended families becoming increasingly common, many parents find it nearly impossible to meet the financial obligations of supporting children from both former and current relationships.

The key to reaching a workable solution—and avoiding huge debts and severe penalties—is communication. Parents who cannot meet their support obligations will have a much better chance of fair, favorable treatment by the court if *they* take the initiative to request a reduction in monthly support payments and keep paying something each month, even if they can't pay the full amount.

Beyond the Child Support Guidelines

In trying to establish a support plan that can work for a period of years, it is important to consider factors beyond the state guidelines. People often forget the everyday details and uncommon expenses that can throw a budget into disarray.

Judy Lawrence, a budgeting counselor and author of several books on financial planning (see the Resources section), notes that people involved in a divorce often forget to take the time to look at the real, total cost of living, especially children's expenses. Although it may not be too difficult to calculate the expenses of very young children, the older a child gets, the more complex such planning becomes.

Lawrence explains that most parents begin by adding up such costs as tuition, day care, orthodontia, and karate lessons, but a complete picture requires a much more detail-oriented approach. She reviews with her clients each of the child's school programs, sports, hobbies, lessons, and general activities, then figures out all the expenses entailed by each activity. It is also essential to include school-related expenses such as yearbooks, class rings, photos, fund-raising activities, letter jackets, uniforms, proms and homecoming, and graduation gifts.

Often, too, sports and organizations require expenditures a parent won't anticipate in assessing the cost of the activity. Besides clothing, shoes, and equipment, there may be entry fees, travel, team photos, coach's gifts, banquets, camp, and trophies. Music activities are full of hidden costs such as private lessons, sheet music, reeds (Lawrence says she has seen reeds alone come to $100 per year), trips, and performance clothing. Dance or gymnastic students need tights, costumes, lessons, and well-fitting, appropriate shoes. The skier, actor, singer, horseback rider, computer buff, or hockey player has a unique set of similar costs. Even if the expenses do not occur every month, Lawrence urges parents to calculate a monthly average, which may be substantial. Parents need to have an explicit picture of the expenses in order to plan how to meet them and avoid having to take the child out of cherished and important activities.

Parents Who Misuse Support

Another factor that makes setting and enforcing child support a difficult task is the sad fact that occasionally custodial parents do misuse the money they receive. Tom Murphy is the devoted father of two daughters. He has never missed a child support payment in the twelve years since his divorce, and he has also been very generous in providing extra benefits and gifts for his daughters. However, he has been continually frustrated by his ex-wife's refusal to abide by the terms of the custody and support agreement, as well as her constant demands for more money.

"I kept up my end of the bargain, but she didn't," he explains. "For instance, I agreed to pay extra at the time of the divorce so the girls could have a private parochial education. I later found out that she was using the tuition money for other things, mostly to benefit her rather than our daughters. Child support should be viewed as *child* support, not another source of income to be spent anyway you please. It's specifically for the good of the children. She used the money for herself, spending it on things like summer cottages and vacations with her boyfriend, while the girls did without. I had to buy them essentials like gym shoes and glasses on my own, in addition to paying child support, if I wanted to be sure they got the things they needed."

Tom's former wife has never been hesitant to exploit the court system. "When I married again, she immediately took us to court and demanded more money because my total household income had gone up, even though my second wife wasn't earning much money at the time, far less than my ex was making. She was driving a new car and taking several vacations a year, while my new wife and I were virtually broke. Yet she manipulated the system to get support payments raised, and I still found myself having to buy the kids things to meet their basic needs. I would advise anyone in a similar situation to keep very careful records, including receipts and accounts for everything bought directly for the children."

Fortunately, laws in many states are becoming more specific as to what can be considered an appropriate change in circumstances to increase or decrease child support. Many now have laws providing that a new spouse's income cannot be considered, yet difficulties and abuses persist.

Murphy believes that part of the problem lies with the legal and judicial system. "Throughout all the wranglings over support, the attorneys on both sides really have been devil's advocates," he says. "I do believe that family courts are slanted in favor of women, though I know both men and women abuse the system. But a lot of things make the system inherently unfair. For example, when I remarried, the judge instantly raised my child support obligations. Yet he didn't consider my ex-wife's total household income. Both she and her new husband make a very good living. The formula that was used looked at my household income, but only my wife's earnings alone. And when I was unemployed for several months after the company I worked for went bankrupt, there was no adjustment in my child support obligation during this time."

Today, men are getting better treatment under current divorce laws. "When I got divorced in the seventies, the system was really anti-male," Murphy continues. "My wife was having an affair, and she demanded the divorce so she could be with her lover. I didn't want the divorce, yet I was made out to be a bad guy and suffered for it financially. There should be some way people could try to avoid adversarial divorces, especially when children are involved. Parents inevitably use kids as pawns, or to spite their spouse, for things that have nothing to do with the kids. You're stuck having to deal with your ex forever. The system should give parents a break somehow."

CHILD ABDUCTION

According to statistics produced by the U.S. Justice Department in 1990, more than 350,000 children were kidnapped by family members during 1988 alone. The most common reason for such abductions is that a person feels that a custody decision was unfair or wants to avoid becoming further embroiled in a custody dispute and decides to take the law into his or her own hands. Sometimes desperate parents view a custody battle as too risky, too expensive, or too time consuming. Some blame the legal system as contributing to the problem by its cost, inflexibility, and inability to address the emotional issues involved in a custody case.

That same Justice Department study, commissioned by its Office of Juvenile Justice and Delinquency Prevention, found that most children abducted by family members were back home in a week or less. Yet even a brief abduction can cause tremendous anguish and terror to both the parent and the abducted child, who may suffer long-term emotional trauma as a result. Of course, when a child is abducted and forced to live on the run for a longer period, the trauma can be very severe.

Many parents who kidnap their children believe they are justified. They feel they were forced into doing so by a system that denied them their rights or by a spouse who deliberately isolated the children and prevented them from maintaining contact. Often they have an idyllic and grossly distorted fantasy of creating a perfect new life with a child who will adjust easily, with the former spouse out of their lives once and for all. Needless to say, this is virtually never the case.

In the past, there may have been some legal basis for such high hopes. When the parents lived in different jurisdictions, and one parent brought the child into the area where he or she lived, judges felt obligated to hold a custody hearing to protect the rights of the citizens they served. Many sincere judges believed they had a duty to fully investigate the welfare of a child brought into their jurisdiction, even if another court had already held a full custody hearing. Today, all states have adopted some form of the Uniform Child Custody Jurisdiction Act, which was designed to eliminate such incidents. The act requires courts to defer to legally binding custody orders from another court in a different jurisdiction.

Ongoing controversy over child support, visitation, or custody arrangements often triggers child stealing. This is especially true when parents try to manipulate or retaliate against each other. The custodial parent who does not receive child support may deny the other parent visitation, or the parent denied visitation may withhold support. It is important to note that these two legal issues are separate. While refusing to pay child support may certainly be considered by a judge setting visitation or custody, the issues really are different. When parents tie the two problems together, it is the children who lose.

Recently, increasing attention has been given to the plight of all kidnapped children, including those abducted by family members. Both greater media coverage of individual stories and broader social concern overall have made finding missing children somewhat more likely. Numerous organizations exist to help locate missing children (see appendix A). Most children who disappear are eventually located.

Yet sometimes even heroic efforts take years to pay off. In one case, a father snatched his son from the mother's home in Spain and returned to the United States. He settled with the child in a small Texas community with the help of his family in California. The mother, with the financial assistance and moral support of her well-to-do family, hired the best attorneys and investigators, invoked the help of the American press, checked every possible government resource and record bureau, and even gained the assistance of Interpol. The family spent thousands of dollars on private detectives, yet the boy and his father were not located until they moved back to California, some four and a half years after the abduction.

Laws against parental kidnapping have continued to evolve to prevent such tragedies. However, the development of law in this area has been hampered by the same attitudes that delayed the adoption and enforcement of laws against domestic violence and other crimes in the home. Some legislators and others in the legal system believed that such occurrences were private "family matters" and that the law should not interfere. As more information on tragedy and trauma wrought by crimes within the family have come to light, such assumptions have, fortunately, become the exception rather than the rule.

The penalties faced by a kidnapping parent vary from state to state. Nearly all states now have their own laws, in addition to the Uniform Child Custody Jurisdiction Act, making child abduction a felony. New federal legislation went into effect in 1988 to enforce the Hague Convention on International Child Abduction, a treaty that set up a system to be followed by member countries to guarantee the prompt return of children taken across international boundaries. The new law, named the International Child Abduction Remedies Act, is aimed at reducing international child snatching, though it still happens far too often. Furthermore, if a parent takes a child into a country that is not a signatory to the law, the other parent's remedies may depend on the justice available in that nation.

A parent who abducts a child may be subject to serious criminal penalties, such as charges of felonious concealment, as well as a civil lawsuit by the other parent to recover legal fees and expenses for locating and recovering custody of the child. In the international case mentioned above, the mother won a civil judgment for her legal and investigative fees to locate her son, which totaled over $76,000.

Others who conspire to assist in a child kidnapping, such as grandparents or other family members, can also be subject to civil and criminal penalties. Those who assist indirectly may become involved as well. In 1983, the Donahue Television Production Company was ordered by a court to pay $5.9 million in damages to a mother whose child had been kidnapped by the father. The father had appeared, in disguise, on the "Donahue" show, while an employee of the company baby-sat the little boy backstage. The mother happened to be watching the show and sued the company for assisting in the criminal behavior of the father.

Such judgments cannot always be collected, however. In the international kidnapping mentioned earlier, the father's lawyers repeatedly delayed enforcement of the $76,000 award through various stalling tactics. Just before the last hearing was finally scheduled, the father filed for bankruptcy. The mother never received any reimbursement for the money she had to spend to recover custody of her son. On a brighter note, the boy involved in that kidnapping was able to reestablish a close relationship with the mother and brother from whom he had been separated, as well as maintain a good relationship with his father.

Numerous individuals and organizations continue to fight child abduction, including the Office of Citizens Consular Services in Washington, D.C. and the National Center for Missing and Exploited Children in Arlington, Virginia (see appendix A). The center also provides advice to parents on how to help prevent potential kidnapping, such as emphasizing to the child how much he or she is loved no matter what anyone else may try to tell them, and teaching children how to telephone them or someone else who is close to them, both locally and long distance. It also advises parents to notify schools and day care centers about custody and visitation arrangements and to keep basic information such as the spouse's Social Security number, passport number, automobile information, and bank account numbers in case this information is ever needed by law enforcement authorities.

Also, parents should keep an up-to-date written description and photographs of each child, taken at least every six months. Under the Federal Missing Children Act, parents can register descriptions of missing children into the FBI's National Crime Information Center computer, even if no crime has been charged. Furthermore, many local organizations sponsor fingerprinting, identification cards, and other programs designed to help keep children safe and locate them if they are abducted.

FINAL THOUGHTS FROM A FAMILY COURT JUDGE

When parents quarrel over their children or criticize the other parent in the presence of the kids, children receive the subtle message that they must choose between the parents, picking one to love and the other to reject. Judge Anne Kass has compared such parental behavior to the movie *Sophie's Choice*. In the movie, Sophie, the mother of two small children, was sent to a Nazi concentration camp. An especially cruel soldier told her she had to pick one child to live; the other would die. When she replied that she could not choose between her children, the soldier said that if she didn't pick one, she would lose both. So Sophie made a choice and suffered lifelong anguish as a result. In the movie, Sophie's life after the war becomes aimless, nonproductive, and alcoholic.

Judge Kass says that parents often force their children into a similar decision that may be nearly as painful. Sometimes the message is blatant, she explains, when a parent makes a child tell the judge which parent he or she wishes to live with. In others, it's more subtle, with one parent moping or acting annoyed when the child tries to enjoy the company of the other parent. "Divorcing parents need to know the most loving gift each parent can give their children is his or her permission for the children to love the other parent and to accept love from the other parent," Kass adds.

When parents battle over custody, they often do not give their children this permission, and may eventually force them to make "Sophie's choice." Says Kass, "These children often self-destruct, as Sophie did in the movie. Theirs is the lifelong anguish of being denied what should truly be an inalienable right—the right to love both parents."

THE EMOTIONAL
CHALLENGES
OF DIVORCE

Even the most amicable divorce is seldom entirely painless. Society still places heavy pressure on everyone to be a part of the perfect, happy, stereotypical family: Mom, Dad, and 2.5 kids securely nestled in their home with the white picket fence. This ideal is held up as a symbol of personal success, and those who do not meet it often feel a sense of failure.

In reality, only about 10 percent of American families today fit the traditional mold, and 50 percent of all marriages end in divorce. Given the obvious shift in society, the children of tomorrow are likely to feel far less pressure to achieve this supposed norm, as they grow up surrounded by many different versions of the secure and successful family. But for most people old enough to be contemplating a divorce, the stigma remains.

I have heard of no more than a handful of divorces that were truly amicable, that were accomplished without any ugly behavior or bitterness. Erica Jong, in her memoir *Fear of Fifty*, described an experience far more typical: "What happens when your partner and best friend becomes your enemy? You scream and hang up the phone in the middle of the night, throw yourself at cars and at men, drink too much, sue and get sued, discharging money—and rage. You can't skip all that—even though it seems so useless at the time. Unlike childbirth, it only ends in emptiness. As with war, you are happy simply to come out alive."

All humans harbor a population of resident demons, and divorce brings them out at their most sinister. Inevitably, there is grief. There are messy emotions. There is fury, rage, and anger of the degree that truly can be called madness. Both the partner who leaves and the one who is left will on some level suffer the tortures of the damned, though the form and timing of their torments may differ. No one gets out entirely unscathed.

Yet many different studies of divorced people have shown that the vast majority are happier after the divorce, or at least see that in retrospect, it was the right decision.

WHETHER AND WHEN TO DIVORCE

The decision of whether to end a marriage that is no longer working is the first and often the most agonizing step in the divorce process. Contrary to what many people believe, most American divorces occur after seven or more years of marriage. Nearly one-third of people divorcing have been married fifteen or more years. By this time, the people in a marriage have established strong habits, identities, patterns, and emotions associated with the marriage. Even if they are terribly unhappy and divorce ultimately proves to be the preferable course of action, changing these patterns will result in tremendous upheaval and require a great deal of personal adjustment. Also, people contemplating a divorce while overwhelmed by an unhappy marriage often expect the divorce to solve all their problems. They do not focus on what they will lose as a result of the end of the marriage and what new challenges they will face as a single person.

This does not mean that divorce should not occur. On the contrary, most professionals believe that the pain and misery of a divorce is far less detrimental than the damage of remaining in an unhealthy, miserable marriage. What it does mean is that the decision to divorce should not be made lightly or in haste, and that it is better to get a realistic picture and make preparations for life as a single person rather than expecting either automatic bliss or inevitable devastation as soon as the divorce papers are signed.

It is not uncommon for one spouse to ask another for a divorce when what he or she is really asking for are major changes and improvements in the marriage. For many people, this leads to marriage counseling or similar professional intervention. For couples who are uncertain, this is often the best step, whether it "works" to restore the marriage or not. Some discover that miscommunication, extreme stress from outside factors, or other solvable problems have distorted their perception that the marriage is not to blame for their unhappiness. They learn the marriage is still supported by a foundation of love, mutual respect, equality, friendship, and a shared desire to rebuild the joy that was there in better times. For others, counseling clarifies what one or both suspected: that the marriage is not salvageable; it has become loveless, miserable, and destructive to both partners.

Counseling can be effective in rebuilding a marriage only if both partners truly want to try to forge a new relationship, are willing to accept some responsibility for the problems, are prepared to work to change behaviors that are detrimental to the marriage, and are willing to put aside anger and misunderstanding to make a good-faith effort to save the marriage. If one partner goes into counseling half-heartedly and expecting failure, this can be another indication that the marriage is already over. Divorce is not determined by the signing of the final decree, but by the emotional certainty in the hearts and minds of one or both partners that the bond that formed the marriage is gone.

"The hardest part of getting a divorce is making the decision," says psychologist Kathryn Lang. "People waver back and forth before the final conclusion, and many start going through the steps of grieving even before the decision is made." Lang, a licensed professional mental health counselor, works with many people who are at various stages in the divorce process.

Many people are surprised to learn that the decision to divorce commonly takes several years. Lang explains that two to three years of uncertainty before the decision to make the divorce is about average. "People barter, bargain, and make excuses to avoid making the final decision. For someone who has been married before, the process is somewhat easier in the second marriage, simply because you've been down the road before."

"Often, the process that leads up to the decision to divorce is not even conscious," continues Lang. "Something is a catalyst, and then the person starts thinking about what they can do and can't do. Once one person or the other decides to leave the marriage, the nuts and bolts of the decision start to fall into place."

Lang emphasizes that while the process of coming to a decision to divorce can be painful, the timing can have a significant effect on the person's future emotional state. "It's best to be sure you have no doubts before you leave. Some people leave a marriage without thinking things through and find that they have traded one set of problems for another. You don't want to look back and say, 'If only we tried counseling, if I'd been more assertive, if we had tried harder to communicate.' If you have doubts, try these things first. Don't leave before taking away all of the 'what ifs.' Otherwise you'll be beating yourself up over your uncertainty, along with everything else divorced people have to experience," she explains.

Lang points out that single life is not easy, and many single people tend to be chronically depressed. "I'm more apt to counsel people who aren't sure about a divorce to try and work it out, to recognize their own issues, as opposed to blaming their spouse for everything that is making them unhappy. First, I advise them to look at how they could change their own lives. For some, there is nothing they can do, and they know then that divorce is the right choice. If you can look back and say, 'I did everything I could,' then you'll know that divorce was the right thing to do."

Lang explains that even when a person has given the divorce careful consideration and determined that it is the only reasonable choice, it is still hard on everyone involved. "When you get divorced, your life is displaced," she says. "This is especially true for the person who leaves the home. The one who retains the home, usually the woman, keeps some familiar structure. In a new home, everything is new. It's especially helpful if children can stay in the home they know."

Lang explains that things go a bit more smoothly when the decision to divorce is unanimous, but she acknowledges this is seldom the case. She believes both parties in a divorce go through a grieving process, even the person who makes the decision to leave. "The one who files for the divorce often feels an initial sense of freedom and elation but will usually go through an emotional transition about six months later. If they have someone else waiting in the wings or begin dating someone right away, this can prevent the grieving process or delay it, which only makes it more difficult and painful in the long run. I believe that you don't go through this essential process unless you spend some time alone. You don't get a real feel for the pain you need to work through. Everyone needs to come to terms with aloneness, and learn to be a one before you can be a two. You need that time to learn who you are."

DIVORCE AND THE EMOTIONAL ROLLER COASTER

Lang believes that emotional upheaval during divorce is to be expected, but the degree of severity depends on the individual. "People walk a fine line between being sane and insane during a divorce," she explains. "Most people feel very fragile, like a china doll, that if you touched it too hard it would shatter into pieces. The emotional roller coaster is very common. There are, inevitably, a lot of ups and downs."

Lang, who is now remarried, went through a divorce as the mother of two young daughters. "I was shocked by the feelings I had. I consider myself an extremely stable person. Not much shakes me. But divorce shakes everybody severely. I honestly had no idea what people felt until I went through it myself. Now, I have a much greater appreciation for the pain that both people suffer in a divorce."

When you make the decision to leave your marriage, you may have a clear, definite idea of why it is ending, or only a vague certainty that due to some combination of factors, the marriage can no longer work. No matter what the perspective, the actual act of separation is always a difficult and emotionally charged time. In the book *Divorcing*, psychologist Mel Krantzler identifies "seven deadly emotions" that he says can turn the decision to separate into a nightmare. These emotions are fear, guilt, self-pity, failure, anger, self-flagellation, and hatred of the spouse. Krantzler warns that these emotions may overwhelm a person after the decision to separate has taken place.

It is not uncommon or abnormal to experience these emotions in combinations that seem to be directly conflicting. For example, hatred toward your spouse may bring about guilt for feeling that way. The key is to understand that such feelings are normal, but not to let them paralyze or control you so that you are held back from making good decisions. The fact that such threatening, complex emotions are common and even normal helps to explain why many people get stuck and cannot come to terms with feelings of failure, bitterness, and anger for years after the divorce has technically ended. This is why most professionals, as well as individuals who have been through a divorce, recommend some form of professional counseling during this difficult transition.

Krantzler emphasizes that no emotions are inherently good or bad, but should rather be seen as signals alerting you to important insights about yourself. He stresses that his "seven deadly emotions" inevitably appear in some form during the early stages of any divorce and are a natural part of the mourning of the death of a relationship with a person who was, at one time, the most important adult in your life. What makes them deadly, he explains, is that if you attach yourself to them rather than letting them go, they can stunt your life permanently. It is the strong person who seeks out counseling, rather than the weak one.

Common Feelings During the Divorce

Psychologist Kathryn Lang describes some common feelings that anyone in a divorce is likely to experience. "Both people participate in a divorce, so there is often anger at yourself, that you allowed it to happen. Anger, grief, depression, crying episodes, remorse, panic, and anxiety attacks are common symptoms."

Lang describes how these emotions are logically tied to the context of a divorce. "For example, anxiety is tied to specific future fears. People are afraid they will be alone for the rest of their lives, which is a big reason many people don't leave unhappy marriages in the first place. Those with low self-esteem may think an unhappy marriage is all they deserve. This is especially true for somebody who is left by his or her spouse. They often feel rejected, whereas the person who initiates the divorce will feel empowered and experience an initial high for six months or so. But eventually, they too will go through a emotional crash," she says. "When I left my first marriage after fifteen years, I was walking on air. I felt unchained after being trapped, like I could finally do whatever I pleased. Then about six months later, the depression hit. There was no looking back or questioning my decision, but I still had to go through the grief of this ending."

In addition to the stark, raw pain that characterizes nearly every divorce, many people either experience severe guilt in which they feel solely responsible for the divorce, or heap all the blame upon their partner, believing he or she is entirely responsible. Seldom does either of these extreme perspectives reflect the truth about the situation. Of course, there are certainly exceptions, as when one partner has been abusive to the other. In most cases, however, it takes two to make a divorce, just as it takes two to make a marriage.

The emergence of no-fault divorce has eased much of the hostility that occurred between spouses when one, "the winner," had to prove the other was a bad person, a "loser." Many psychologists believe, however, that the emotional realities of divorce remain essentially the same. Krantzler, who has written extensively on divorce and founded one of the first divorce recovery seminar programs in the early 1970s, observes that certain psychological reactions to divorce are universal and transcend nations, cultures, and social differences.

Krantzler reports that he sees virtually every client, male and female, experiencing many of the same feelings he went through during his own divorce. Fear is one such universal emotion, as even those well equipped for single life face change and uncertainty. Divorcing parents always suffer anguish over the upheaval they are causing in the lives of their children, and worry about how the relationship with them will continue. A sense of failure, or perhaps that the marriage was a mistake, is also nearly universal.

Krantzler and other psychologists emphasize that people in the midst of the divorce not only need to accept that such feelings are normal, but also need to forgive themselves and look at the divorce as a learning experience leading to a better future, rather than a personal failure. It is also important to realize that every marriage that eventually ends in divorce was not a "mistake." Most involved a wonderful, healthy, positive relationship for at least a part of their duration.

It is perfectly normal to feel overwhelmed during a divorce, even if everything else in your life is running smoothly. If other problems crop up, as they often do, involving family, health, work, or money, it may seem as though it will be utterly impossible to cope with all the chaos. Remind yourself that it can be done, and people do it successfully every day. This, too, shall pass.

There are several things you can do to help make such times more bearable. Try to separate emotional reactions from rational decisions. It is all right to feel guilty, angry, or sad, but if you let these emotions override your common sense you can make bad decisions that will affect you the rest of your life. For example, if you feel guilty for leaving your spouse, don't give in to a desire to appease your guilt by giving away your fair share of the property and things you need for your own support.

Assess your level of fear. Many people are terrified during a divorce, especially if they are confronted with difficult tasks, such as important financial decisions, that make them nervous even when things are not in a state of upheaval. Others are overwhelmed by a fear about the future and may experience a feeling that nothing they do matters anyway, because the future is out of their control. Overwhelming fear signals a need for expert assistance, whether in the form of financial advisers, mental health counseling, or other types of help. Talk to your attorney or other professionals and get the help you need.

Don't spend wildly, but avoid being too frugal. Sometimes people believe they are being economically wise when in fact they are causing themselves more trouble and expense in the long run. Don't be afraid to spend some money, even if you have to borrow, in order to protect yourself and your interests. Get a good attorney who knows the family law field. Don't try to do too many things yourself, even if you are an expert. You need an objective viewpoint. This does not mean that you can't cut corners or that you shouldn't do a reasonable part of the work. But make sure everything you do is at least reviewed by an objective, qualified expert.

Try to be patient. Understandably, many people want to get a divorce over with as soon as possible. But too much haste can have devastating effects in the future. At the very outset of your case, ask your attorney how long it is anticipated the divorce will take. This way, you will at least have some idea of what to expect and can focus on that date in the future when everything is likely to be over.

Don't become paralyzed. Some people are so overwhelmed they feel immobilized, as though they can't ever imagine getting out from under the burden of all the tasks and emotionally trying responsibilities hanging over their head. If this happens to you, try to make realistic lists and schedules of a few things to be accomplished each day, rather than focusing on the huge mountain of responsibilities. Break big tasks down into small steps, and stick to a few things to accomplish each day. A professional counselor, organizer, or time management consultant may be able to help.

The Siege Mentality

Couples often get stuck on one or more points when trying to settle issues of custody, property, or support. Sometimes couples enter into a siege mentality in which one or both become entrenched and refuse to budge, often over a seemingly trivial matter. This sticking point is actually a symbol of the battle for emotional control, a desire to hurt the other party, or an attempt to cover up sadness with anger and blame.

This type of stalemate never accomplishes anything positive. Results of the siege can range from mild irritation to ludicrous posturing to heartbreaking tragedy. Sometimes both people refuse to leave the family home and draw literal battle lines to mark territory. Others go through elaborate, destructive vendettas, as in the movie *The War of the Roses*. The film was a satire, but unfortunately it scarcely exaggerated the warfare some couples go through and the degree of destruction that can result. When custody is the sticking point, the innocent victims suffer the most.

Couples who are able to put an end to their games of control and get past the siege are generally able to achieve a satisfactory resolution to their lives and get on with a new beginning once the divorce is final. But when a bitter custody battle has been played out, couples can continue these struggles for years. Such relationships are inevitably no-win situations.

There are few universal truths in matters as individually varied and emotionally charged as a divorce. However, virtually everyone, including those who have been through a divorce, agrees that hostile and vituperative behavior toward the other party accomplishes nothing and does more harm than good. This does not mean that you should not be assertive and insist on your rights to a fair property settlement and good custody arrangements, as well as reasonable support if required. Assertive does not mean aggressive, though. Calm, persistent, mature behavior by both lawyer and client encourages a favorable outcome in any type of legal case, far more than anger and bitterness.

Renowned trial attorney Melvin Belli, himself divorced four times, states in his book *Divorcing*, "As a general principle, the way you act toward your ex-spouse will determine whether or not you will be scarred with hate and vengefulness or feel renewed as a better person, and this is something you should be seriously concerned about."

Based on his own personal and legal experience, Belli advises clients, especially those with children, to cool their anger and never let it show in front of the children. Instead, they must reassure the children that both parents still love them and will continue to have a regular relationship with them.

Recovery Takes Time

Psychologist Genevieve Clapp, author of *Divorce and New Beginnings*, an excellent book on divorce recovery, states that on the average it takes people about two years after a divorce before they feel they have gained their equilibrium. More time is required before a person will feel completely detached from the divorce and have a real sense of stability and satisfaction.

Divorce often gives rise to unexpected feelings. Men often miss daily contact with their children more than they thought they would. Disentangling a family is a complex process. Any change in the routines of a household causes stress and upheaval, even when the basic structure of the family remains unchanged. For those divorcing, the little things, such as the added responsibility of car care or cooking, can be almost as frustrating as the larger changes.

Clapp believes that those who are the most devastated at the breakup often recover more quickly and completely. This may be due in part to the willingness of people who are in great emotional pain to seek professional help.

Counseling and Therapy

Psychologist Kathryn Lang feels that different types of mental health counseling, or combinations of types, work for different individuals. "Individual therapy is usually more important at the beginning," she says. "Many people need to heal on their own first, to take time to recover from their anger and pain. Then group therapy can be very helpful. There are different types of divorce adjustment groups and divorce recovery groups available. But many people right out of a divorce are too angry, emotional, and self-absorbed to benefit from the group process. They can't see beyond themselves. Also, different types of therapy work for different people. Some of my patients, especially older women, find it hard to be in a recovery group. They may be ashamed that their marriage ended. Many people, especially those who are deeply religious, believe that marriage was supposed to be for life. They simply are not comfortable sharing their feelings in a group, at least not until they have had some individual help first."

An Overview from a Family Therapist

Stephen Feher, Ph.D., is a family psychologist who has worked with individuals, couples, children, and adolescents for many years. His practice has focused extensively on couples trying to work on their marriage or come to a decision about divorcing. "Over time, I gradually began working with a greater number of couples who were stuck or getting ready to divorce, before they had come to the final decision and gone to see attorneys," he remarks. "As this part of my practice grew, I began getting interested in mediation and took mediation training through the University of New Mexico Law School. It's interesting how things seem to happen simultaneously. As I've begun to do more formal mediation, I've been seeing more and more couples who are in this dilemma."

In a related area, Feher has also found himself counseling an increasing number of couples who are already divorced but need to learn how to be better parents together. "Many divorced parents want to learn better communication skills, and they need help in creating a united front so the children have the same rules in both households. Recently, I worked with two couples and four children in this situation. Everyone in the group learned better ways to get along, but it was primarily a parenting problem."

Feher believes divorced parents today are more focused on their parenting. "People are becoming more open, and more concerned about being good parents. Yet I still see couples who are openly hostile to one another," he says. "I agree with other professionals who believe that hostility between parents is one of the most damaging things a child can endure, second only to direct abuse of the child. While I work primarily with parents, the emphasis is on the needs of the children for better parenting."

Although most families can overcome their difficulties, Feher cautions that in some, the individual problems of one of the people involved make it very difficult. "Where there is psychopathology, that's another issue," he explains. "Not everyone who gets divorced is mentally healthy enough to work with their kids. A person with a severe pathology of their own needs significant individual treatment. Sometimes they do respond, and then we can get to work on the family. But unfortunately, so many people with this type of problem are in denial, or they face several problems heaped on top of one another. I worked with a mother who had serious emotional problems and had been ordered into counseling by the court. Her husband had been given sole custody of their young child, although there had been no abuse on the part of the mother. There is such a stigma, especially for a woman, when joint custody is denied. She faced tremendous problems and felt terrible anger. The best we could really hope for was to help her to the point where she could convince the court to award joint custody."

Feher explains that among people who are essentially normal, emotional reactions to divorce varies between individuals. "The absolute worst comes out in people," he notes. "So many of us don't deal with conflict well. We put things aside over and over, then divorce opens the floodgate to all those things that haven't been dealt with over the years. Tremendous anger, bitterness, self–doubt, grief, loss, and depression often pour out."

For other people, he says, "There is a great sense of relief, at first. Then they are surprised to experience feelings of loss after the first wave of satisfaction wears off. It's not so much loss of the spouse, but of the ideal."

Feher cautions against the tendency of those who experience profound relief soon after a divorce to jump into another relationship. "People feel fine, so they find another partner right away, but these rebound relationships hardly ever last. It's not conscious, but people often seek out someone else right away just to avoid facing the pain. They get very involved with the new person, yet later they will have to deal with their bad feelings about the end of the marriage. Inevitably, there will be pain."

Feher believes that while some people can come to a well–reasoned decision to leave a marriage and carry out the necessary steps to end it and move ahead on their own, some form of therapy is helpful for most. "It's a painful process for most people," he says. "A few come to a decision and know it's right, and don't really have any problem with it. But especially when there are children, it's difficult not to have a divorce that's troubling in significant ways. It requires a major adjustment in identity for everyone involved. It's like a fabric that's been woven together. You can't just take the scissors and cut out a piece and expect what's left to be whole. You have to pull out the threads one by one, and weave a new tapestry from them."

Some people Feher has counseled did not realize they were facing unresolved problems until long after what appeared to be an amicable divorce. As Feher points out, "Denial and repression are common in a divorce. People push their feelings aside, but they don't just go away. I worked with one couple who did very well for five years after the divorce, worked together as parents, and were friendly enough that they had lunch together on a regular basis. Then, out of the blue, everything hit the fan. It seemed they had been pushing things down the whole time, ignoring negative feelings in their efforts to have a good relationship."

Feelings may often become confused, with unfamiliar emotions coming out as anger, for example. "So many people are only able to express a few emotions. They feel powerless and helpless, feel they can't do anything about what is happening to them, and these feelings manifest as anger. This sometimes happens when people believe they were treated badly by the court system, especially in custody matters. They feel helpless against a system that can affect their lives in such a big way, and it comes out as extreme anger," he explains.

"Also, few people know how to express anger in healthy ways in our society," he adds. "We have no training in anger management or how to get along in relationships, yet we're expected to know. I'm really glad to see communication skills, anger management, and alternative dispute resolution being taught in the schools today. Some schools even have mediation, beginning in the lower grades. I think that's a great idea."

Feher emphasizes that different types of mental health services work for different people, and that a variety of programs are available. "There is individual therapy, couples therapy, and groups or seminars. The main thing is to talk to others who are going through or have gone through the same thing and had similar feelings and experiences." Feher also believes self-help groups can be effective, "as long as the group takes a positive direction and doesn't just become a complaint session." Various materials and guidelines are published for people forming such groups, and these can be valuable resources.

"People need support, but not necessarily the type they get from family members or friends. There is an element of taking sides. Relatives or friends act as advocates for the 'good guy,' and this perpetuates the notion that one is right and the other wrong," he explains. "People going through a divorce need support, but they also need more objective input. As long as the couple keeps blaming each other, they will stay stuck. They need to look at themselves, too. The place to get to is forgiveness—of others, and of themselves."

Reaching this point takes time. "You can't just jump into it. There's a rejection factor that makes divorce, in some ways, harder to cope with than the death of a loved one. For children, especially, it takes them a long time to come to terms. They see the parent as not wanting to be with the family or with them. Death and divorce are both tumultuous, and there's a difficult grieving process for both."

In his practice, Feher has seen many people suffering from depression during a divorce. "It's very common," he says. "There are many types of depression, and divorce often brings on reactive or exogenous depression. This type of depression can occur due to some circumstance or situation in a person's life which affects the brain in a way that causes the symptoms. Fortunately, this kind of depression is generally temporary and responds well to treatment, with the best treatment often combining therapy and medication." As a clinical psychologist, Feher cannot prescribe medication, but he can refer patients to a psychiatrist or their own physician for recommended drugs.

Anxiety, though not as common as depression, is also a problem for many people facing divorce. "We all have our pathologies of choice," Feher explains. "Our temperament pushes us in one direction or another. Women often experience anxiety because of the reality of the unbalanced financial situation they face. They're quite naturally anxious about the future. We are still in a patriarchal society, and this affects the way people react. Men still derive much of their sense of self-worth from work, and often use workaholism as a coping mechanism, sometimes to a health-threatening extreme. I see this in women, too, to a lesser degree, but executive women sometimes cope this way."

Feher believes that it is not so much gender, but how individuals are psychologically structured, that is the biggest factor in how people react to the stress of divorce. "It's more personality than gender. Also, socioeconomic factors play a part, so it's hard to generalize. The people I see tend to have the resources and mind–set that let them ask for help."

Anxiety is common among children. "They are used to viewing the family as one entity, and see parents as one being, in a way. When the family they know breaks down, its natural for children to experience fear, especially, `Who's going to take care of me?' This is very normal." Feher also sees many problems in children caused by parents who try to use their children as a source of their own emotional support, especially if they speak badly about the other parent. "It's hard for parents not to do this, but it's really detrimental. The divorce itself is very traumatic for kids of all ages, because they lose their solid base of support."

Feher says some of the most exciting work he is doing at the moment came about through serendipity. "You never know how referrals happen," he says. "But lately, I've had many blended families referred to me. So I've been doing more and more work with divorced couples and their new families, to help them better coparent their children. This is so important, because if parents can change their communication with each other, the kids can regain what is essential for them—support, boundaries, structure, and consistency." He receives tremendous satisfaction from this aspect of his work. "When I can help parents put their own stuff aside in favor of the kids, they learn to be in control as parents. Parents must both provide support and set limits. Kids need limits to feel secure."

He explains that parents, especially those who do not have primary custody, sometimes overindulge or won't discipline children because of the limited time they spend with them. "They fear that if they are too strict, the child won't want to spend time with them, so they go too far the other way," he explains. "This is especially common when the custodial parent is poisoning the mind of the child against the other parent. As a reaction against this, the other parent feels they have to prove themselves, and make every moment they spend together like a trip to Disneyland."

Feher is concerned that sources of mental health assistance for people and families at lower socioeconomic levels are diminishing in some areas. He recommends those with limited resources to talk to clergy, if they have a religious affiliation, or to contact a local hospital with a mental health department, as many maintain referral services. "I would strongly advise anyone in distress during a divorce to keep trying until they find some professional support. Above all, get help. There are agencies that provide services on a sliding scale according to income. Friends and relatives are important, but they're not enough. You need to look at what's going on within yourself as well, with the help of a more objective person. Most people need to find some resource they can utilize before they really get over it."

Use Caution in Locating Help

Professionals caution that some sources purporting to help actually do more harm than good. "There are some bad therapists out there who only contribute to the hostility and pain of a divorce," cautions mediator Roberta Beyer. Some basic standards to follow include avoiding anyone who tells you that the divorce is all your fault, that you are a failure, that you just need to work harder on the marriage, that you should fight harder against your spouse, or, especially, that you should accept unkind or abusive treatment.

One danger sign to watch for in you or your children is a persistent, unchanging sense of hopelessness. People who feel this way are at the greatest risk for suicide, either directly or indirectly through high-risk, self-destructive behavior. If you notice hopelessness, persistent depression, or a persistent lack of caring about yourself and your future, seek professional counseling immediately.

People also may become their own worst enemy. Be wary if you see your own behavior changing in negative ways, such as increased drinking or drug use, sexual promiscuity, overeating or undereating, workaholism, or extreme expression or suppression of emotions. Also be aware of changes in your physical health. It is not uncommon for people suffering from the stress of the divorce to experience symptoms ranging from headaches and lethargy to serious physical illness. Your medical doctor can help you attend to your physical health as well as making recommendations for counseling or therapy.

Depression

Clinical depression is common among people going through the divorce process. The symptoms of depression, as well as the disease itself, can be utterly debilitating. However, many forms of effective treatment are available today, and depression can be successfully managed in most cases by counseling, medication, or a combination of both.

Stephen Feher explains that finding help is especially important when symptoms of depression don't go away. "Sadness and grief are normal, but people have to assess their symptoms, which can be hard with clinical depression," he says. "It's an insidious illness, because it attacks our sense of self. You notice that people don't say, `I have depression,' they say, `I am depressed.' This tells a lot about the nature of the problem."

Feher advises those who don't seem to be progressing to be on the alert for symptoms that can indicate serious depression. Common maladies include loss of energy, change in sleep patterns, withdrawal, isolation from others, changes in eating habits, an inability to enjoy things that used to give you pleasure, and waking up too early and not being able to go back to sleep.

Nearly everyone suffering from depression has problems sleeping. Difficulty concentrating, impaired reasoning, and a limited attention span are also experienced by many people. These symptoms can be especially troubling when you need to be functioning at an even higher level than usual, in order to cope with your everyday duties as well as the added stress and responsibility of dealing with the divorce.

CHAPTER 7

Sleep disorders contribute to the depression by adding the burden of constant exhaustion. "Depression is especially problematic during the divorce process, because people have to make extremely important decisions. Yet at the same time, the inability to make decisions is a characteristic of depression. Intense emotions cloud judgment. And the pressures that come to bear, to make good decisions, are so immense. People feel like they're in a pressure cooker—the stress is horrible. They're being asked to make decisions that will have an impact for years to come, under circumstances that are not conducive to decision making. People must get the help they need and do whatever it takes to get clear with their situation and overcome the symptoms so that they are making good decisions, instead of letting the symptoms make decisions for them."

It is important to seek treatment for depression as soon as possible. Some people start with their medical physician, others with a psychologist, psychiatrist, or other mental health professional. Often, the two professions will work together, with the physician providing medication and a counselor conducting therapy.

Some people are hesitant to use antidepressant drugs, either out of fear of becoming dependent, or because they see medication as a sign of weakness. Others are concerned that drugs may mask the symptoms that need to be dealt with in therapy. Yet drugs can be extremely valuable tools that are safe when administered and monitored by a physician, and many people suffering from depression have found them to be, quite literally, life savers. Most therapists emphasize that drugs are best used on a short-term basis in combination with counseling to address the underlying causes of the depression.

Stress

Divorce can also bring on severe stress. Not only is this an emotionally miserable condition, but it can also lead to physical disorders. Headaches, abdominal problems, chest pains, dizziness, and other symptoms may be caused by stress or can signal that you have a more severe physical problem. These physical symptoms should not be ignored. Most stress–related problems can be treated effectively by medication, counseling, changes in lifestyle and diet, or some combination of one or more approaches. Anytime you suffer from recurrent or serious physical symptoms, you should see your physician and tell him or her everything that is happening in your life. If you do have a serious health problem, this will need to be taken into consideration as you structure a divorce settlement and plan for your new life.

Stress is often brushed off as an inevitable part of modern life, but in severe forms it can cause serious physical and mental damage. People under severe stress are at far greater risk for illness, auto accidents, substance abuse, suicide, and homicide. In a divorce, many of the outside factors contributing to stress will disappear eventually. But life is full of the changes and frustrations that produce stress, and it is extremely valuable to learn skills for coping with stress both in the present and in the future. Many good books can help, and mental health providers, clinics, and classes offer assistance. Professionals advise that such simple things as having a good cry, practicing deep breathing techniques, getting physical exercise (especially outdoors), and writing in a journal can help tremendously.

Psychologist Genevieve Clapp advises that it is important to remember that everyone experiences feelings of rejection, worthlessness, failure, and craziness. She advises avoiding a common tendency to put all of the blame for bad feelings on either yourself or your spouse. She says, "Anger and divorce go together about the same as do love and marriage." Clapp's book *Divorce and New Beginnings* contains a wealth of self–help techniques to combat stress, as well as information on how and when to realize that self–help is not enough.

Lorraine Parker, D.C., a chiropractor and nutritionist, teaches classes in stress management. She explains that certain physiological reactions occur when a person experiences stress from either positive or negative changes in life. "People are surprised to learn that the body goes through the same reactions when a person gets married, gets divorced, experiences a birth or death in the family, or wins or loses a million dollars. Stress is not a thing; it is a process that happens inside the body because of an outside influence, which can be perceived as either negative or positive. The body doesn't differentiate."

Parker explains that the physiological reaction to stress involves the entire body. "It's a throwback to cave people," she says. "At the time modern humans were developing, people would encounter something such as a wild animal and have to prepare to either fight or flee. They would follow through with one behavior or the other, expending tremendous physical energy. Afterward, they were exhausted and would sleep for a long period of time, then awake restored."

In the 1970s, Dr. Hans Selye identified the steps that occur in the body in response to a "fight or flight" reaction. "The adrenal glands release hormones, heartbeat increases, muscles tense, digestion slows, breathing changes, blood flows to the extremities, and the blood clotting mechanism becomes more active," Parker explains. "In primitive societies, these physical reactions served an important purpose for survival, and people nearly always went through the usual steps of fight or flee and rest that we're programmed to follow. But in modern society, we can't go through these steps because we need to maintain our lives according to the norms and practices of today. This tension builds, but we don't get the opportunity to expend the energy and then rest and recuperate. Plus, primitive people faced this reaction on only an occasional basis. People today encounter stressful situations that can trigger the fight–or–flight reaction up to twenty times a day."

Single parents may go through this process even more often. "For example, a mother may have to get the children up and ready for school, then rush to drop them off, then fight traffic to get herself to work, deal with the pressures and stresses of the job, then the child support check doesn't come. It goes on and on. People under these circumstances don't have the opportunity or take the time to react to the stress. It would be healthiest to drop everything and run around the block a few times, but instead we keep the energy all inside," Parker remarks. "This causes enormous wear and tear on the body. It can do real damage in different ways. In my stress management classes, I use a rubber band as an example. Stretch it a little at a time, further and further, until it's stretched out to the maximum. Then when you let it go it flies around the room, in the same way people can fly off the handle."

Parker explains that while the outside factors that can trigger stress change all the time, the internal reaction is always the same. "Stress is caused by changes or frustrations in life, and divorce is full of both," she says. "The people who suffer the most from stress are those who feel they have no control over their situations. Some people are surprised to find that it is not so much the high-powered executives who get severely stressed, as it is their secretaries. The executive can go to the secretary with a report he has been mulling over all night and say, 'I need this typed in an hour.' But the secretary has no control. She has to accomplish a lot of work under high pressure. People going through a divorce often feel a similar loss of control over their circumstances," she points out.

One thing that can help break the cycle of stress is to achieve some small measure of control. "One work situation that causes high stress is that of people working on assembly lines in factories," Parker says. "Some experiments have been done in which these people are given some measure of control to stop the line if a problem arises. This really helps temper the stress. People need to gain a sense of empowerment during a divorce. If you can gain back control over any little portion, this will help."

Parker also emphasizes that exercise and good nutrition are absolutely essential for people in stressful situations. "Exercise is important both psychologically and physiologically," she says. "It's important to dissipate that buildup of energy from the fight-or-flight response, so it doesn't stay in the body and cause physical wear and tear. People used to get more physical release through their work. Today, we work harder and often longer hours, but we don't use nearly as much physical energy. Therefore, everyone needs to find a physical outlet. It's essential for good health."

Good nutrition is crucial for people in stressful situations for several reasons. "High stress compromises the immune system," Parker explains. "As stress accumulates, white blood cells and other immune system cells don't function as well to protect the body. This increases the likelihood of illness, just at a time when people can least afford or cope with being sick. It doesn't mean that a catastrophe is inevitable, it simply means that people need to be more diligent about caring for their health. It's important to eat good, balanced amounts of protein and complex carbohydrates, and to avoid excessive junk food. Rewards and treats are good in moderation—if I couldn't have cheesecake or Haagen–Dazs ice cream once in a while, there would be no point in living! But the key is moderation. It may be tempting to eat a whole pint of ice cream instead of dinner, but this can really set a person up for problems. Plus, eating a lot of sugar causes that familiar sugar rush that can make you feel flighty and irritable. This can add to the sensations that are already there with stress and aggravate the negative feelings that people are trying to avoid.

"People sometimes overeat to get a false sense of relaxation, but this is temporary and more damaging in the long run," she continues. "The key is to use common sense and eat a balanced diet. It's important to have whole grains, pasta, bread, and potatoes (the complex carbohydrates), but people need to remember that they can't eat too much of any one food. Carbohydrates that are not used by the body as energy are stored as fat, so a varied diet is important."

People facing stress from a particular source, such as a divorce, can benefit greatly from a regular dialogue with people enduring similar challenges. "Support groups can really help deal with the problem head–on," Parker remarks. "There are groups to deal with every sort of personal problem available today, from addictions to lost children to cancer. There are many divorce groups that I'm aware of. It helps a lot to discuss your feelings with those who have experienced the same thing before. Support groups can be very helpful for kids, too. There are groups of different sizes and formats—prayer groups, classes, all types of programs to help people learn to cope with their stress. And that's really the key. You can't avoid stress; it happens in a situation like divorce. But you can develop positive coping mechanisms. Some people turn to negative coping tools, such as alcohol, drugs, escaping into excessive television, or overeating. It's important to channel the stress energy into more positive directions. This can also give a person a sense of gaining control over his or her life."

Parker also advocates exploring new hobbies and activities, provided they are not related to daily work activities, which may contribute to the overall accumulation of stress. "For example, I wouldn't advise a person working in the computer field to take a computer class. They should take a class in something like painting or swimming, so they have to think about something else and get a respite from the rest of their life."

She emphasizes that a wealth of opportunities to learn new hobbies and skills, as well as classes specifically addressing stress management, are available in most communities today. "I teach a stress management class through a continuing education program at the local university. Some corporations offer stress management programs for employees, as do hospitals and HMOs." She also points out that many books and self-help programs offer assistance. Simple day-to-day activities such as journal writing can be tremendously helpful as well. "Writing gets feelings from the inside out," she explains. "Also, meditation and other simple relaxation techniques can be easy, free, and effective tools to reduce stress. These activities quiet the mind. Just like stress, relaxation is cumulative too. Simply taking ten to fifteen minutes each day to concentrate on your breathing while focusing on one word to occupy the mind and keep worries away can make a big difference. Tapes for guided relaxation are available in any bookstore."

Don't forget the importance of enjoying simple pleasures. Parker says, "Buy yourself flowers, or something that makes you smile. Do something silly. People don't play enough anymore.

Taking a few moments to pet a cat or dog can be very calming. It focuses your energy outside yourself. Studies have shown that petting an animal actually lowers the heart rate and blood pressure. Anything pleasant and simple can break the tension of the moment. I keep a jar of bubbles from the dimestore—the kind that comes with a little wand—on my desk. When I start to get overwhelmed, I just sit back and blow bubbles for a few minutes. One of the best ways to relax when you have a little more time is to take a long, warm bath, with candles and a glass of wine. There are many simple and inexpensive ways to deal with the stress that we all have to face. It's often just a matter of getting into the habit of doing this for yourself. But it's really essential. It's a major part of taking care of your health."

Support Groups

More and more support groups for people coping with divorce, both under the leadership of a professional and self-help groups, are cropping up all over the country. Some focus on one particular stage of the divorce process, such as recovery after the divorce, or on one issue in a divorce, such as parental custody rights. Others deal with a broader range of topics at all stages of the process. As divorce has become more common, some schools and churches have formed divorce adjustment groups for children.

Group seminars often address topics as diverse as communication skills, anger management, intimacy, self-esteem, trust, friendship, self-discovery, stress, health, grief, forgiveness, sexuality, living single, letting go of old patterns, freedom, fear, and parenting. Many place heavy emphasis on learning to build healthy new relationships.

Information on groups available in your area can be found through local help and information hotlines, the Internet, mental health organizations, churches and synagogues, attorneys, counselors, college catalogs, and ads or community information bulletin boards in the local newspaper. Some of the organizations listed in appendix A of this book make referrals to local affiliates. Others provide materials and assistance to those wishing to start their own self-help group.

Substance Abuse and Divorce

It is undeniable that alcoholism or drug abuse plays a major role in the demise of many marriages. Some professionals have compared one partner's chemical dependency to an extramarital affair because it is, in effect, a different type of third-party interference. There are certainly similarities. An unhealthy relationship outside the marriage, whether it is with another person or a substance, can become more important than the relationship within the marriage.

If an addicted partner is willing to recommit to the marriage, to accept responsibility for the problem, and to seek professional intervention, the marriage can often be rebuilt. However, "drunkenness" was one of the earliest recognized grounds for divorce, following adultery and desertion.

The stress of divorce may lead those who tend to overindulge in alcohol or drugs to lean more heavily on a convenient chemical crutch. If you are concerned that you may be misusing intoxicants, talk to a private counselor or someone from one of the many groups, such as Alcoholics Anonymous, for information, assessment, and help (see appendix A).

Divorce and Spirituality

Religious faith or other forms of spiritual foundation can be one of the most important sources of comfort and stability for a person facing any major life trauma. Until fairly recently, many religious groups forbade or condemned divorce. A few still do, in varying degrees. Some fundamentalist sects still prohibit their members from divorcing except when one spouse has committed adultery, and counsel even those in a violent marriage to stay. However, most churches today have a more enlightened and humane point of view. Many now offer divorce recovery assistance through counseling, workshops, group sessions, and self-help materials. Psychologist Kathryn Lang emphasizes that many churches are beginning to offer excellent support programs. "There are good counseling programs through various churches, focused on both saving marriages and helping people whose marriages end," she remarks. "The Catholic church has a program called The Beginning Experience for people who are at least one year out of a divorce or the death of a spouse. This group sponsors weekend retreats, which can be extremely valuable and healing."

In fact, religious congregations and organizations are often at the forefront in helping families cope with divorce and begin healing. Many provide direct counseling services, as well as more indirect help through discussion groups and classes, in an atmosphere that encourages spiritual growth. For example, the church I attend offers both one-on-one counseling with volunteers trained by the associate pastor, who is also a psychiatrist, and classes and seminars on such diverse topics as building self-esteem, overcoming fear of intimacy, and coping with anger. Thus, a spiritual or religious affiliation can provide comfort and guidance as well as practical assistance.

Some Good News

There is no getting around the fact that divorce is traumatic. Even the most amicable divorce will have its unpleasant aspects and leave a residue of hurt over everyone involved—partners, children, and those who care about them. Yet in almost every case, healing comes sooner or later. Most therapists estimate the time required to recover completely at one and a half to five years.

Constance Ahrons, Ph.D., is a professor of sociology and associate director of the marriage and family therapy program at the University of Southern California. The title of her book *The Good Divorce* may sound like an oxymoron. But Ahrons believes that while no divorce is actually "good," we must accept that divorce is a fact of our society that acts as a safety valve for bad marriages. Nearly everyone seems to agree, particularly if he or she has been through an unpleasant marriage, that the temporary pain of a divorce is far more bearable than the endless suffering of a bad home life. Yet, Ahrons believes that a "good divorce" is one in which couples part without destroying their lives or the lives of those they love, especially the children. She feels that one of the key factors is to assure that divorced parents both continue to have close relationships with their children and that they remain a family.

Ahrons was the first social scientist to study *normal* divorced families. She coined the term *bi-nuclear family* to refer to a family that spans two or more households. Her study included both ex-spouses and the relationship between them, again a first.

In a good divorce, a family with children remains a family, with the former spouses developing a parenting partnership that is cooperative enough to permit the bonds of kinship to continue with and through the children. Ahrons emphasizes that with so many people today involved in divorces and remarriages, our society must begin to sanction the process and incorporate it into our concepts of good and normal lives.

Divorce is often the best and healthiest solution for everyone involved when a marriage has become miserable. Ahrons urges that we must change both the negative image of divorce and our expectations that it must always be an adversarial event. Rather, we should expect and encourage ex-spouses to be and remain as civilized as possible during and after the marriage. Unfortunately, the myths that label divorce as a shameful and pathological event continue. Even when society and its demographics change drastically, the myths persist well beyond the reality.

There are a number of reasons why such outmoded ideas resist change. Scientific studies emphasizing the negative impact of divorce are frequently cited, but many are seriously flawed. For example, those emphasizing the financial decline faced by many women and children after divorce often ignore the fact that while many women do experience a short-term drop in actual income after divorce, many ultimately find greater financial satisfaction due to the increased control and access over the money they earn.

Likewise, studies focusing on the negative consequences of divorce for children may focus on the short-term only, when children are naturally experiencing distress and upheaval, instead of taking a look ahead to the point when most children recover from the effects of divorce. Also, such studies usually do not include a control group of children from nuclear families, both stable and unstable. Nor do they consider the vast differences in how people handle divorce and its impact on children; for example, whether custody was disputed, whether the parents are hostile to each other in front of the children, whether the children received therapy, and whether the children were able to maintain a stable relationship with both parents.

According to Ahrons, in a recent study of divorced, middle-aged women, over half reported feeling better about themselves after the divorce was over. Many also reported an improved relationship with their children. Adolescents in particular can appreciate what their mothers go through in accomplishing and starting a new life after a divorce and often gain a new admiration for their parents. Attitudes have begun to change, albeit slowly. It is a healthy reflection of our society that most people have come to accept that divorce is normal, and a family restructured after divorce is far healthier than a family that stays together despite misery, abuse, or general unhappiness in a home.

Although difficult, efforts to redefine a life and develop a new image of the family can be rewarding. Ahrons stresses the importance of a career, friends, and the opportunity to interact with people in similar situations. She believes that family, friends, and support groups are important to both women and men, especially fathers who have lost the opportunity to have daily contact with their children.

The Importance of Ritual

Rituals have been followed throughout history to symbolize major transitions: to focus on the exit from one phase of life into another, and to provide reassurance to the person facing a difficult change that it is a normal part of life.

Modern society has abandoned many of the ceremonies that were once common in nearly all cultures to mark an important passage in a person's life. We still follow social customs to celebrate birth, marriage, and graduation, to observe holidays, and to mourn death. Some other rituals survive to a lesser extent, such as housewarming, birthday, and retirement parties.

Unfortunately, there are no established rituals to mark either divorce or the beginning of a new family after the structure of the family has changed. Many people report feeling bereft, a sense of letdown. "No rights of passage exist to help mourn the losses, to help healing, to help solidify newly acquired roles. Entire sections of greeting card stores are given over to reminding couples and those around them that it is time to celebrate another year of togetherness, but only a few stores offer cards designed to cheer up those who have parted ways," Constance Ahrons points out in *The Good Divorce*.

Perhaps part of the reason for this lack of attention to this extremely important transition is the discomfort and uncertain feelings that often result when we learn of a divorce. I have often asked acquaintances who told me they had been divorced whether I should say "Congratulations" or "I'm sorry." Responses varied, but many people said "Both." Divorce is, if nothing else, a situation in which some ambiguity and mixture of feelings are almost inevitable.

Many psychologists and therapists who attempt to help people heal after divorce believe that ritual can be a crucial part of the process. Ahrons states, "I'd like to see us get to a time when a parting ritual for divorce is part of our culture." There does appear to be a growing trend, as divorce becomes more common throughout the world, to mark the occasion, not with mourning but with the recognition that it is an important life passage that can lead to positive new beginnings.

Rituals may be in the form of a shared ceremony or a private event. Lynn Peters, a jeweler and the owner of a graphic design company, came up with a unique idea several years ago when she noticed her old wedding band collecting dust in a drawer. She now runs a business called Freedom Rings: Jewelry for the Divorced. "The idea came from my own divorce," she explains. "The ring laid in the drawer for three years. One day I realized what a waste it was—I should recycle it." She decided to invite a group of friends to join her in a ceremony to smash the old ring, which she would then fashion into a new piece of jewelry. Thus a new tradition was born, complete with humorous yet encouraging words, supportive friends, and champagne to celebrate the new beginning.

A poll of Peters's divorced friends revealed great enthusiasm for the idea and inspired an amusing collection of stories about old wedding rings. "People pawn them, give them away, throw them in the nearest sewer or lake—or at their ex!" Peters cringed at the waste of precious metal and gemstones and saw a need for a healthier outlet for both the jewelry and any lingering anger. She offers both the ceremony and creation of a new piece of jewelry. Clients smash the old ring with a sledgehammer on an anvil as a part of a ceremony, in preparation for meltdown into the new design, and exorcise a few emotional demons in the process.

Peters's own divorce was difficult, and ended with litigation. Yet she felt a lack of finality. "One day my divorce decree just arrived in the mail. I remember thinking, this is it? After all this shit, all this misery, this big trial, this is all there is to it?" From this, the idea for her new business, Freedom Rings, was born, "I never really put the divorce behind me until I bashed my ring in my own divorce ceremony," she explains. "In bashing my past, I recreated a symbol of freedom with my old wedding ring."

Levity and laughter are inevitably a part of the event, but Peters is quick to respond to those who accuse her of trivializing divorce. "It's a fun way of dealing with a serious issue," she explains. "The humor is very healing, and the jewelry becomes a symbol of recovery, confidence, and feeling good about being single. Some clients say a few words of their own before the ceremony, sometimes there are tears. But in the end, the focus is always on making a fresh start with a positive outlook."

Clayta Spear was one of Peters's early clients. Unlike Peters, Spear felt her divorce happened too quickly: The entire process was completed in six months, after she filed for no-fault divorce, "before I really knew what had happened." Yet she, too, felt a lack of completion from a different perspective. "I still had both wedding rings five years after the divorce when I saw Lynn on television in an interview about Freedom Rings. I knew instantly that was what I wanted to do with them. Going through the Freedom Rings ceremony with my friends present was really an experience," she notes. "It provided a ritual which was therapeutic for me, and the opportunity to do something creative with my anger and sadness. I wanted to turn it into something positive, entirely new and beautiful. We designed a pendant using the gold from both rings and a pearl from the Philippines. The rings and the pearl represented the two most dramatic and important times in my life, and I love the final product—it's an original, and people always notice it."

Freedom Rings' clients are as diverse as their jewelry choices, but all seem to share similar feelings. Sam Trevino Sustaita, a forty-five-year-old manager, exclaimed, "What a release!" as he smashed his gold band, which was made into a golf ball marker.

Pat Mathews, an accountant and writer, spoke of "turning the bad vibes into something new and positive." Her old ring and other unworn jewelry were transformed into matching pendants for her daughters as an expression of family continuity.

Marilyn Morgan, a labor relations worker, added two Australian sapphires to her wedding jewelry to create a symbol of growth. Peters fashioned a piece that she can wear as a pendant or brooch. Freedom Rings has garnered international media attention throughout the United States, Europe, South Africa, Australia, and Japan.

Others working through divorce healing have created their own personal rituals. M. Carol Curtis, whose husband always cooked her a special dinner on her birthday, revived the tradition by recreating the event with her daughter. She also held a "wake" on her wedding anniversary. She lit incense and candles, put on music from the era, and donned clothing from the time of her marriage. The fact that the clothes no longer fit comfortably added to the theme. "For me, this was a good physical reminder that many aspects of the marriage and the old life were restrictive and did not fit the new me."

Curtis also created a collage with pictures symbolizing both the good and bad aspects of her marriage, which she later burned in her fireplace. This, she says, helped her make peace with the past. She now celebrates a new anniversary commemorating the date she resigned from her career to be a full-time mother by receiving wishes from friends and enjoying a special day or weekend with her child. "Building a new life after divorce involves building new memories, new occasions to celebrate, and a new happy history about which to reminisce. We have the opportunity to create rituals that suit our special situations and ease our transition into a new life," she says.

Looking Ahead as the Divorce Concludes

Psychologist Kathryn Lang feels that one of the most important functions of therapy is to help people take a realistic look at their lives and future. "I often ask my patients, what's the worst thing about him leaving? When they say being alone, I ask them, what's the worst thing about being alone? People are afraid they will always be alone, so I ask them what's different being alone now than being alone when you were married? People come to see that now when they are alone they can do something about it and change what they're doing if they want to. They look at the positive side of being alone. This is such a big fear. So many people have abandonment issues. Yet many look back on the marriage and realize that the person they were married to was emotionally unavailable, so their life isn't really that different and they are, in fact, in a better place now."

Lang explains that the fear of abandonment and betrayal tend to be universal themes that span the life spectrum. "Marriages are made in the unconscious, and often people who are the most afraid of abandonment or betrayal actually marry someone who won't give them what they need. Going through a divorce can actually make people become more flexible, learn how to communicate, raise their self–esteem, and, from this vantage point, realize that they overlooked traits that now seem obvious in their mate. They change in positive ways along with the negative changes of the divorce."

Many of her divorced patients feel they have no identity of their own when they leave a marriage. "I have to remind them that they still exist whether the other does or not," Lang says. "Many people can't see the future, can't visualize any new partner who would want them. Their perceptions are distorted by the past relationship, especially if they were put down by their former spouse. Many people can't look at reality as it is now. When people realize they have already been alone for years, by being with a person who is emotionally and sometimes physically unavailable, the light turns on."

Lang believes it is important to reinforce the notion that one parent and children living in a home does constitute a family. "Over and over, I hear clients say, 'We don't have a family now.' People must realize that yes, one person or two people *are* a family. I have to remind people that they don't have to wait until they are back into a traditional nuclear family again through remarriage or whatever to get on with their lives. One, two, or three of you can go on and enjoy life on your own. So many people put their life on hold until another partner comes along. During my own single years, I did plenty of things with my daughters. We traveled through Europe, drove across the United States, and took trips to New York City. Some of my friends were horrified and shocked. They were so unfamiliar with the idea of a woman traveling alone and without a man. They would ask, 'Aren't you afraid?' I told them there was nothing to be afraid of."

Women often have a difficult time shaking this preconceived notion. "I have to remind people that they *can* get out and do things as a divorced woman. I ask them to consider what they want to do with their life. Men, to some degree, have different fears. Many are afraid of not being good single fathers, especially if they never took on an active parenting role during the marriage. Yet some become better fathers after the divorce as a result of this, because they are actually more available to their children," she points out.

Lang agrees with other professionals who say that the language we use to describe families who have been through a divorce needs to be changed. She proudly describes her own daughters' response when their friends commented that they came from a broken home. "They would say 'What's broken about us? We're not broken.' "

THE STAGES OF RECOVERING FROM DIVORCE

In most cases, the divorce comes as something of a surprise, even if the marriage has not been functioning well for a long period of time. Over and over we hear people say, "I never thought this would happen to me." Almost as frequently, we hear those outside the divorce say, "She just up and left him!" or "He walked out on her!" In reality, however, it is almost never that simple.

Emotional upheaval may come at unexpected times. "I thought I was doing fine. We had been miserable together for a year and a half, and it was a relief when my husband moved out and we started planning the divorce," said one woman. "But when I got the papers in the mail, it really tore me up. I don't know why, but that really got to me." Such reactions are far from uncommon, and different events trigger an emotional response for different individuals.

The stages of divorce have often been compared to the stages of grief after the death of a loved one. This comparison seems appropriate, since psychologists generally rate the trauma of divorce as second only to that of the death of a loved one.

Depending on individual circumstances, divorce may even be more stressful than death. A person who is divorcing often feels abandoned, rejected, or betrayed. He or she not only loses an old role, but is faced with the necessity of adopting one or more new roles. The change is more than simply going from married to single and frequently involves other awkward and uncomfortable transitions in identity as well. It brings about change in family structure, holiday observances, job or place of residence, and other changes that also rank high on the list of stressful life events.

Many of the same stages that are necessary to survive mourning the loss of a loved one who has died are also essential to moving beyond the grief of the divorce. Such stages include protest and denial, often accompanied by physical upheaval; despair, in which you are hit by the reality of what has happened; detachment, in which an apathetic, zombie period makes you isolate yourself from others and simply go through the motions of living; and recovery, in which you become detached from the old self-image of a married person and begin to rebuild your life with a new outlook.

This mourning process is an essential part of healing. Some people take longer to go through the process than others. This is perfectly natural as long as the person does not become stuck in one stage and unable to move on to complete the process. Some people go through all the stages before the divorce is even final. For some it may happen before they even separate from their spouse. For others, especially those who were anxious to escape from a bad marriage, the feelings may not arrive until the initial exhilaration from getting free wears off.

Contrary to popular stereotype, men suffer the pain of divorce just as much as women do. Both men and women experience a sense of loss and failure in divorce. Both may view themselves as victims or want vengeance against their ex-spouse. Men and women often do have different ways of expressing their emotions, because we are socialized in American society to believe that men and women should behave in certain ways. Men are not urged to express emotions freely, so they are more likely to wall up the pain inside themselves. It may later explode in indirect ways, such as an outburst of rage at a third party.

People are often surprised to learn that truly terrifying feelings are normal during any divorce. Some of the most common feelings people express are a sense that they and the world have gone crazy, that they are going to die or already feel dead, that they are frightened and feel helpless regarding the future, that they are depressed without knowing why, that they are angry enough at their ex-spouse to want to kill, or that they feel like a stranger to themselves and don't know who they are. Such emotional disarray is inevitable, and some psychologists believe it is necessary before you can start building a new life as a single person.

Artist, businessman, and *bon vivant* Gerald Murphy coined the phrase "Living well is the best revenge." There's a lot of truth in this saying when it comes to dealing with the anger that often lingers after divorce. Those who indulge themselves in favorite pleasures, enjoy the social support of old and new friends, enjoy their children, their accomplishments, and their new lives demonstrate to their spouses, themselves, and others that there is life, a very good life, after divorce. Psychologists encourage people not to put off doing things they enjoy until after they feel totally healed, make a move, get the final papers, or find a new mate.

As psychologist Mel Krantzler has stated, divorce can be an adventure instead of a disaster. Krantzler explained that after his own divorce, he learned that the valuable components of the marriage are not lost after the divorce, but rather become part of the bank of experience which enable an individual to become a more mature, capable, and wise human being. Divorce, he explains, is a process rather than a label. He identified four steps in the process as:

1. terror time, involving the initial separation and feelings that life is out of control;

2. mourning time, in which the past marriage is laid to rest in the same way the loss of a loved one to death is mourned;

3. living in the present time, in which each new day is viewed as a challenge with the best in life yet to come;

4. self-renewal time, in which the person arrives at a stage in which it seems truly possible to survive happily, physically, and emotionally, as a single person.

Many people have preconceived notions about when they should "get over" the emotional upheaval that follows a divorce. They have stern talks with themselves on specific dates: "Okay, it's been a year now since the decree was entered. It's time to get over this. I'm going to be okay from here on out!" However, the mourning process can't be rushed. Unless a person feels mired in one stage and is not moving forward at all, it's best to let it progress naturally. Comparing experiences with others who have been through a divorce can help.

THE FAMILY IN TRANSITION: HELPING CHILDREN COPE WITH THE TRAUMA OF DIVORCE

Although all children suffer stress and anxiety when parents divorce, the experience does not always leave permanent psychological scars. In the book *Divorce Without Victims*, author Stuart Berger, M.D., explains that two loving parents can help kids survive the trauma of divorce, and that in the process both parent and child can grow. He also advocates abolishing the term *broken home*.

The Unique World of a Child

Berger urges parents to realize that each child is a unique individual with his or her own personality and temperament. Also, because of the stages of child development, children live in a universe different from that inhabited by adults. Young children ages two to six often have trouble distinguishing between thought and action and may believe that they cause all of the things around them to happen. Furthermore, Berger believes they may feel an Oedipal rivalry with the same-sex parent and tend to be very egocentric. For this reason, young children need special, repeated reassurance that nothing they did caused the divorce.

Children ages six to twelve still have an exaggerated perception of the effect they have on the events around them and remain self-centered. This egocentrism persists through adolescence, when it is complicated by the natural rebellion of that age as teenagers test new roles and try new behaviors to discover their own personalities. Stability at home is especially important for kids who are testing the waters of the world outside, so divorce is very threatening to adolescents. Some mental health professionals think adolescents are more likely than any other age group to suffer problems as a result of their parents' divorce.

Berger explains that children of all ages often feel that they can take steps to get their parents back together. Some even misbehave to encourage contact between the parents. Such fantasies often persist long past the time parents believe the children should have recognized that reconciliation won't happen.

However, children tend to react differently to the breakup of a marriage that has been violent. For many, their first preference is to see harmony restored in the home, but departure of the violent parent is the next best alternative. Kids are usually relieved to see the constant terror and tension end.

Berger advises parents to tell their children about the divorce only when the decision is definite, and to tell them together if possible. This can be a powerful reinforcement to the child that although the parents are parting, they can still talk to each other and focus on the children. Berger also feels the entire family should be told together, as siblings can often support and help one another.

Berger and other experts stress that kids need constant reassurance that although the parents no longer love each other, both still love the children, and the divorce is not the children's fault. He suggests that parents state the real reason for the divorce, because children are very perceptive of dishonesty, and they may hear the truth elsewhere. Avoid lurid details, but keep the explanation simple and straightforward.

Virtually all experts who have studied children of divorcing parents agree that excessive conflict between the parents is one of the most traumatic things children can face, and that such hostility is often the cause of ongoing or extensive psychological trouble after the divorce, as opposed to a reasonable recovery. Parents who feel guilty about divorcing should remember that it is much worse for a child to be in a home filled with constant tension, strife, and conflict, than to be in a peaceful environment with one parent. Likewise, anything parents can do to minimize the hostility during the divorce, such as avoiding custody battles, will go a long way in assuring normal recovery of the child.

Sometimes youngsters seem to behave in peculiar ways when reacting to the news that parents will be divorced. Berger explains that such behaviors as disinterest, denial, and other seemingly bizarre reactions are no cause for alarm as long as they do not persist indefinitely.

Parents sometimes believe that children are being selfish when kids focus on personal or trivial concerns, such as whether they will still have their own room or still have a birthday party that year, while their parents are trying to get through the trauma of divorce. Berger and others who work with children point out that such concerns are not selfish, but rather an attempt by the child to gain some control over his or her world at a time when it is going through a frightening upheaval. Professionals stress the importance of addressing these concerns patiently, as well as dealing with what parents perceive to be the more important issues. It is essential to discuss honestly the divorce process and what will happen with all children, including those as young as two. Youngsters usually know if they are being lied to or if information is being hidden from them. This can cause tremendous anxiety about what is really happening, and also cause children to lose faith in parents, which can be devastating.

Kids need to know in concrete terms what changes will happen and when. They should be told where the parent who is moving will live, when they will see them, and how often. If one parent has abandoned the family, honesty is still the best policy. Berger reassures parents that it is okay to tell children when they don't know the answer to a question, such as where the absent parent has gone. In such a case, it is important to emphasize that the behavior of the parent is his or her own problem and was not caused by something the child did. Emphasizing that the youngster was wanted and was a product of love can provide some comfort in this difficult situation.

Berger urges parents to try to avoid any extreme or contrived displays of emotion around children. Unnatural calm or cheerfulness may be confusing when the child knows something is very wrong in the home. However, it is especially hard for small children to see a parent fall apart or fly off the handle. Controlled expression of honest feelings may be hard, but it is the best middle ground.

Anything that creates a feeling of conflicting loyalties in children can be detrimental. This can include everything from forcing a child to choose which parent he or she wants to live with to questioning a child who has been to the other parent's home about that parent's habits, companions, and so forth. Most agree that children should never be placed on the witness stand during a trial under any circumstances. In most courts, the child will talk either to the judge in the judge's chambers or to a court-appointed professional, such as a psychologist or social worker, in a less intimidating setting.

When the Child's Home Is in Two Places

Some psychologists feel strongly that parents must agree on certain consistent rules for a joint custody system to work well, especially when the child spends large blocks of time in both homes. In reality, specific household rules may have to vary somewhat, yet parents who are willing to put their own discomfort aside in the interest of the child can usually develop a consistent plan as to major expectations, responsibilities, and limitations. When serious problems arise with the child, it's best if the parents can present a clear and united front. Both parents need to remain legitimate authority figures. Again, if there are differences in the rules or expectations in the households, one parent should never belittle the other. Instead, the parent should explain to the child that that's simply how things work when you spend time in more than one home.

Psychologist Kathryn Lang cautions that children need boundaries when spending time in two homes. "Kids tend to manipulate and divide the parents when they don't like something one is doing. That's another reason parents need to work together, so that the kids can't take advantage of the conflict between them," she explains. "Parents need to make it clear that it's okay to have different rules in different homes. Consistency would be ideal, but it probably won't happen. If people were that amicable, they probably wouldn't have divorced in the first place. Kids simply need to be taught that just because the rules are different at one house, this is not a problem, it's just the way things are. This can actually help kids learn to be flexible."

Lang advises parents to look below the surface to determine the motive behind any major changes in children's behavior. "Parents are often worried when children say they don't want to go to the other parent's home. Often, the child may be trying to spare the parent's feelings, to be the emotional caretaker for that parent. Children frequently exhibit signs of depression, changes in school performance, and fighting in school when their parents are divorcing. One key thing to watch for is how they are doing in their social life—how happy is the child in other settings."

In Lang's experience, boys have a much harder time adjusting to divorce than girls. "Girls tend to be more verbal and mature faster, socially and emotionally. They tend to do better. For both sexes, teens and young adults have the hardest time coping with a parent's divorce, harder than people expect. Parents worry more about the little ones. Yet young children, five-year-olds for example, are really flexible. Plus, we tend to be more careful about children that age. There are many books for little kids to help them cope with their parent's divorce, but not a lot for those in the middle school years and up," she says.

"When young adults watch their parents divorce, they are horrified and really angry. They tend to be very protective of the parent who was left and think terrible things about the parent that did the leaving. Teens especially may get hostile in different ways. They don't have the ability to temper their anger like adults, yet we expect them to be mature. Adolescent boys tend to have a really hard time, especially when their mothers leave," she adds.

Lang advises parents of adolescents to watch for signs of anger, resentment, and depression, and to help their children seek counseling or therapy if needed. "Counseling can help normalize things for adolescents, help them realize that they are not alone and their feelings are normal," she explains.

Either group or one-on-one therapy may be best, depending on the individual. "Like people of other ages, some adolescents simply aren't comfortable in groups," says Lang. "Some just sob and sob and are too devastated to share their feelings with others. But it helps them to hear from an individual counselor that this is typical. Sometimes we can almost give people a script for their lives because the patterns are so similar. They know the beginning of the drama, and we can offer them the rest. Recognizing that they will survive and recover is one of the biggest things that helps people."

Visitation, Shared Time, and Schedules

Another reason communication and cooperation between parents is essential is to accommodate for some flexibility in visitation schedules, particularly as the child gets older and involved in more activities. Even though the parenting plan filed with the court should be very specific, it is better for the child if the parents can agree to minor modifications from time to time, especially for special events such as homecoming, a concert or ballet in town, or an important sports event.

It can be devastating to a child when a parent fails to arrive for a visit or is repeatedly late, or when the custodial parent sabotages the schedule of the visiting parent. Parents may slip into such habits, consciously or unconsciously, in order to irritate the other parent, but again, the child is the victim. Children may believe that the parent doesn't care about spending time with them or may feel guilty for "causing" an argument between the parents. If visitation schedules are disrupted by legitimate problems, the parent should call the child immediately, explain what happened, and make alternate plans.

Experts who work with children also emphasize the importance of spending some unstructured time with the noncustodial parent. Many parents feel bad about leaving the child and try to make up for it by filling each visit with special activities and events. This can be detrimental for several reasons. First, it tends to feel artificial and may prevent the parent and child from focusing on each other. Second, many children today are run ragged by the demands of school, chores, sports, hobbies, and friends. They may need a low-key weekend to relax and simply hang out with the parent, with nothing planned. Third, children are sometimes hesitant to say what activities would truly please them if the parent constantly meets them with a detailed schedule. It can be beneficial to ask the child if there is anything special he or she would like to do, and to consider including some of their friends in outings or activities. Small amounts of time, focused on the child and spent comfortably and creatively, seem to mean the most. Think back to moments you remember as special in your own childhood. Attention to the child is everything.

Psychologist Mel Krantzler advises fathers to beware of falling victim to a belief that they are bad fathers because they are not in their children's lives every day. Parents must eliminate preconceived notions about there being one and only one way to be a good parent. The noncustodial parent can show a child that they love and care for him or her by treating the child as a unique individual and simply spending the time to learn about his or her life. Overindulgence, inconsistency, and constant gifts of material goods can actually work against this by preventing the natural development of genuine caring.

It is common for teenagers to want to move back and forth between the homes of different parents. Most experts believe that it is best to allow the teens to do so, unless there is a problem in one home. Most teens have a mind of their own and may run away or simply pick up and go to the other parent's house if their wishes are denied. Many parents negotiate a trial period for such changes before filing any official change with the court.

Parents also face a restructuring of their own roles after divorce. For example, a mother who always left discipline up to the father may suddenly feel uncomfortable when she finds she must take on this responsibility. If you feel overwhelmed or uncertain in your new role as single parent, check into counseling, self-help groups, or parenting classes. Many are offered through local colleges, public agencies, social service groups, and private organizations. The national organizations listed in the appendix can refer you to local chapters or other sources of help.

Helping Children Heal

Therapists emphasize that children need to talk about their feelings of anger, sadness, worry, loneliness, resentment, guilt, and shame. "Children need help talking about each of these feelings more than one time," says Dino Thompson, director of the Northland Crisis Nursery and Center Against Domestic Violence in Flagstaff, Arizona. "They need help exploring feelings, sorting them out from one another, getting labels on them, and having permission to feel that way. They also need to get the strong message that it is not okay to hurt yourself or others when you're angry or upset. Kids need help managing their feelings in order to feel better at some point."

Thompson recommends parents acknowledge that it's normal to feel such emotions as anger—"the big mad," as she calls it—and that parents should explain what behaviors are acceptable and not acceptable to work it off. She encourages offering such outlets as running together, hugs, and physical activities. She also recommends the use of "guessing statements" such as "I'm guessing that having Mom and Dad getting a divorce could feel really awful for you. You might be feeling (angry, sad, worried)." This can help children label feelings they can't identify for themselves, and move toward feeling better as time passes. Thompson encourages parents to repeat such conversations often.

Professionals stress that it is vital for each parent to avoid criticizing the other in the presence of the child, with one exception: If the other parent has been abusive toward either the custodial parent or the children and could pose a danger to the family, the child should be made aware of the facts. In such situations, sole custody is often granted to the nonabusive parent, and no contact with the abuser allowed. These cases require special, careful handling by a parent who may have the difficult duty of explaining to the child why he or she cannot see the other parent. Fortunately, more and more sources of help for families facing this type of crisis are becoming available, often in the form of group therapy offered by domestic violence shelters and other social service providers. It can be powerful reassurance for a child to know that he or she is not the only one who has suffered this type of trauma, and that others have survived.

If you truly believe your child is being exposed to genuine danger during time spent with the other parent, speak with your lawyer, a social worker, or a state-employed family services agent. Such agencies go by different names, such as Child Protective Services, the Department of Children and Family Services, or something similar. Legal or social service hotlines can provide information as well. Professionals can intervene and investigate to determine whether there is truly a serious problem. For disagreements that are not immediately threatening, mediation or family counseling can be extremely helpful.

Unfortunately, child custody battles give rise to some of the saddest, ugliest behavior ever witnessed in a courtroom. While relatively rare, false accusations of child abuse or inappropriate sexual behavior are sometimes made in an attempt to gain custody or otherwise manipulate a parent. Conversely, a parent who is able to put up a deceptively credible front may calmly and convincingly deny real abuse, making the other parent appear hysterical or unstable.

If you are falsely accused of misconduct by the other parent, get expert legal advice immediately! A child psychologist or social service professional should be brought in to clear your name and determine whether a custody change is required. Such misuse of a child as a weapon is one of the most damaging things a parent can possibly do. It may warrant a change granting sole custody to the other parent.

Family rituals and familiar routines are important to children and should be preserved as much as possible. New traditions often form naturally to replace the unconscious family rituals that are lost when a relationship ends. Constance Ahrons explains, "For a divorce to be a good divorce, family rituals around birthdays, holidays, dinnertimes, and vacations need to be redesigned to accommodate the new bi-nuclear family, and the loss of this portion of our lives must be balanced by its satisfactory reconstruction."

Some families are able to continue old rituals in a new context, as long as the divorced couple have remained reasonably friendly. For example, some families reunite to celebrate a child's birthday, often with new family members in attendance. Professionals caution that children should never be forced into a position of taking sides, such as choosing whether to spend Christmas or Hanukkah with one parent or the other. The parents should make the decision, keeping the feelings of the children in mind. Some families preserve important traditions such as hanging up Christmas stockings in the home where the children lived before the divorce, then establishing a new ritual such as delivering food to the homeless at a local mission the next day.

Again, the feelings of parents must sometimes take a backseat to the children's needs. Kathryn Lang often counsels divorcing couples with children who cannot work out their anger and resentment or who make unrealistic demands. "Frequently, one of the two hasn't let go of the relationship, so they try to control the other. They set all kinds of rules, such as the ex can't bring anyone new around that he or she is dating when the kids are visiting, or they won't let the child bring gifts from the other parent's home," she says. "In a typical case, couples need help in knowing when to let go and how to sort things out and reorganize their lives. Many need help in figuring out what is worth battling about and what is not."

Lang agrees with others who feel that continued hostility between parents is tremendously damaging to children, second only to abuse directed at the child. "Children are often forced into a situation of divided loyalties," she explains. "They love both parents, then hear the parents attack each other. It can ruin lives for years. Sometimes parents still fight openly at their children's weddings and graduations. People can stay angry forever, with the kids caught in the middle. I've heard of more than one instance when battling parents have ruined a grown child's wedding day."

When counseling such couples, she tries to get them to look at the realities of their lives. "When people divorcing are parents, 'till death do you part' becomes a given. People must accept this for the sake of the children. People have to realize they can't control what happens when the child is with the other parent, and realize that it is none of their business what goes on at this time, as long as it is not endangering the kids. The sooner people accept this, the sooner they can let go of their own anger about injuries of the past. People simply have to commit to not doing things that are detrimental to their children."

The most important thing a child can have, during divorce or any other time, is unconditional love by both parents. Sensible rules, consistency, and an ongoing dialogue that goes both ways can go a long way in helping a child remain secure during the upheaval of a divorce. Remember, the parents are probably the most important role model a child will ever have. Do your best to set a good example, especially by listening to your child as well as talking to him or her.

Grandparents, aunts and uncles, friends, cousins, and other people important in the children's lives can also help give them a sense of security. Be sure they are given plenty of access to these people during and after the divorce. All states now have laws providing for the visitation rights of grandparents. The AARP publishes a brochure on grandparents' rights (see appendix A).

Be empathetic. Put yourself in your child's shoes, perhaps by looking back on difficult times you went through in your own childhood. Remember that you healed, and they will too. Try to prepare them for changes in advance. For example, talk to them about dating before you become involved with another person who may be important in your life. Explain that this is normal and that it is what parents do after a divorce.

Share the difficult realities, such as the money situation if it is tight, without expressing any insecurity or panic you may feel yourself. Set a good example for them as to how difficult situations can be overcome.

At the other extreme, custodial parents, too, often fall into the Disneyland syndrome by trying to buy and do everything for the children. Parents often run themselves ragged trying to earn enough money to keep up the lifestyle they enjoyed before. This is not what kids need most. They need love, attention, and reassurance far more. Other single parents can be a fount of ideas on how to cope, as well as provide practical assistance such as carpooling, shared baby-sitting, and so forth.

To address another myth that persists even today, divorce has nothing to do whatsoever with the sexual preferences a child will develop later in life. Whether a person will become homosexual, heterosexual, or bisexual is determined some time between prebirth and the first two years of life. The lack of either a male or a female role model in the home has nothing whatsoever to do with homosexuality. Some sexual confusion is not uncommon during later childhood and adolescence, as children struggle to figure out who they are in all aspects of life. But ultimate sexual preference is determined much earlier.

Diverse role models for a child are important, but gender is not as important as having a variety of good people from different walks of life and varied backgrounds to demonstrate to the child that all kinds of people can be successful and admirable. If you do not have a lot of other adults available to your children through social and neighborhood contacts, consider organizations such as Big Brothers and Big Sisters, the YWCA or YMCA, scouting, and other groups that can help your child interact with different adults on a positive level.

Some parents lean on their children as emotional crutches. This can be bad for both parent and child. Parents need to tend to their own emotional needs through professional help or support from other adults. Never say to a child, "You're the man of the house now" or other similar expressions. While such remarks may seem innocuous, children often take them to heart and believe they are responsible for the welfare of the family. This may cause a child to take on more burdens, experience more anxiety, or feel that they are accountable for your happiness. It is a good idea to allow a child to take on additional, appropriate responsibilities, such as a few more chores or, for an older child, a part-time job to earn their own pocket money. But some children tend to worry too much anyway, and even casual comments can add to their burden.

Gay Parents

Unfortunately, some courts still consider sexual preference as a factor of parenting fitness in determining custody issues. In 1995, the Virginia Supreme Court ruled that a lesbian mother was unfit because her gay relationship would bring a burden of social condemnation on her child, and granted custody of the child to his grandmother. However, while the cases are still all over the board, sexual preference is no longer considered an automatic reason to deny primary custody in most courts. There are an increasing number of attorneys who specialize in the rights of gay individuals. These lawyers may or may not be well versed in other issues of family law, though, so it may be necessary to employ a matrimonial attorney and ask him or her to consult with another lawyer with expertise in this specialized area.

In most places today, parents are free to live their private lives as they see fit. Any sexual behavior between consenting adults will usually not affect custody, unless it is flaunted in front of the child.

WHAT "CAUSES" DIVORCE?

There are so many reasons that people divorce that it would be impossible to catalog them all. For many people, it is a combination of factors. Preconceived ideas of what marriage should be are often unrealistic or change as the years go by. The dynamics of a marriage naturally change as two individuals live and grow in a complex relationship. Career shifts, children, changing interests, attraction to other people, disappointment in the perceived drudgery of everyday life, and the simple reality that human beings are not static but grow and change may all contribute to either the strengthening or deterioration of a marriage. Plain, dumb luck may play a large part as well. For many couples, unexpected upheaval or tragedy seems to bring out previously hidden personality traits that contribute to incompatibility. There is no easy formula to determine why some marriages last and others don't.

Many outside factors, too, have been blamed as the cause of more and more frequent divorce in modern American society. Economic upheaval, changing gender roles, greater emphasis on individual fulfillment, and many other factors have been blamed. While these elements may indeed contribute to the demise of some relationships, each combination of individuals is so unique and complex that very seldom can any one factor inside or outside the marriage be held responsible for causing it to end.

Jane Foster met and married her husband Ron when they both worked for a government firm. The marriage was happy for several years, but the relationship changed when Ron was laid off from his job shortly after she left the firm to start her own design business. "There are two sides to every story, and this is only my perception," she emphasizes. "But it seemed that his self-esteem was greatly affected when he lost his job. At the same time, I had to start working long hours and weekends to get my business off the ground. He was negative and unsupportive, and hoped I would go back to the big company, regular paycheck routine. For a long time I believed it was just a stage of insecurity that would pass, but it didn't, and things just got worse."

Eventually the couple decided to divorce. "We thought we had everything worked out," Foster recalls. "We didn't have children, and we made a written agreement dividing most of our property. We verbally agreed to keep our cars and the stock we each owned in our own names, as these things were fairly equal in value. It wasn't important to me that we split everything fifty–fifty, I simply wanted each of us to get back what we had put into the partnership," she explains.

Unfortunately, events did not follow the simple scenario the couple first envisioned. "As things progressed, we began to disagree about how to divide the equity in the house, some loans, and my new design firm," she says. "He wanted his initial, larger investment in the house back, and I wanted what I had contributed. At that point our attorneys entered the picture and it became apparent that things were not going to end quickly or easily."

As the relationship continued to deteriorate, Foster recalled things her husband had said about his first marriage. "I worried that some unresolved anger and possibly a desire for revenge was being transferred to me during our divorce," she explains. "I hoped this wasn't the case, but sometimes his actions and the emotions he displayed didn't seem to make sense. It was painful for both of us."

As the divorce dragged on, Jane and Ron Foster separated within their home, while the house was up for sale. "At the outset we agreed I would stay in the home, and he would move," she recalls. "But then he refused to leave. Things kept getting worse, and one day our fighting became physical. That was it—I was scared of all the anger, so I proceeded to find a new home for myself." However, even this became difficult. "The realtor we were working with made it clear to me that she considered my husband to be the owner of our house. So I found another realtor as soon as the contract with her expired and urged him to expedite the sale of the house. Too much time was passing and I wanted this divorce to be over."

Unfortunately, however, the Fosters' case eventually went to litigation. "The courtroom was the last place I thought we would have to go to settle the division of the house and loans," she remarks. "We had no kids, nothing of extreme value. My business and most of our property had been settled at that point, but we just couldn't reach a final agreement on these issues."

Foster remembers the pain of appearing in the courtroom as a litigant against her husband. "How sad that it had come to this with the man I had married, loved, slept with, and traveled with. He seemed so desperate—and so was I. It was even sadder when Ron resorted to lying on the witness stand. My attorney proved he was not being honest, and the judge was not kind to him at the end of the trial."

Looking back years later, Foster emphasizes the importance of both personal and professional support for anyone going through a difficult divorce. "I've always made sure I had good friends in my life and their support was absolutely essential," she says. "I was seeing a counselor too, who told me about the stages of grief and pain I could expect to experience. At first I told her, 'no—that won't happen to me.' But everyone goes through it. Naturally, you don't want to endure pain, conflict, and bad decisions, but you can't avoid it. At least if you know what to expect, then you can remind yourself that you're normal, there's nothing wrong with you. Absolutely everyone should get some kind of counseling, group therapy, or other outside support."

Foster urged her husband to get counseling both before their separation to try and save the marriage, and after they decided to part. But he chose not to do so, insisting that Jane was the only one in need of counseling. "I agreed to accept 50 percent of the responsibility for the failure of the marriage, and through counseling I learned from past mistakes," she says. "I realized I had become self-destructive and very angry. But one of the most valuable things my therapist told me was that it was okay to be angry, even to visualize hitting someone in the head—any thought you want is all right as long as you don't act on it. For me, professional assistance was a must, and I feel sorry for anyone who doesn't get help."

Foster felt that one reason her divorce was so difficult was the time it took to reach a final conclusion. "Maybe the worst part was that some of the love was still there," she recalls. "I kept wondering, why does he have to resort to actions that cause us both more pain, like stalling the process and arguing about issues that were never important before? It was a year of pure hell. I think the more time that passes before a divorce trial is held, the greater the potential for damage to the people involved. It gets more expensive and more emotionally difficult as time goes by." Having to go to court also contributed to the misery. "The trial was a nightmare," Foster comments. "I sometimes wonder if it was worth it, and yet a part of me could not just be a doormat, just let things happen when I felt something was wrong. Looking back, I'm glad I stood up for what I knew was right, but I wish there had been a better way to get through it, for both of us."

BUILDING A NEW LIFE

THE DIVORCE IS FINAL: NOW WHAT?

There's an old saying, "It's not over 'til it's over." In a divorce, the more accurate saying would be, "It's not over even when it's over." As discussed previously, when parents divorce, ties will likely remain between them for the rest of their lives or at least until the children are grown and on their own. Yet even in a divorce without children, in which all the financial, legal, and other tangible matters are resolved, emotional as well as practical baggage may remain.

Experts advise caution in all areas of life immediately after a divorce. The exhaustion or exhilaration many people experience can lead to bad decision making. It may be tempting to toss everything aside, move to a new state, and start a new life. This can be a wonderful adventure, but certain business must be taken care of first.

Wrapping Up Financial Business

When joint accounts are closed, it is best if both spouses can sign a mutual letter to be sent to the account holders, stating the account is to be closed, so that there is no doubt. This should be double-checked later to make sure that the instructions were carried out correctly. If you have any lingering questions or doubts, sit down one last time with attorneys and other advisers and get everything straight.

If your former spouse refuses to carry out the terms of the settlement agreement, such as paying debts that were not refinanced in his or her name alone, the court that supervised the divorce can enforce the agreement without requiring another lawsuit. However, a judge will rarely change a settlement agreement except to modify ongoing payments such as alimony or child support, or to change the terms of child custody or visitation. Anytime you and your ex agree to a voluntary change in one of these matters, it should be put in writing and taken to the same court for approval and filing.

Most experts advise that it is best to wait until you are in a comfortable financial and emotional situation and settled into your new life before making major life changes such as investments, moves, or purchases. Psychologist Constance Ahrons describes the aftermath of divorce as a separate stage of the process. The point at which the aftermath stage is reached, as well as the nature of the transition itself, is very different for couples and individuals. This stage is defined by emotions rather than by any outward event, such as the final signing of papers. Some people feel they have reached the aftermath almost as soon as the decision to divorce becomes definite, while for others it takes years. Naturally, various factors affect the timing, such as whether there are children, the ages of the ex-spouses, new relationships or remarriage, and whether all the issues of the divorce are resolved in a satisfactory way.

Once a divorce is over, many people are surprised to have ambivalent feelings. Even if you are thrilled to be out of an unhappy marriage, you may find yourself missing small, everyday things, such as dinner routines, regular contact with in-laws, security, and companionship.

Many professionals recommend that people experiencing such feelings look for the opportunities they present. For example, if you have been wanting to move, redecorate, take some time alone for introspection, get a new job, make new friends or reconnect with old ones, or get involved with new hobbies or activities, this may be the time to do so. This is also the time to take stock of the healing that will begin. Remember, it may take several years before you really feel comfortable with your new life and your new identity. But if feelings that interfere with your everyday life, such as depression, anger, a desire for vengeance, or feeling victimized persist without getting better, you may need some professional counseling in order to move forward.

Relocating After Divorce

Moving is always stressful, especially when it's done in response to a situation fraught with emotional upheaval. Whether you, your partner, or both of you will be moving, you will be faced with the task of creating a new home.

This work can be made easier in several ways. First, you may want to have a friend or family member help you sort through your belongings, if you are unable to do so with your partner. Many people turn the packing and sorting process or the moving day itself into a social event. Once you know what is going to stay or go, consider asking several friends to help you pack and move everything that won't be transported by professional movers, then treat them to food and drink in a casual housewarming party.

The packing and transportation process usually takes at least a few days. It can help to set up a schedule and a definite date for the move. Many of these tasks, especially the emotionally difficult ones, such as dividing up photos, are best accomplished a little at a time. Many people recommend starting with the easier chores and working up to the harder ones.

Things that can be accomplished even before the actual packing process begins include accumulating labels, trash bags, boxes, packing materials, and marking pens. Get everything set up with professional movers, including confirmation of costs, date, and time. Send out cards with changes in name, address, and telephone number to friends, neighbors, professional associates, health care professionals and organizations, your church, credit card companies, organizations you belong to, health clubs, sports and social clubs, magazines and newspapers, catalogs, book, record, and video clubs, insurance providers, and anyone else who needs to know of the change.

Professionals such as Kathleen A. Kukor, president of Nest Builders, Inc., a company specializing in preparation before a household move and organization of the new home, are becoming more and more available. They can provide not only practical assistance but emotional support as well. Kukor says that people need to realize that healing takes time, and it helps to gradually begin making the new or changed home a special, individual place. She urges clients staying in the old house to buy things for the house that they never purchased before, change wall coverings and other decorating details, and consider adding house plants and a pet to the family. As a contributor to Margorie Engel's *Divorce Help Sourcebook*, she advises, "At a time when you have to face so much change, surround yourself with your favorite and familiar things to give yourself some sense of continuity in your life."

Child Support Enforcement

Collecting child support is often the most vexing problem after a divorce. Support requirements usually continue for years after the divorce is final. Changes in circumstances may require both parties to return to court or renegotiate again and again. It is uniquely subject to abuse by both sides, and, sadly, parents sometimes view child support not as a duty to their child, but as a means of manipulating, punishing, or annoying the former spouse. Fortunately, there is increasing help available for the custodial parent whose former spouse refuses to pay or simply disappears.

As discussed in chapter 6, every state has a special agency to enforce child support. The federal government also maintains agencies in different regions, which deal in large part with child support enforcement when parents live in different states. These agencies are listed in appendix B at the back of this book. A call to the state or federal agency serving your area can provide information on the types of services provided.

There are various methods of collecting child support, and more are becoming available as the government looks for additional ways to force parents to meet their obligation of support so that the government does not have to take care of children with public funds. In addition to withholding wages, income tax refunds, lottery winnings, and other payments due can be intercepted by a local prosecutor's office or child support enforcement agency. In some states, a lien can be placed on property and a foreclosure sale ordered to collect the amounts due. Some courts will order self-employed parents to post a bond with the court to assure that payments are made. If a parent is behind $1,000 or more of child support obligations, a report can be made to a credit bureau by a child support enforcement agency. In fact, such agencies are required by law to make these reports. This can interfere with the nonpaying parent's ability to borrow or get other benefits of credit. Some states are refusing to renew professional or driver's licenses when parents do not pay child support.

Anytime a court order is violated, several options are available. Either civil or criminal contempt of court may be imposed by the judge for a violation that is deliberate or flagrant. This process begins by filing a motion for an "order to show cause." This motion tells the judge that the other party is in violation of the court order and gives them a chance to respond. The judge will generally order them to appear in court and "show cause" as to why they did not obey the court order in force. If they do not have a good reason, they can be fined or even jailed.

Wages may also be garnished in a procedure slightly different than that of simple withholding of child support. In garnishment, a percentage of the check rather than a set amount is withheld by the employer. Some states publish

Most Wanted lists with names and pictures of deadbeat parents. Various methods of foreclosure may be used against property such as money in the bank, boats, cars, real estate, and stocks. The district attorney's office or local child support enforcement agencies can help and advise on the options available in your area.

Dealing with an Ex-Spouse: What to Expect

When a childless marriage ends, it can truly end, and the couple may choose never to see each other again for the rest of their lives. Others take the opposite extreme and become friends, reporting that they get along better than ever once the stress of an unworkable marriage is removed. Yet, in our culture, divorced couples are expected either to ignore one another or to be openly hostile. Such stereotypes are both inaccurate and highly detrimental, especially when the couple has children.

Those who have studied divorced couples have found that the relationships between these individuals span the spectrum of possibilities, with most somewhere in the middle between bitter enemies and best friends. Constance Ahrons has studied coparenting couples extensively and found that the largest group consists of what she terms *cooperative colleagues*, in which the individuals do not consider each other to be close friends but cooperate reasonably well on issues concerning their children. Ahrons also emphasizes that relationships between former partners often improve over the years, especially if both individuals are committed to the loving support of their children. She noted the benefit of more positive role models in both fictional portrayals, such as the popular movie *Mrs. Doubtfire*, and in real–life examples. She praised the increasing attention to the cooperative parenting efforts of celebrities; encouraging advice of columnists and other commentators; and more and more written accounts by people who have found a way to make their own painful situations work.

"The good news is that eventually you do recover from the divorce completely," says Laura, now divorced a dozen years and remarried. "Sometimes I literally forget that I was married before," she laughs. "But it took a long time to get here. My marriage was really bad at the end, and I lost perspective. I was so insecure when I came out of it, I was a different person. Now, I don't know who that person was."

Psychologists and sociologists who have studied the effects of life events on human emotions have ranked the stress of divorce as equal to the stress caused by the death of a child or spouse. Certain words are heard again and again by professionals working with people involved in a divorce: frustration, helplessness, anger, failure, hurt. In the words of Emily Couric, author of *The Divorce Lawyers*, "Sadness, disappointment, pain, and anger are the handmaidens of divorce, and their presence makes it difficult to behave with dignity."

For this reason, interaction with others who have been through and survived divorce can be tremendously helpful in overcoming the initial pain as well as beginning the long-term healing. Many find it especially helpful to talk to others who went through a divorce several years ago, and know that perhaps the ultimate tool in healing is the passage of time. The reassurance that the pain will pass with time is more meaningful if it comes from someone who has been in a similar situation. My mother, herself divorced, has often quoted the philosopher Friedrich Nietzsche, who said, "What doesn't kill me makes me stronger." I have many friends who have assured me that in the context of the breakup of a marriage, these words are indeed true.

ONE WOMAN'S EXPERIENCE

"My emotional state during my divorce was like being stuck in a nightmare. I felt lost, as though I was stumbling in the dark. I was terrified I would never find myself again," says Clayta Spear, a second-grade teacher who has now been divorced for ten years. "Actually, my divorce was a lot easier than most I've heard about. I really made an effort to keep it as simple as possible. I waited until I realized and accepted that there was no hope, that I was the only one trying to save the marriage, and you can't do that by yourself. I never wanted the divorce, but I felt defeated. So I accepted it was time to move on, so we could both have a life. I decided to file under the new no-fault law. I thought that would make it easier to divide up our possessions. Besides, I wanted to move away and leave the house where we had been living for ten years. Yet it was hard to build up the courage to take the step."

On the surface, Spear's divorce indeed appeared simple. The couple had been married for eleven years and had no children. They owned a townhouse and a condominium, as well as assorted personal property, but nothing that required complex division. However, as in most divorces, outward appearances failed to tell the whole story. "For the last two years of the marriage, things were no good," she says. "I see now that I stayed about one year too long. But, like everyone, I never expected this to happen. And I didn't learn what was going on until the divorce was almost final."

Spear suspected her husband was involved with another woman, but he refused to admit it. "The last year was just a matter of waiting. I think he was waiting to see if the other woman was going to leave her husband and commit to him; while I was waiting to see if we could work things through. I encouraged him to see a psychologist before we made any decisions, and he did, for several months. But when I finally figured out what was up, I felt a tremendous sense of disappointment and betrayal. That was what created the nightmare. I think the hardest type of breakup is when one person feels rejected and betrayed by the other," she explains.

At the same time her marriage was crumbling, Spear's father was dying of Alzheimer's disease and she was seeing a psychologist to help her through her grief. She continued to work with the psychologist on divorce issues. He advised her to join a divorce support group. "I wish I had joined a group then, but at that time there weren't any in my own town, and I would have had to drive thirty or forty miles to Boston to join one. So I thought it would be too much effort. Also, I know now that I was too ashamed to join a group then and talk about my pain and feelings of rejection with strangers."

Eventually, Spear moved across the country, revitalized her career, and started building a satisfying new life. Even several years after her divorce, however, she realized that many of the issues that had arisen were not yet resolved. "I got a flier in the mail promoting a seminar on separation, divorce, and personal growth that would be held in the town where I was now living. It was an eleven-week program, and I recalled what my psychologist back in Massachusetts had recommended. I knew I had lots of feelings buried inside. I didn't even know it was anger. I was brought up in a New England family in which anger was not considered feminine, and any expression of anger was forbidden. Denial was the lifeblood of my family. Plus I always had the role of peacemaker. When I got divorced I kept my anger suppressed and it was still there after five years.

"I was reluctant to join the group at first because by that time I had been divorced seven years, even though a volunteer who screened me before I signed up told me she thought it would be helpful to me and others in the group. Most of the people were newly separated or divorced. Some of them were still in relationships and trying to decide whether to leave. But the psychologist who ran the program wanted me to join, in part to show other people of the importance of facing and dealing with the issues of a divorce, whether it be sooner or later. I was a living example that the pain and confusion doesn't go away until you are willing to confront it," she says.

Spear found the seminar immensely helpful in both identifying her feelings and learning how they had naturally occurred because of the events that led to the end of her marriage. "My husband didn't treat me with respect or trust. He kept things from me and blamed all the problems we were having on me alone. As things deteriorated, he became emotionally abusive, telling me I was stupid and so on. I think a lot of this came from his own guilt," she explains. "For him to leave me for another woman was absolutely the last thing I expected, because his first wife had left him for another man. He was so insecure, he made me promise I'd never leave him. This made the betrayal doubly hard. I was even more surprised when he was so unfair to me in our settlement negotiations. It was easy to divide up the furniture and possessions, but we had a hard time with the money and some things that seemed small at the time, like his refusal to give me any of our photographs. I had chosen a beautiful set of drapes to be custom made for our home, which I had carefully decorated over a period of years. He insisted that the drapes stay in the house. He wanted to impress his new girlfriend by bringing her to a showplace. It felt like the drapes had become more important to him than I was. That was such a shock—it really hurt."

Although she had a successful career of her own, Spear, like many people, saw her marriage as the main focus in her life. "My childhood was bad, my parents were both alcoholics, and I never felt secure. So it was very important for me to have security and stability in my home and through my marriage. When it ended I lost the whole focus of my life. I really expected my life would just end. I felt I had no reason to go on, so I didn't fight over the divorce settlement. I was never suicidal, but I was in such terrible pain I fully expected to die. All I could feel was rejection, shame, loss, and betrayal," she recalls.

"I learned a lot in group therapy," adds Spear. "Besides dealing with my own problems, I realized that although my husband had been divorced for seven years when we got married, he had not dealt with the baggage from his past relationship. Some of the problems in our marriage were a direct result of this. I think everyone needs some kind of therapy or support group when he or she is going through a divorce. My attorney strongly recommended I get professional help and I'm grateful that I did."

As in many support groups, the seminar Spear attended included weekly sessions that combined structured activities with a chance for people to talk and share their thoughts informally. Each session built on topics covered in previous weeks. "The psychologist in charge of the group led us in different discussions and activities. Volunteers, usually people who had been members of previous groups and had some additional training, would assist. Additionally, we would have assignments to do during the week, such as keeping a journal or using a workbook we were given. The volunteers called group members every week, both to check on how we were doing and to give us someone to talk to. They also set up social events that members could attend or not, as they chose. Loneliness was a real problem for a lot of people, not so much for me because I had always been independent and had my career and friends, but it was still good to become a part of a social group with common issues."

The people in the group, who were at different stages of the breakup process, were able to learn from one another. "Days like Christmas, the wedding anniversary, and other special times brought up a lot of emotions," says Spear. "People also reported how their moods and attitudes changed. Most found that their spirits and hopes really lifted between the beginning of the seminar period and the end. The community was really important. A lot of people started to experience real anxiety toward the end, when they faced more loss—separation from the group. Sharing a traumatic time of life really brings people close together. The social events that took place during the seminar period helped everyone to get into the habit of meeting informally, so in nearly every seminar group some of the participants continued getting together afterward. Many new friendships and a few relationships occurred."

After completing her seminar, Spear continued as a volunteer with a subsequent group. "The psychologist asked me to volunteer, and others in group recommended me, so I was pleased to give it a try. I don't think I'll volunteer for another one due to the emotional drain and the responsibility. But it was really good for me to see how much I had learned and how far I had come. You also see the advantages and disadvantages in your own situation when you compare it with that of others," she explains. "For instance, I had a much easier time than many people making the transition to single life because I'd always been independent and had other interests. My career as a teacher, strong friendships, and work with local dramatic players groups were important things that had always been a part of my life. But the healing still takes a long time. I'd keep giving myself deadlines, thinking I should be over it by a certain period. But you never really get over it, it's always a part of your life. Those years are a component of your experience, you deal with it, and you go on. But you can't remove a block from the foundation that built your life. People have to realize that the marriage was a part of what made the life they have today. They should also realize that everyone is different, and everyone heals at different rates. I was my own worst and harshest critic. I would advise others to be patient with themselves and to realize that even after you do feel good there will be things that will cause emotional upheaval. Going through this roller coaster of emotions is very upsetting but typical."

While the secondary purpose of the seminar group was to meet new people with common issues for support and form new friendships, some people went into the group seeking immediate contact with potential new mates. "The psychologist warned us about this at the outset. He recommended we not date anyone else in the group until after the seminar was over. However, several people did date in both of the groups I worked with. These seemed to be troubled relationships, though, because the wounds were still raw from the other relationship."

Spear found an unexpected bonus in the communication skills taught in the seminar. "This part really struck me, because of the weakness I've seen in my own relationships and as an educator. Communication skills are critical in all our interactions, but training is lacking in our society," she says. "People are expected to know how to communicate effectively with one another, but we are never taught the techniques. Children, parents and children, and men and women especially, all tend to communicate on a totally different level. In the school where I work, I'm pleased to say that we teach communication skills and effective dispute resolution techniques at the elementary level. We start training kids to be mediators at the third- to fifth-grade level so they can help others resolve their disputes without violence. It's a pilot program, and I'm pleased to see it catching on throughout the country."

The seminar Spear attended also included sessions on accepting the grief process, managing anger, building self-esteem, learning to love and trust again, discovering new opportunities, intimacy, sexuality, and friendship. An optional session on helping children adjust to divorce was offered for those participants who were parents. She gained new insights into her own experience and emotions, as well as greater insight about other people. "The sexuality part was really interesting," she remarks. "There was such a broad range of reactions, from "I never want anyone to touch me again," to "I'm ready to jump on anybody!" It was sad to see how many people had been so abused or put down by their former spouse that they felt unattractive and unlovable. But I know how that can happen. You get such a sense of failure. You know you're intelligent and that you're attractive and lovable on an intellectual level. But on an emotional level you remain convinced that you are not."

Despite the passage of time, Spear found that she had a hard time letting go of the past relationship and still felt a persistent concern about her husband's well-being and happiness. "Even today, I still worry about him. But that's just the way I am about any friend. And I've learned it's okay to be this way. When you look at it logically, you wouldn't love someone if there was nothing about them to love. That part doesn't go away. In the seminar I learned that this is normal, and it can make you want to either embrace or kill someone. But the history you shared, with its bittersweet memories, is important."

She also gained a different perspective about the extreme labels we tend to place on relationships as a total success or a total failure. "Americans are so success–oriented. We don't deal well with the realities of life. We expect absolute success or failure in relationships and don't recognize what's in between," she says. "We still believe that a marriage is supposed to be forever, and if it doesn't last, you've failed. It's very shameful and completely devastating in our society to fail. Moving out of a marriage, for many reasons, is not a failure; it means you're taking another path in life. People need to support those who are divorcing, not reject them or place blame."

Although the seminar process helped her tremendously, Spear cautions that people should not expect an immediate cure-all from this type of therapy. "I'm still afraid to trust, and to be vulnerable again to the risks in a relationship. I just don't want to deal with it or risk it, because betrayal has been a pattern in my life," she explains. "But in the seminar, we covered a lot about our future and our goals, both actual planning of activities and imagining our dreams and our future life. I know now that I will not marry again, but I am open to new relationships. I've done some casual dating and I don't want to let the damage from my divorce make me bitter and unhappy. I've always been a survivor and a strong individual. I was independent from an early age. I taught with the Peace Corps and traveled around the world. This really helped me to have the courage to start over after my divorce. I never dated much as a young woman and don't believe you have to have a man to be a whole woman. It would be nice to have the love and understanding of a partner, but it's not something I require to have a happy and fulfilling life. I know now I can go on living a meaningful life just for myself."

DATING AFTER DIVORCE

When to start dating after a separation or divorce is a subject of some controversy, both among professionals who work with those healing after the breakup of a relationship and the people who have been there. Many strongly urge waiting until some specified time period has passed. Others believe people should go with what feels natural and right. "I know it's probably not a good idea to be involved with another man so soon," said one woman who began dating another man almost immediately after breaking up with her husband. "But I really enjoy being with this person. Should I turn away from something good, someone special, just because others tell me the timing isn't right?"

During what some experts have labeled as the "walking wounded" stage immediately following a divorce, extreme views toward the opposite sex are not uncommon. Many people feel bitter, believing that all men or all women are alike, and they want nothing to do with the opposite sex ever again as long as they live. Others feel desperate to find another partner immediately so they won't have to be alone.

It is important to remember that while both of these extremes are normal, actions taken in response to either can be detrimental. Those who feel they must find a new relationship immediately may feel that theirs is the healthier attitude, but it is actually the more dangerous. Desperation is a big turnoff to those who would be good partners. Too often, people who seek out new relationships immediately become entangled with others whose problems are as great or greater than their own.

Moreover, hostility tends to dissipate in a healthy person more quickly than dependence. According to psychologist Mel Krantzler, these extreme attitudes are mirror images both based on fear. He and many other professionals emphasize the importance of time alone to renew a sense of self-worth, let extreme feelings heal, and learn to be a whole and content person on your own.

"People who go into a new relationship too soon after a divorce take the same problems with them," says psychologist Kathryn Lang. "In the long run, it usually doesn't work well. Often, two dependent people get together, and you end up with two halves trying to be a whole."

Lang feels it is important for people divorcing to take some time to heal and be alone before moving on to a new relationship. "For several years after I went through my divorce, I slept with only one pillow on the bed, to remind me that I had to learn to be a one before I could be a two. I realized, in hindsight, that I'd never learned who I was before. I needed that time alone to discover my wants and needs, to figure out who I was."

Lang believes that the period of time people need to fully heal after a divorce varies, but for many it may take up to five years. "The majority of people remarry within five years, and it seems that those who wait longer are less likely to remarry," she remarks. "But likelihood of whether a person will remarry often depends on whether he or she liked the state of marriage itself, rather than the quality of the marriage. It depends on the individual. Some feel constrained by marriage. To others, family is extremely important."

Lang herself waited ten years before she married again. "I was a lot more cautious the second time around," she says. "I would find myself taking inventory of a person when I went on a date, which people often tend to do on a subtle basis. Sometimes I wished we could just exchange lists of our characteristics and traits, what we were looking for, information about our past, and be on with it," she laughs. "But I believe that it is really important to know who you are and to be whole before you can have a healthy relationship."

Krantzler warns that those who remarry too quickly—say within two years—after a divorce are more likely to experience problems in the subsequent marriage. Four out of five divorced people do remarry, and those who take some time before jumping into another marriage have the best chance of having a better marriage than the first. It is essential to get some perspective and wisdom on the former relationship, experience self-discovery, heal, grow, learn new ways of relating to people, and to set new goals.

Krantzler believes that most people go through four phases of reacting to the opposite sex during the first two years or so after divorce, which reflect a process of mourning and rediscovery. During the first, the "walking wounded stage," people commonly feel dazed, terrified, and disoriented. This is when the feelings of wanting to find another person immediately or never wanting to have another partner are common. Krantzler and others advise that such feelings of helplessness and being out of control are normal anytime we face a significant ending and new beginning in our lives. All human beings, however, have a strong instinct for survival and self-renewal, and these feelings will not last forever. If they do last for more than six months, professional counseling should be considered.

In the second stage, which Krantzler calls the "sex-is-everything-stage," people begin testing the waters. People are often anxious to connect with new partners, yet fearful and confused. Many are unsure about the rules of dating etiquette today, as the roles of men and women have changed in recent years. Yet the good old Golden Rule, flexibility, open communication, simple consideration, and respect for the other person go a long way in overcoming any awkwardness. It takes a while for most people to make the transition from married to single, and difficulties are usually temporary. Krantzler advises that sexual problems at this stage are not uncommon. Most people experience a lot of enjoyment when they begin dating again, and the attraction of someone of the opposite sex is great medicine for a wounded ego. However, most eventually get weary of the dating whirlwind and enter a normal winding-down period. Krantzler emphasizes that this stage can be a time of important learning, as well as recovery.

In stage three, which Krantzler calls "come close but go away," the person may have met someone he or she feels is special, but still experiences lingering fear. He urges people to take chances and to remember that there can be no gain without risk. This stage may include a series of "ninety-day wonders"—short, intimate relationships that eventually end. He advises against making quick commitments such as living together during this phase, as another breakup can be extremely painful. He also cautions against becoming involved with someone who is married or otherwise not completely available, or treating a companion unfairly by keeping them as a "stand-by" while dating others. He emphasizes that a healthy commitment will not be possible until you are ready for an equal partnership with an equal balance of power, communication, and the compromise required to establish a committed monogamous relationship. Emotions may still run wild during this phase.

When a person becomes ready for the fourth stage, "intimacy without fear," they are prepared for deeper emotional involvement. Krantzler advises that a good deal of solitude may accompany the entry of this stage, as a person figures out what he or she wants and needs. He emphasizes that people who are relatively happy with their present lives will be much more likely to find a healthy relationship with a partner. We must make our own happiness, not depend on others to "make" us happy, he points out. At this stage he advises people to be open-minded and to realize that they may meet a special person when they least expect it, perhaps someone they knew long ago.

Krantzler also emphasizes that anxiety about making a commitment when contemplating remarriage is very common, and that many people about to enter a second or subsequent marriage experience an attack of anxiety or even call off the wedding a night or two before. This fear is brought about by the persistent image of another marriage just like the one they left. But these feelings usually pass and are nothing to worry about. One of my friends, who tried to call off her second wedding three nights before the scheduled event, has now been happily married to her second husband for eleven years.

Bear in mind that no rules are absolute, especially in the untamed arena of human emotions. Psychologists acknowledge that a person who has been emotionally divorced for several years before the physical separation may have already gone through the stages of grieving.

Many people divorcing today are part of the baby boom generation. Those coming out of a long marriage may find that the world of dating and sex is a whole new frontier. Many of us grew up in what has been called the "PPPP" (post-pill, pre-plague) generation, in which we could enjoy the freedom of sex without the fear of either unwanted pregnancy or life-threatening disease. Needless to say, things are considerably different today. Be sure you know how to protect yourself if you have been in a monogamous relationship for many years and aren't familiar with the health precautions that have become essential today.

Dating and Children

Divorced parents often feel awkward when they begin dating again, and wonder how or whether to bring new partners around their children. Most experts believe that a casual approach is best, and that children need not be included in activities with the new partner until the relationship becomes at least somewhat serious. Many caution against making every new acquaintance a part of the child's life, because they often form swift emotional attachments and become confused or hurt if the relationship doesn't last. On the other hand, it's both unwise and dishonest to try and hide essential facts about your life from either your children or your dating partners. Telling your partners about your children early on, and your children about those you date, makes the transition easier and avoids awkwardness later.

It is also natural for children to be curious about sex. Most believe you should answer their questions honestly, within the context of the parent's own sense of privacy. It is worse for children to have less information than more, as they tend to have vivid imaginations and may misunderstand or be frightened by sights or sounds they can't identify.

When a dating relationship becomes serious, your children and your new partner should begin to spend time getting to know one another in a gradual and natural way. Blending a family is a long, often challenging process, and if forced can cause insecurity, anxiety, and suspicion.

Stuart Berger, M.D., author of *Divorce Without Victims*, recommends that serious dating partners be introduced to children in settings where there is low pressure and little interaction required. An evening at home where strangers sit around the living room staring at each other can be extremely awkward for everyone involved. Berger recommends a group outing to a place such as a zoo, movie, or other recreational event where the people can interact but have somewhere else to focus their attention and something besides themselves to talk about. He and other experts advise a parent's new partner to let friendship with the children develop gradually and not to overdo such gestures as gifts, which may be seen as bribes by the children.

Berger also says that despite the best efforts of the parent and the new partner, children may remain intransigent and even profess utter hatred of the person. Such reactions may not be based on a genuine dislike of the individual, but rather on a continued denial of the divorce or an ongoing reconciliation fantasy. He advises that sacrificing an important relationship for the sake of the children is generally a mistake, and that older children often feel tremendous guilt in later years if they believe the parent stayed alone and suffered a lonely life on their behalf. Parents of children who reject a new partner must listen carefully to the children's objections, because occasionally there may be a legitimate concern. If there are signs of unkind or abusive behavior, then this is of course quite a different matter, one which must be addressed by the parent. On the contrary, however, children who object to their parent's new partner for inappropriate reasons can often find only inconsequential things to complain about, such as the person's appearance, petty habits, or that they compare unfavorably in the child's eyes to the absent parent. Berger and other experts reassure parents that kids nearly always come around eventually to establish a relationship with the new partner that is at least civil, although it may take a year or even longer.

REMARRIAGE AND STEPFAMILIES

According to sociologist Constance Ahrons, approximately 85 percent of divorced men and 75 percent of divorced women marry again within three years. These numbers demonstrate that most who divorced are not left bitter toward the institution of marriage in general, and retain the necessary hope and optimism to try again. Yet any remarriage brings challenges, especially when children and parents must form blended families or stepfamilies.

Like many professionals in the field of family therapy, Ahrons strongly believes that the terminology by which we refer to family members is vitally important. She deplores such phrases as *broken home* because of its negative connotation. Ahrons refers to families no longer living in one household as "bi-nuclear."

There is, unquestionably, a lack of appropriate terminology for many modern relationships. Children asked by teachers to tell the class about their families often have to spend ten or fifteen minutes describing not only stepparents, stepbrothers, and stepsisters, but also half-siblings, stepparent's brothers and sisters, those who function as grandparents but are not related by blood, or people with whom their parents cohabit. Not only is the lack of labels confusing, but degrading, prejudicial phrases such as *living in sin* and *illegitimate children* are also still heard.

Roles among these new family members may also be uncomfortable and suffer from a lack of guiding norms. Most believe the best approach is to let kinship relationships develop naturally according to the feelings of the people involved. In most cases this does seem to occur with time. As blended families become more common and require more thoughtful consideration on the part of their members, families are coming up with their own solutions. Constance Ahrons and other family therapists warn against unrealistic expectations of the ideal, "Brady Bunch" instant family. In explaining that caring relationships take time to evolve, and that expectations of immediate love between stepparents and stepchildren can lead to disappointment and difficulty, Ahrons quotes Emily and John Visher, founders of the Stepfamily Association of America: "If the stepfamily relationships are allowed to develop as seems comfortable to the individuals involved, then caring between steprelatives has the opportunity to develop."

Ahrons adds that the formation of a new family by one spouse often gives rise to conflicts with the ex-spouse. She counsels avoiding abrupt changes of old schedules and patterns to the extent possible, so the ex-spouse can have time to get used to the new arrangement as well. Couples should bear in mind also that while remarriage is one of the "changed circumstances" that courts will consider when determining whether to make a revision in child support, remarriage usually is not viewed as a valid reason for reducing child support. On the contrary, as in Tom Murphy's experience discussed in chapter 6, it may be viewed as grounds to increase support obligations, especially in the case of a dual-career, childless couple. State laws vary on how remarriage affects child support.

Fortunately, as blended families are becoming more and more common in American society today, both attitudes toward and services for such families are improving. More and more family counselors are developing special programs and therapies to help blended families improve communication and build good relationships. Today, stepparents can receive a good deal of support from others. Stepparent support groups have helped members educate themselves and band together to encourage state legislatures to pass new laws protecting their rights, and for judges to be more enlightened in the way they look at stepparents and their ties to their stepchildren. National organizations, such as the Stepfamily Association of America, provide information and support, and many have local branches (see appendix A).

When blended families break apart, stepparents and children often face a wrenching dilemma. Traditionally, stepparents were generally not recognized as having any special right to continue a relationship with stepchildren under the law. Today, all fifty states have either statutes or binding case law dealing with custody, visitation, and support by stepparents. The American Bar Association has drafted a model act regarding stepparents, which will likely be adopted in its current form or as modified by many of the states. However, while special arrangements are generally left up to the individual court, it is becoming more and more common for courts to facilitate a continued relationship between stepparents and stepchildren, if it will be beneficial to the child. In a few rare cases, custody may even be granted to a stepparent rather than the biological parent. This generally happens when there is a strong showing that this would be far better for the child, especially if the couple married when the child was young, the child has never known another father or mother than the stepparent, and the marriage was of long duration with a close bond between stepparent and child.

As more and more emphasis is placed by the courts on the key determination in child custody cases—the best interest of the child—less attention is being paid to biological ties and more to the individual circumstances of the child and the adults with whom he or she has formed important relationships.

BLENDING A NEW FAMILY

A childless person who marries a parent is faced with learning a whole new set of skills that may be completely unfamiliar. Experts advise such people to take some time to read books and learn about children, their development, and their behavior.

Although it is important for the authority of the new adult in the family to be established, and household rules consistently enforced (generally by the biological parent with the support of the stepparent), change should be minimized and ultimatums avoided. Stepparents should never try to be the same as a biological parent, but rather develop their own individual role in the child's life. Parents who try to force the children to accept a stepparent as a replacement for the biological parent are putting a terrible burden on the child. For example, children should not be forced to call the stepparent Mom or Dad, but instead be allowed to use the person's first name or develop an alternate name that is comfortable to everyone. Likewise, a stepparent who moves in with a set of strict new household rules is courting disaster.

The parents must compromise, reach an agreement on boundaries and ground rules, stick with it, and back each other up. Direct orders to the children, such as to do chores, homework, or go to bed, should generally come from the biological parent, at least during the adjustment period. Most agree that while expressions of direct authority and any type of discipline should come from the biological parent, a stepparent must have the authority to enforce rules in the other parent's absence and should support the biological parent if there is a conflict.

Stuart Berger advises parents and stepparents to be sensitive to small issues which may be tremendously important to a child's sense of stability. Small rituals and routines, such as having a particular blanket, toy, or pajamas every night may seem trivial, but a child needs predictability and security. Stepparents often have to be extremely patient, persistent, and loving toward a child. This may be difficult, especially when the child seems to be critical and rejecting. Youngsters are often confused about how to treat the stepparent. They may worry that loving and accepting a stepparent means abandoning the biological parent.

One of the most common problems stepfamilies face is unrealistic expectations. These new relationships are extremely complex, involving everything from rearranging deep emotional ties to the logistics of more people sharing a bathroom. As Berger says, "Stepparenting is not for the timid at heart." Building a stepfamily requires patience, flexibility, love, determination, and a constant sense of humor. Perfect harmony all the time is not a realistic expectation. Stepfamilies tend to deal with all of the problems faced by biological families, and then some. Bonding does not have the force of history and biology behind it. Yet, as the many successful stepfamilies demonstrate, great love and wonderful relationships can and do develop over time.

Berger advises new stepparents to look for common ground and shared interests with their stepchildren. He reminds the family to laugh and relax and keep things in perspective. While the time for a new family to become bonded varies with the individuals involved, it is not uncommon for one to three years to pass before the family feels entirely comfortable together.

These years may be very trying. It is common for children to idealize the absent parent even if that parent has abused, abandoned, or never been close to the child. Biological parents must be especially cautious not to take this tempting opportunity to criticize the other parent. In all probability, the children are fully aware of the parent's shortcomings and may be using this constant praise to appease their guilt over what is in fact a growing fondness for the stepparent.

It is also essential for the child's well-being that the noncustodial parent try to help the child adjust to the new situation. It is extremely hard on children when that parent is hostile toward a stepparent. All the adults in the child's life need to encourage and reassure them that the new development is positive and will bring more love and richness into their lives, not less.

Stepparents, especially those without children of their own, also need to remember that children are not thoughtful, considerate, or grateful by nature. It is especially important for a stepparent to acknowledge the special bond between the biological parent and child and allow them some time alone. Children may fear that a parent who remarries will transfer to the stepparent the affection formerly reserved only for the child. Biological parents need to reassure the child that they have plenty of love to go around, and to make some special efforts to show the child that he or she is still a very important part of their life.

At the same time, the biological parent is dealing with the delicate process of adjusting to life with a new spouse. It is important for the couple to attend to their own relationship, for example, by taking a traditional honeymoon away from the children, and through communication and consideration for each other's needs. It can be very beneficial for everyone in the family, especially the new stepparent, to have some space that is theirs alone, if at all possible. This is helpful to stepsiblings as well if virtual strangers must now share a room. Even in a large home, everyone is apt to feel crowded, both emotionally and physically, until the settling-in period has passed.

Berger and other experts warn that clashes between stepsiblings are especially common between those close in age. Berger advises parents to let the kids try to reach their own solutions to problems. Of course, they should not be allowed to brawl with one another or act in ways that are hostile or destructive, but petty squabbles are best ignored and usually resolve themselves.

Constance Ahrons points out that entry into a family which includes children and an absent parent is complex, and she offers advice for anyone facing such a challenge: First, stay out of any conflicts between your spouse and his or her ex. Second, don't compete with the ex. Third, don't try to replace the ex as parent, but rather form a new relationship with your stepchildren that is different.

Ahrons recommends looking to other cultural systems to learn new ways of coping with the changes in the family structure today. She points out that African–American families have developed more flexible kinship structures over the centuries, in what social scientists refer to as a pedi–focal family system. In this type of system, child rearing is a task of the community, and all the adults who are a part of the child's world may contribute to the child's well–being and share the responsibility of raising him or her. Taking part in the upbringing of a child is considered a privilege, not a burden. This philosophy and practice is echoed in many other cultures around the world. It is seen in the Israeli kibbutz and in other settings, where people believe that it takes a village to raise a child.

One of the best ways to build a feeling of family is to

share enjoyable activities together and to create new family rituals—shared pleasures that will become a part of the history of the new family. These should be balanced with special times alone between the biological parent and child. Yet something as simple as a day trip to a park can be a memorable way to create a bond between the family, as can a move to a new home that the family works together to decorate, or the addition of a new pet to the family. Adding a new child into the family is a more complicated matter. Many believe that it is best to wait until the new family has achieved some stability before introducing a new member, if possible.

In a recent article in *Parade* magazine, several teenagers who had experienced the trials of adjusting to life in a stepfamily shared their insights on how to make the experience better. Many of their ideas paralleled the advice of the experts. For example, several talked about the importance of a personal space to call their own, such as a bedroom where they can find privacy and be as messy as they like. Others emphasized the importance of direct access and personal time alone with the biological parent. Some discussed the importance of communication between all members of the family, in which the stepparent and stepchild listen to each other. All emphasized compromise and sharing by family members, and drawing appropriate lines so that mean or rude behavior between stepsiblings is not allowed. Open and clear communication about rules, with agreement between the parents, was also noted as essential. Some of the teens emphasized the positive aspects of the stepfamily, such as finally getting a big brother or sister they'd always wished for before. One young woman said she resented having to share her room at first, but eventually she and her stepsister became as close as biological siblings.

Help for Stepfamilies

For stepfamilies who can't work out their problems because one or more members of the family have significant emotional or behavioral problems, more and more help has become available. Family counselors and support groups exist which specialize in helping stepfamilies cope and build good relationships. The Stepfamily Association of America (see appendix A) can offer advice and assistance.

Different family members may need individual or another type of group therapy. For example, play therapy can be very effective in helping young kids communicate and reveal their feelings in a way that is comfortable and familiar to them. Local mental health associations, medical associations, clinics, nonprofit organizations, Parents Without Partners, churches, and social service organizations offer or can make referrals to special services for stepfamilies.

Building a stepfamily can be an arduous process. However, with patience, optimism, respect, tolerance, help, and naturally increasing affection, most stepfamilies do succeed and flourish in time. Many experts today believe that living in a stepfamily can provide positive and important lessons, including how to accept and grow to love people different from oneself, how to adjust to a new and unknown environment, and how to establish new and meaningful family bonds.

Also, in an increasing number of stepfamilies, people are learning through necessity how to become friends and forge strong relationships with potential enemies or competitors. Many families report that a relationship with an ex-spouse improves after one or both remarry, and it is not uncommon for biological parents and stepparents to become good friends, based on their common love for the child or children involved and desire to see that the children have happy and stable family lives.

INNOVATIONS IN THE DIVORCE AND FAMILY RECOVERY FIELDS

As more and more people divorce one or more times, new options to deal with divorce and try to prevent its increasing frequency are being developed. One of the most innovative is a satellite broadcast, interactive television program. It is a unique effort to educate teenagers about divorce, child custody, and how to resolve conflicts between couples and is now under way in more than forty high schools across the nation. This program, with the goal of lessening the frequency of divorce, was the brainchild of Lynne A. Gold-Biken, a divorce lawyer and divorcee. Students, generally seniors in psychology classes, learn relationship skills by working in pairs to set budgets, to fight fair, and to deal with other challenges couples face. Local family lawyers visit classes to discuss the divorce system and answer questions.

Gold-Biken, 1994 chair of the ABA Family Law Section, founded the program because she wanted to make a difference, both in helping preserve marriages and in improving the image of family attorneys plagued by popular images such as Arnie Becker, the lecherous lawyer from the TV show "L.A. Law." With the help of experts in broadcasting, curriculum, relationship skills, and family therapy, she put together a series of programs. The money came from a variety of sources, including the ABA and individual matrimonial lawyers, who buy the tapes and donate them to local schools.

The schools participating are linked by satellite dish, television, and telephone. Gold-Biken appears with a family therapist on a live program to answer questions, discuss issues raised in previous programs, and work with student actors who portray young couples facing various dilemmas. Callers from the schools can ask questions. Students then continue with exercises presented in the programs, such as fair fighting. While teaching relationship skills and divorce law together may seem peculiar, Gold-Biken believes the two combine well. The students learn what it takes to make relationships work, and what they can expect to face if they don't.

Education for adults has expanded remarkably in recent years as well. Santa Fe Community College in Santa Fe, New Mexico, serves a progressive yet relatively small community and offers an astonishing array of credited and noncredited adult classes of interest to people experiencing divorce. Included are practical training classes such as computer technology, job hunting skills, financial planning for women, starting a business, art training, and photography, along with personal growth classes such as peer counseling, coping with anxiety, overcoming fear, health care, setting personal boundaries, and healing old hurts. A special program called Women in Transition provides free workshops for single mothers and other women facing personal, financial, or employment difficulties as a result of divorce, widowhood, or other changed circumstances. The workshops assist women in meeting the challenges of transition, developing goals, establishing a positive self–image, and preparing to reenter the workforce.

Women in Transition is unique in its approach. "There are other programs to help displaced homemakers learn job skills, but the ones I am familiar with are not organized like ours," explains Anita Shields, Director of the Women's Resource Center at Santa Fe Community College. "Many focus on job hunting, résumé writing, and interview techniques. We deal with self–esteem and building healthy relationships first."

The program began with the more traditional structure, but it soon became apparent that a different approach was needed. "We discovered that the women could learn the skills to interview or prepare résumés, but because they weren't feeling good about themselves for a variety of reasons, they wouldn't follow through with pursuing work. So today, the essential goal of the workshop is to help the women gain self–esteem and learn to be in charge of their lives, so they can discover where they want to go and how to get there. Then they are motivated, they want to go out and pursue their new goals," Shields explains.

Women in Transition also grew to serve a broader group of participants. "When we started the program in 1985, we focused on displaced homemakers—women who had been in the home and out of the workforce—but we have evolved since then to serve a wider range of people. Most of the women attending the program do have limited education and are struggling with financial problems, and many come from abusive situations. But everyone facing a transition into single life after marriage experiences trauma and grief, even women with successful careers and financial stability. We teach that the grief process doesn't happen overnight. Most people take between eighteen months to four years to work through it completely, depending on how much grief there is," she says.

When the women complete the twenty-four-hour program, which is scheduled flexibly on weekdays, weekends, and evenings to meet the participants' needs, each woman is assisted in taking the next step that is right for her. "The help we give them varies, according to each individual's needs," Shields remarks. "Some go on to take specific courses at the Santa Fe Community College, some go to job training programs, and others get free career counseling from Student Services. The women also share an incredible amount of information and ideas among themselves."

The camaraderie that occurs in the group is one of the program's most important aspects. "There is so much support and encouragement among the members of every group— sometimes I think I could leave these thirty or forty women in a room by themselves, and they would end up in the same place as at the end of the class," she laughs. "So many people think they are the only one going through this. When they find out they are not alone, it is such a relief. A lot of long-lasting relationships and small support groups form after the program."

Women who have completed the program often maintain ties with the program itself, as well. "The first day of each new workshop, women who have been through the program come back and do testimonials. It has changed lives," she comments. The view of life as a continuing work in progress is an important component of the program. "These women always emphasize where they are in their own journey, and not that they have 'made it,' " Shields explains.

WORDS OF WISDOM FROM THOSE LOOKING BACK

Ernest Hemingway once said, "The world breaks everyone and afterward many are strong at the broken places." Divorce is different for everyone who experiences it. However, in reading and hearing the words of people who have been through a divorce and now look back years later, certain insights are heard over and over.

Contrary to the myth that many people leave marriages impulsively and then live to regret it, few people divorce in haste. People often spend months or even years trying to resolve the problems and keep a troubled marriage afloat; many struggle with conflicting feelings for long periods before finally coming to the agonizing decision that it is time for the marriage to end. One of the most common sentiments expressed is a wish that the couple had taken steps to end the marriage earlier. "I wish I hadn't hung around so long hoping it would get better," one man reflects. "I'm a romantic by nature, so I always believed that if you love someone, everything had to work out in the end. But some people just aren't meant to stay together, and I can see that now."

The wisdom of such hindsight is supported by scientific research. Psychologists are learning that many children who suffer long-term problems, which are often blamed on the divorce itself, were in fact more damaged by spending several years in a troubled home with unhappy parents.

Not surprisingly, the more civilized the parting, the better the relationship between the former partners is likely to be. "My first wife and I were only twenty when we got married. We were just too young to know what we were doing," one man explains. "We figured out that we made a mistake, but there was no hostility. We both agreed to part, we did all of the paperwork on the agreement ourselves, and we've remained good friends. In fact, when my second wife learned she was pregnant, my ex was the first person she told!"

Mental health professionals often caution that divorce is not a panacea that solves every problem and immediately ends a frustrating old life in favor of a sparkling, exciting, new freedom. People sometimes report still feeling married even though a divorce is over, both because of the necessity of continued contact with the former spouse, and because they sometimes remain mired in old habits that were expected to change automatically as soon as the final decree was issued. It is often difficult to create a new reality and identity. People are sometimes shocked to learn that they are still unhappy, even though their spouse, who they saw as the sole source of their unhappiness, is no longer there to blame. As Mel Krantzler states, "Freedom means taking personal responsibility for one's own behavior, which is the difficult but necessary demand that divorce imposes on every man or woman who separates from a spouse."

One divorced woman explains, "Many people do learn something from previous divorces. Unfortunately, we frequently focus on what's wrong with the other person. By blaming someone else, it relieves an individual of responsibility for their part in the failed relationship equation. The real learning process comes from an individual taking personal responsibility for what contributions he or she made to the failure of that relationship, and then not repeating it in the next relationship. Part of this process is identifying the individual patterns— usually hidden in the subconscious—that we developed throughout our lifetime. The one common denominator in every failed relationship of mine is ME! I finally realized that at age thirty-five and went on a quest to discover how I was sabotaging my own life and why."

Therapists who work with those recovering from a divorce often emphasize that it truly is possible to view a cup as half empty or half full, and the way a person looks back on the divorce and forward to the life ahead can make a tremendous difference in his or her future. Most people eventually look back on former marriages with mixed emotions, including regret, nostalgia, and a bittersweet wisdom born of survival and growth. While the loss of identity and status as a married person can be devastating, it also opens the door to discovery of a new identity as a unique individual.

People are often, quite naturally, fearful of intimacy immediately after a divorce, but most find a place for it in their lives eventually. For others, the learning that comes out of a divorce is that marriage is simply not the best arrangement for their lives, and that they would be happier remaining single. These individuals are in the minority, but society is becoming more accepting of this option.

Most people who have been through one or more divorces learn and may bring new knowledge of themselves as individuals and the nature of their relationships to new involvements. Mel Krantzler, speaking of his second marriage to a woman who was also previously divorced, says, "We have learned from our past, not repeated it."

Resources and Suggested Readings

Ackerman, Mark J., and Andrew W. Kane. *Psychological Experts in Divorce, Personal Injury, and Other Civil Action.* Somerset, N.J.: John Wiley & Sons, 1993.

Adler, Robert E. *Sharing the Children: How to Resolve Custody Problems and Get on with Your Life.* Chevy Chase, Md.: Adler & Adler Publishers, 1988.

Ahrons, Constance R. *The Good Divorce.* New York: HarperCollins, 1994.

Ahrons, Constance R., and Roy H. Rogers. *Divorced Families: A Multi-Disciplinary Developmental View.* New York: W.W. Norton, 1988.

American Association of Retired Persons. *Divorce After Fifty: Challenges and Choices.* Washington, D.C.: AARP, 1987.

Anderson, Keith, and Roy MacSkimming. *On Your Own Again: The Down-to-Earth Guide to Getting Through a Divorce or Separation and Getting on with Your Life.* New York: St. Martin's Press, 1992.

Bartholet, Elizabeth. *Family Bonds: Adoption and the Politics of Parenting.* New York: Houghton Mifflin, 1993.

Bauer, Jill. *From "I Do" to "I'll Sue": An Irreverent Compendium for Survivors of Divorce.* New York: Plume/Meridian, 1993.

Beall, Edward W., and Gloria Hochman. *Adult Children of Divorce.* New York: Delacourte Press, 1991.

Belli, Melvin, and Mel Krantzler. *Divorcing.* New York: St. Martin's Press, 1988.

———. *The Complete Guide for Men and Women Divorcing.* New York: St. Martin's Press, 1990.

Berger, Stuart. *Divorce Without Victims.* Boston: Houghton Mifflin, 1983.

Berman, Claire. *Adult Children of Divorce Speak Out.* New York: Simon & Schuster, 1991.

Berner, R. Thomas. *Parents Whose Parents Were Divorced.* Binghamton, N.Y.: Hawthorne Press, 1992.

Bernfield, Lynne. *When You Can You Will: Why You Can't Always Do What You Want to Do and What to Do About It.* Los Angeles: Lowell House, 1992.

Berry, Dawn Bradley. "Let Freedom Ring!" *Healing Your Life After Divorce,* newsletter, June 1991.

———. *Equal Compensation for Women: A Guide to Getting What You're Worth in Salary, Benefits, and Respect.* Los Angeles: Lowell House, 1994.

———. *The Domestic Violence Sourcebook.* Los Angeles: Lowell House, 1995.

Bienenfield, Florence. *Helping Your Child Succeed After Divorce.* Alameda, Calif.: Hunterhouse, 1987.

Biracree, Tom. *How to Protect Your Spousal Rights.* Chicago: Contemporary Books, 1991.

Blakeslee, Sandra, and Judith Wallerstein. *Second Chances: Men, Women and Children a Decade After Divorce.* New York: Ticknor & Fields, 1989.

Blau, Melinda. *Families Apart.* New York: Putnam, 1993.

———. "What Every Woman Must Know About Divorce." *McCall's,* June 1994, p. 90.

Blume, Judy. *Letters to Judy: What Your Kids Wish They Could Tell You.* New York: Today Reader Service, 1987.

Bradford, Laura. "The Counterrevolution: A Critique of Recent Proposals to Reform No-Fault Divorce Laws." 49 *Stanford Law Review,* February, 1997, p. 607.

Briles, Judith. *The Dollars and Cents of Divorce: The Financial Guide for Women.* New York: Master Media, 1988.

Brown, Laurene Krasney, and Marc Brown. *Dinosaurs Divorce.* Boston: Little, Brown, 1988. (A book for kids.)

Brown, Ronald L., and Michael J. Albano. *Bankruptcy Issues in Matrimonial Cases: A Practice Guide.* Englewood Cliffs, N.J.: Prentice Hall Law and Business, 1992.

Buckman, Sid. "Ghosts from Your Past." *Healing Your Life After Divorce,* June 1991.

Burns, Bob. *Through the Whirlwind: A Proven Path to Recovery from the Devastation of Divorce.* Nashville: Oliver–Nelson Books, 1989.

Carlson, Linda. *Everything You Need to Know About Your Parents' Divorce.* New York: Rosen Publishing, 1992.

Carpenter, Krista. "Why Mothers Are Still Losing: An Analysis of Gender Bias in Child Custody Determinations." *Detroit College of Law at Michigan State University Law Review.* Spring 1996, p. 33.

——— . "Child Support Payments Increase by 27 Percent." *Albuquerque Tribune,* Jan. 9, 1998, p. A7.

Chiriboga, David, and Linda S. Catron. *Divorce: Crisis, Challenge or Relief?* New York: New York University Press, 1991.

Chused, Richard H. *Private Acts in Public Places.* Philadelphia: University of Pennsylvania Press, 1994.

Clapp, Genevieve. *Divorce and New Beginnings.* New York: John Wiley & Sons, 1992.

Coleman, Gerald D. *Divorce and Remarriage in the Catholic Church.* Mahwah, N.J.: Paulist Press, 1988.

Commerce Clearinghouse Staff. *Divorce and Taxes.* Chicago: Commerce Clearinghouse, 1992.

Couric, Emily. *The Divorce Lawyers.* New York: St. Martin's Press, 1992.

——— . "'Covenant Marriage' Laws Could Trap Women in Bad Marriages." *HipMama Hot Flash* (www.hipmama.com/hflash_disp.asp?S=9), May 20, 1998.

Crown, Bonnie. *D-I-V-O-R-C-E-S Spell Discover: A Kit to Help Children Express Their Feelings About Divorce.* Pimbrough Pines, Fla.: Courageous Kids, 1992.

Crumbley, D. Larry, and Nicholas G. Apostolou. *The Handbook of Financial Planning for Divorce and Separation*. New York: John Wiley & Sons, 1990 (Cum. Suppl., 1993).

Curtis, M. Carol. "Rites of Passage—Rituals of Release." *Healing Your Life After Divorce*, June 1991, p. 2.

DeAngelis, Sidney M. *You're Entitled! A Divorce Lawyer Talks to Women*. Chicago: Contemporary Books, 1989.

Defrain, John, Judy Fricke, and Julie Elmen. *On Our Own: A Single Parent's Survival Guide*. Boston: D.C. Heath, 1987.

Depner, Charlene E., and Charles H. Bray. *Non-Residential Parenting: New Vistas in Family Living*. Newbury Park, Calif.: Sage Publications, 1993.

DiFonzo, J. Herbie. "Alternatives to Marital Fault: Legislative and Judicial Experiments in Cultural Change." 34 *Idaho Law Review* 1, 1997.

Donahue, William A. *Communication, Marital Dispute and Divorce Mediation*. Hillsdale, N.J.: Lawrence Erlbaum Associates, 1991.

Dorf, Paul A., and Russell G. Alion, Jr. "Louisiana Marriages—Your Choice of Marriage." *Lawatch Online* (www.ardhs.com/pubs/marriage.htm) May 20, 1998.

Dubin, Murray. "Teens Get Early Shot at Marriage Skills." *Knight-Ridder Newspapers/The Albuquerque Journal*, Nov. 11, 1994, p. B10.

Emerick–Cayton, Tim. *Divorcing with Dignity: Mediation—The Sensible Alternative*. Louisville, Ky.: Westminster/John Knox Press, 1993.

Engel, Margorie L. *Divorce Help Sourcebook*. Detroit: Visible Ink Press, 1994.

————. *Weddings for Complicated Families*. Boston: Mount Ivy Press, 1993.

Engel, Margorie L., and Diana D. Gould. *The Divorce Decisions Workbook: A Planning and Action Guide*. New York: McGraw Hill, 1992.

Ewald, George R. *Jesus and Divorce: A Biblical Guide for Ministry to Divorced Persons*. Stockdale, Pa.: Harold Press, 1991.

Fassler, David, Michele Lash, and Sally Blakesley Ives. *Changing Families: A Guide for Kids and Grownups*. Burlington, Vt.: Waterfront Books, 1988.

Fintushel, Noel, and Nancy Hillard. *A Grief Out of Season: When Your Parents Divorce in Your Adult Years.* Boston: Little, Brown, 1991.

Flosi, James V. *Lives Upside Down: Surviving Divorce.* Anaheim, Calif.: ACTA Publications, 1993.

Forer, Lois G. *What Every Woman Needs to Know Before (And After) She Gets Involved with Men and Money.* New York: MacMillan/Rawson Associates, 1994.

Galper, Miriam. *Joint Custody and Co-Parenting.* Philadelphia: Running Press, 1980.

Gardner, Richard A., M.D. *The Boys and Girls Book About Divorce.* Northvale, N.J.: Arenson, Jason, 1992.

————. *The Boys and Girls Book About One-Parent Families.* Cresskill, N.J.: Creative Therapeutics, 1983.

Genasci, Lisa. "Working Mothers: Courts Often Hold Them to Higher Standards in Custody Battles, Legal Experts Say." *The Albuquerque Journal*, Jan. 23, 1995, p. E8.

Golabuk, Phillip. *Recovering from a Broken Heart.* New York: Harper and Row, 1989.

Gold, Lois. *Between Love and Hate: A Guide to Civilized Divorce.* New York: Plenum Publishing, 1992.

Gottlieb, Dorothy Weiss, Inez Bellow Gottlieb, and Marjorie A. Slavin. *What to Do When Your Son or Daughter Divorces: A New Guide of Hope and Help for Parents of Adult Children.* New York: Bantam Books, 1988.

Greif, Geoffrey. *The Daddy Track and the Single Father.* New York: Lexington Books, 1990.

Greif, Geoffrey L., and Rebecca L. Hegar. *When Parents Kidnap: The Families Behind the Headlines.* New York: The Free Press, 1992.

Grizzard, Lewis. *Lewis Grizzard's Advice to the Newlywed . . . and the Newly Divorced: I Can't Remember the Names of My Ex-Wives: I Just Call Them Plaintiff.* Marietta, Ga.: Long Street Press, 1989.

Gumz, Edward. *Professionals and Their Work in Family Divorce Court.* Springfield, Ill.: Charles C. Thomas Publishers, 1987.

Hardie, Dee, and Tom Hardie. "Grandparenting." *The Albuquerque Journal*, Feb. 26, 1995, p. C9.

Heatherington, Mavis, and Josephine Arasteh, eds. *Impact of Divorce, Single Parenting and Stepparenting on Children*. Hillsdale, N.J.: Lawrence Erlbaum Associates, 1988.

Hendrix, Lorraine. *Caught in the Crossfire: The Impact of Divorce on Young People*. Summit, N.J.: PIA Press, 1991.

Hill, Gerald. *Divorced Fathers: Coping with Problems, Creating Solutions*. Cincinnati: Betterway Publications, 1989.

Hirschfield, Mary. *The Adult Children of Divorce Workbook*. Los Angeles: Jeremy P. Tarcher, 1992.

Hyde, Margaret O., and Elizabeth Held Forsyth. *Parents Divided, Parents Multiplied*. Louisville, Ky.: Westminster/John Knox Press, 1989.

Ives, Sally B., David Fassler, and Michele Lash. *The Divorce Workbook: A Guide for Kids and Families*. Burlington, Vt.: Waterfront Books, 1992.

Jensen, Geraldine, and K. Jones. *How to Collect Child Support*. Stamford, Conn.: Longmeadow Press, 1991.

Johansen, Frances. *The Financial Guide to Divorce*. Irvine, Calif.: United Resources Press, 1991.

Johnson, Colleen Leahy. *Ex-Familia: Grandparents, Parents and Children Adjust to Divorce*. New Brunswick, N.J.: Rutgers University Press, 1988.

Jones, Thomas F. *The Single Again Handbook*. Nashville: Oliver Nelson Books, 1993.

Jong, Erica. *Fear of Fifty: A Midlife Memoir*. New York: HarperCollins, 1994.

———. *Megan's Book of Divorce*. 1984. (For kids, currently out of print, but available at some libraries and used bookstores.)

Kaith, Pat M. *The Unmarried in Later Life*. New York: Praeger Publishers, 1989.

Kamm, Phyllis. *Remarriage in the Middle Years and Beyond*. San Leandro, Calif.: Bristol Publishing Enterprises, 1991.

Kaslow, Florence, and Lita Linzer Schwartz. *The Dynamics of Divorce: A Life Cycle Perspective*. New York: Brunner/Mazel, 1987.

Kass, Anne. "A Word from the Bench: Dispelling a Few Myths About Divorce Court." *The New Mexico Verdict* 1, no. 4, Aug./Sept. 1994, p. 16.

————. "Don't Give Children a Sophie's Choice." *Albuquerque Tribune*, Oct. 8, 1989.

Kiley, John Cantwell. *Self Rescue*. Los Angeles: Lowell House, 1992.

Krantzler, Mel. *Creative Divorce*. Chicago: Signet NAL, 1974.

Krementz, Jill. *How it Feels When Parents Divorce*. New York: Alfred A. Knopf, 1988.

Lansky, Vicki. *Divorce Book for Parents*. New York: Penguin/New American Library, 1989.

Larson, Hal, and Susan Larson. *Suddenly Single: A Lifeline for Anyone Who Has Lost a Love*. San Francisco: Halo Books, 1990.

Lawrence, Judy. "Children, Divorce and Budgets." *The New Mexico Verdict* 1, no. 4, Aug./Sept. 1994, p. 5.

————. *Common Cent$: The Complete Money Management Workbook*. Albuquerque, N.Mex.: Lawrence & Co., 1989.

————. *The Budget Kit*. Chicago: Dearborn Financial, 1992.

Lebowitz, Marcia L. *I Think Divorce Stinks*. Woodbridge, Conn.: CDC Press, 1989.

Leonard, Frances. *Money and the Mature Woman*. Reading, Mass.: Addison-Wesley, 1993.

Leonard, Robin, and Steven Elias. *Family Law Dictionary*. Berkeley, Calif.: Nolo Press, 1990.

Lewin, Elizabeth S. *Financial Fitness Through Divorce*. New York: Facts on File, 1988.

Lowe, Peggy. "McDonald's Meets L.A. Law at Chain of Drive-Up Legal Stops." *The Albuquerque Journal*, Dec. 20, 1992, p. D7.

Maccoby, Eleanor. *Dividing the Child.* Cambridge: Harvard University Press, 1992.

McMillan, Terry. *Waiting to Exhale.* New York: Viking Penguin, 1992.

Margulies, Sam. *Getting Divorced Without Ruining Your Life.* New York: Simon & Schuster, 1992.

Marston, Stephanie. *The Divorced Parent: Success Strategies for Raising Your Children After Separation.* New York: William Morrow, 1994.

Mayle, Peter. *Why Are We Getting a Divorce?* New York: Harmony Books, 1988. (A book for kids.)

Miller, Mary Jane. *Upside Down.* New York: Puffin Books, 1994. (A book for kids.)

Minton, Lynn. "Fresh Voices: Getting Along with Stepparents: Teenagers Talk Frankly." *Parade,* Feb. 26, 1995, pp. 24–25.

Moss, Anne E. *Your Pension Rights at Divorce: What Women Need to Know.* Washington, D.C.: Pension Rights Center, 1994.

Murphy, Patricia A. *Making the Connections: Women, Work and Abuse.* Winter Park, Fla.: GR Press, 1993.

——— . *Making the Connections Workbook: A Career and Life Planning Guide for Women Abuse Survivors.* Winter Park, Fla.: GR Press, 1995.

National Center for Women in Retirement Research. *Women and Divorce: Turning Your Life Around.* Brooklyn, N.Y.: Long Island University Press, 1993.

Nelson, Jane, L. Lott, and H. Glenn. *Positive Discipline A–Z: 1001 Solutions to Everyday Parenting Problems.* Rocklin, Calif.: Prima Publishing, 1993.

Neumann, Diane. *Divorce Mediation: How to Cut the Cost and Stress of Divorce.* New York: Henry Holt, 1989.

NiCarthy, Ginny. *Getting Free: You Can End the Abuse and Take Back Your Life.* Seattle: The Seal Press, 1986.

Nichols, J. Randall. *Ending Marriage, Keeping Faith: A New Guide Through the Spiritual Journey of Divorce.* New York: Crossroad Publishing, 1993.

O'Dell, Larry. "Lesbian's Mother Wins Custody of Grandchild." *The Albuquerque Journal*, Apr. 22, 1995, p. C4.

Pitzele, Sefra K. *Surviving Divorce: Daily Affirmations*. Deerfield Beach, Fla.: Health Communications, 1991.

Pruett, Kyle D. *The Nurturing Father: Journey Toward the Complete Man*. New York: Warner Books, 1987.

Quello, Dan. *Safely Through the Storm*. Eugene, Oreg.: Harvest House Publishers, 1992. (A book for kids.)

Reidy, Thomas J., Richard M. Silver, and Alan Carlson. "Child Custody Decisions: A Survey of Judges." *Family Law Quarterly* 23, no. 1 (Spring 1989).

Reske, Henry J. "Domestic Retaliations: Escalating Violence in Family Courts." *ABA Journal*, July 1993, p. 48.

Reynolds, Randy. *Divorce Recovery: Putting Yourself Back Together Again*. Grand Rapids, Mich.: Zondervan Publishing, 1992.

Ricci, Isolina. *Mom's House, Dad's House: Making Shared Custody Work*. New York: Collier MacMillan, 1982.

Robertson, Christina. *A Woman's Guide to Divorce and Decision Making: A Supportive Workbook for Women Facing the Process of Divorce*. New York: Fireside/Simon & Schuster, 1989.

Robinson, Margaret. *Family Transformation During Divorce and Remarriage*. New York: Routledge Chapman & Hall, 1993.

Rosenberg, Maxine B. *Living with a Single Parent*. New York: MacMillan/Bradbury Press, 1992. (A book for kids.)

———. *Talking About Stepfamilies*. New York: MacMillan/Bradbury Press, 1990.

Rosenberg, Stephen M., and Ann Z. Peterson. *Every Woman's Guide to Financial Security*. Atlanta: Capital Publishing, 1994.

Rosenstock, Harvey A., Judith D. Rosenstock, and Janet Weiner. *Journey Through Divorce: Five Stages Toward Recovery*. New York: Human Sciences Press, 1988.

Russo, Francine. "Can the Government Prevent Divorce?" *The Atlantic Monthly*, October, 1997, p. 28.

Sadler, Judith Deboard. *Families in Transition: An Annotated Bibliography*. Hamden, Conn.: Archon Books, 1988.

Schilling, Edwin, and Carol Ann Wilson. *Survival Manual for Men in Divorce*. Boulder, Colo.: Quantum Press, 1992.

Schoichet, Barbara. *The New Single Woman: Discovering a Life of Her Own*. Los Angeles: Lowell House, 1994.

Shapiro, Robert B. *Separate Houses: A Practical Guide for Divorced Parents*. New York: Fireside/Simon & Schuster, 1989.

Splinter, John P. *The Complete Divorce Recovery Handbook*. Grand Rapids, Mich.: Zondervan Publishing, 1992.

Stinson, Kandi M. *Adolescence, Family, and Friends: Social Support After Parents Divorce or Remarriage*. New York: Praeger Publications, 1991.

Strater, Carole Sanderson. *Finding Your Place After Divorce: Help and Hope for Women Who Are Starting Again*. Wheaton, Ill.: Harold Shaw Publishers, 1992.

Sugarbaker, Geneva. *Nice Women Get Divorced: The Conflicts and Challenges for Traditional Women*. Deaconess Press, 1992.

Sullivan, Maria. *The Parent/Child Manual on Divorce*. New York: Tor Books, 1988.

Tangvald, Christine Harder. *Mom and Dad Don't Live Together Anymore*. Elgin, Ill.: Chariot Books, 1988.

Teyber, Edward. *Helping Children Cope with Divorce*. New York: Lexington Books, 1992.

Thompson, Dino. "Working Off the Big Mad." *Healing Your Life After Divorce*, June 1991.

Thrash, Sara A. *Dear God, I'm Divorced!: Dialogues with God*. Grand Rapids, Mich.: Baker Book House, 1991.

Trafford, Abigail. *Crazy Time*. New York: Harper Perennial, 1992.

Trump, Ivana. *The Best Is Yet to Come*. New York: Pocket Books, 1995.

Ungar, Alan B. *Financial Self-Confidence for the Suddenly Single: A Woman's Guide*. Los Angeles: Lowell House, 1993.

Vigeveno, H.S., and Anne Clire. *No One Gets Divorced Alone: How Divorce Affects Moms, Dads, Kids, and Grandparents*. Ventura, Calif.: Regal Books, 1987.

Virtue, Doreen. *My Kids Don't Live with Me Anymore*. Minneapolis: ComCare Publishers, 1988.

Wallerstein, Judith S., and Sandra Blakeslee. *Second Chances: Men, Women and Children a Decade After Divorce*. New York: Ticknor & Fields, 1989.

Wallman, Lester, and Sharon McDonnel. *Cupid, Couples, and Contracts: A Guide to Living Together, Prenuptial Agreements, and Divorce*. New York: Master Media, Ltd., 1994.

Walther, Anne N. *Divorce Hangover*. New York: Pocket Books/Simon & Schuster, 1991.

Watson, Jane Werner, Robert E. Switzer, and J. Cotter Hershberg. *Sometimes a Family Has to Split Up*. New York: Crown Publishing, 1988.

Watson, Rita E. *The Art of Decision Making: Twenty Winning Strategies for Women*. Los Angeles: Lowell House, 1994.

Weitzman, Lenore J. *The Divorce Revolution*. New York: The Free Press, 1985.

Wilson, Carol Ann, and Edwin Schilling III, Esq. *The Survival Manual for Women in Divorce*. Boulder, Colo.: Quantum Press, 1990.

Wilson, Patricia. *Beyond the Crocodiles: Reflections on Being Divorced and Being Christian*. Nashville: The Upper Room, 1990.

Woodhouse, Violet, and Victoria Felton–Collins. *Divorce and Money*. Berkeley, Calif.: Nolo Press, 1993.

———. "Woman's Work." *People*, December 22, 1997, p. 72.

Zipp, Alan S. "Divorce Valuation of Business Interest: A Capitalization of Earnings Approach." *Family Law Quarterly* 23, no. 1 (Spring 1989).

National Organizations

Many of these organizations maintain international websites. A search using the group's name will take you to the current site.

ABA SECTION OF DISPUTE RESOLUTION
740 15th Street NW
Washington, DC 20005-1009
(202) 662-1680
E-mail: dispute@abanet.org
This division of the American Bar Association provides information, services, library, and numerous publications.

ACADEMY OF FAMILY MEDIATORS
5 Militia Drive
Lexington, MA 02173
(781) 674-2663
E-mail: afmoffice@mediators.org
This organization promotes mediation as an alternative to the adversarial system and publishes various periodicals, audiotapes, and videotapes.

ACKERMAN INSTITUTE FOR FAMILY THERAPY
149 E. 78th Street
New York, NY 10021
(212) 879-4900
Various clinical, educational, professional, and research programs, including a library and speakers' bureau.

ALCOHOLICS ANONYMOUS WORLD SERVICES
475 Riverside Drive
New York, NY 10163
(212) 870-3400

ALTERNATIVE DISPUTE RESOLUTION COMMITTEE OF THE ABA FAMILY LAW DIVISION
740 15th Street NW
Washington, DC 20005
(202) 662-1690
This group of lawyers supports family mediation and arbitration. It conducts various educational programs.

AMERICAN ACADEMY OF MATRIMONIAL LAWYERS
150 N. Michigan Avenue, Suite 2040
Chicago, IL 60601
(312) 263-6477
This organization is composed of attorneys specializing in the field of family law. It provides various publications, including lists of members.

AMERICAN ASSOCIATION OF MARRIAGE AND FAMILY THERAPY RESEARCH AND EDUCATION
1133 15th Street NW, Room 300
Washington, DC 20005-2710
(202) 452-0109 or 1-800-347-AMFT
Provides referrals to marriage and family therapists in local areas and publishes a consumer's guide to marriage and family therapy.

AMERICAN ASSOCIATION OF RETIRED PERSONS
601 E Street NW
Washington, DC 20049-0001
(202) 434-2277
Publishes Divorce After Fifty: Challenges and Choices, *and provides a broad range of information on related issues, including a brochure on the visitation rights of grandparents.*

AMERICAN BAR ASSOCIATION
Section on Family Law
750 N. Lakeshore Drive
Chicago, IL 60611
(312) 988-5000 or 1-800-621-6159
National association of attorneys practicing in family law field. Numerous publications.

AMERICAN DIVORCE ASSOCIATION OF MEN (ADAM)
1519 S. Arlington Heights Road
Arlington Heights, IL 60005
(708) 364-1555
This organization promotes reform in the divorce laws and encourages counseling, mediation, education, and related services. It maintains lawyer referral lists and publishes a periodic newsletter.

AMERICAN FAMILY THERAPY ASSOCIATION
2020 Pennsylvania Avenue NW, Suite 273
Washington, DC 20006
(202) 994-2776

AMERICAN INSTITUTE OF STRESS
124 Park Avenue
Yonkers, NY 10703
(914) 963-1200 or 1-800-247-RELAX
Professionals from various disciplines provide information, workshops, and consultation for individuals, institutions, and organizations.

AMERICAN SELF-HELP CLEARINGHOUSE
Northwest Covenant Medical Center
Denville, NJ 07834-2995
(201) 625-7101
Publishes a sourcebook.

AMERICAN SOCIETY OF APPRAISERS
P.O. Box 17265
Washington, DC 20041
(703) 478-2228 or 1-800-ASA-BALU
This society is composed of professional appraisers of all types of property. It offers consumer information materials and produces numerous publications.

ASSOCIATION FOR CHILDREN FOR ENFORCEMENT OF SUPPORT, INC.
2260 Upton Avenue
Toledo, OH 43606-4300
(419) 472-6609
This organization is composed of parents seeking enforcement of child support awards. It advocates improved enforcement, and sponsors education, research, and a speakers' bureau. Various publications.

ASSOCIATION OF FAMILY CONCILIATION COURTS
329 W. Wilson
Madison, WI 53703-3612
(608) 251-0604
This organization is composed of judges, attorneys, mediators, counselors, family court personnel, teachers, and others concerned with the resolution of family disputes and the effect on children. It publishes a newsletter, a directory, a journal, and other documents.

BIG BROTHERS/BIG SISTERS OF AMERICA
230 N. 13th Street
Philadelphia, PA 19107
(215) 567-7000
National program with many local chapters to provide children from one-parent homes with adult volunteers to act as friend, mentor, and role model.

C. HENRY KEMPE NATIONAL CENTER FOR THE PREVENTION AND TREATMENT OF CHILD ABUSE AND NEGLECT
1205 Oneida Street
Denver, CO 80220
(303) 321-3963
This organization is associated with a similar international society.

CENTER FOR DISPUTE SETTLEMENT
1666 Connecticut Avenue NW, Suite 501
Washington, DC 20009
(202) 265-9572
This organization promotes and evaluates mediation and similar programs, offers consulting and training, and manages a complaint center.

CENTER FOR LAW AND SOCIAL POLICY
1616 P Street NW, Suite 150
Washington, DC 20036-1434
(202) 328-5140
This public interest law firm works toward making improvements in family law policy and publishes Family Matters, *a newsletter. It also publishes manuals on various issues, including opportunities for AFDC recipients, team parents, and child support enforcement.*

CHANGES
229 E. William, Suite 200
Wichita, KS 67202
(316) 263-1166
Occupational consulting, employment network, business funding alternatives, and other information for divorcing women.

CHILD ABUSE LISTENING MEDIATION (CALM)
P.O. Box 90754
Santa Barbara, CA 93190-0754
(805) 965-2376
This is a program designed to prevent and treat child sexual, physical, and emotional abuse, offering intervention, referrals to other organizations and resources, and volunteer and emergency assistance. It also maintains a 24-hour bilingual listening service at (805) 569-2255. Various publications.

CHILD FIND OF AMERICA
P.O. Box 277
New Paltz, NY 12561-0277
(914) 255-1848 or 1-800-I-AM-LOST
This organization works to prevent child abduction and locate missing children. It conducts mediation and counseling programs for parents involved in, contemplating, or worried about child abduction, and produces various videos, children's games,

publications, and other tools for information and education. Call 1-800-A-WAY-OUT for mediation information. Children who have been abducted and those who can identify missing children can call 1-800 I-AM-LOST.

CHILDREN'S DIVORCE CENTER
88 Bradley Road
Woodbridge, CT 06525
(203) 387-8887
Services, information, and publications for individuals and professionals to help children and parents deal with divorce and remarriage.

CHILDREN'S FOUNDATION
725 15th Street NW, Suite 505
Washington, DC 20005-2109
(202) 347-3300
Assistance and information for child care providers. Numerous publications.

CHILDREN'S RIGHTS COUNCIL
200 Eye Street NE, Suite 200
Washington, DC 20002-4362
(202) 547-6227 or 1-800-787-KIDS
This organization supports joint custody, harmony between divorced parents, and mediation, and conducts various programs and services to achieve these goals. Maintains computer databases, resource and information lists, and numerous publications for those working to promote the rights of children.

CHILDREN'S RIGHTS OF AMERICA
8735 Dunwoody Place, No.6
Atlanta, GA 30350
(770) 998-6698
Provides information, services, and brochures to families of missing and exploited children. Also assists lawyers working on parental abduction cases, conducts seminars, sponsors runaway and child prostitute outreach programs, and maintains speakers' bureau.

COMMITTEE FOR MOTHER AND CHILD RIGHTS
210 Ole Orchard Drive
Clearbrook, VA 22624
(540) 722-3652

CONSUMER INFORMATION CENTER
8th and F Street NW, Room G-142
Washington, DC 20405
(202) 501-1794
General information of interest to consumers. Publishes catalog including publications on credit and divorce.

CUSTODY ACTION FOR LESBIAN MOTHERS (CALM)
P.O. Box 281
Narberth, PA 19072
(610) 667-7508
Provides free legal and counseling services for lesbian mothers seeking child custody.

DADS AGAINST DISCRIMINATION
P.O. Box 8525
Portland, OR 97207
(503) 222-1111
Information and services for divorced fathers, publications, and referrals.

DEBTORS ANONYMOUS
P.O. Box 400, Grand Central Station
New York, NY 10163-0400
(212) 642-8220
Coordinates self-help groups, and publishes various materials.

DEPRESSIVES ANONYMOUS: RECOVERY FROM DEPRESSION
329 E. 62nd Street
New York, NY 10021
(212) 689-2600
Publishes brochures, pamphlets, and a newsletter.

DIVORCE SUPPORT
5020 W. School Street
Chicago, IL 60641
(773) 286-4541
Support and assistance for members, as well as an information network.

DIVORCED PARENTS X-CHANGE
P.O. Box 1127
Athens, OH 45701-1127
(614) 664-3030

ELISABETH KÜBLER-ROSS CENTER
South Route 616
Headwaters, VA 24442
(703) 396-3441
This network serves families and individuals in personal crisis, including divorce, sponsors programs, conducts a lecture series, and produces various publications.

EX-PARTNERS OF SERVICEMEN FOR EQUALITY (EXPOSE)
P.O. Box 11191
Alexandria, VA 22312
(703) 941-5844
This group of former military spouses maintains a hotline, (703) 255-2917, and

publishes a newsletter as well as a booklet entitled A Guide for Military Separation or Divorce.

F.A.I.R.
322 Mall Boulevard, Suite 440
Monroeville, PA 15146
1-800-722-FAIR
This group focuses on fathers' advocacy, rights, responsibilities, and relationships between divorced parents, other family members, and children. Educational programs, videotapes, and materials are available.

FAMILY LAW COUNCIL
P.O. Box 217
Fair Lawn, NJ 07410
This organization seeks reform in current systems of divorce. It supports arbitration and mediation in settling family disputes.

FAMILY RESEARCH COUNCIL
801 G Street NW
Washington, DC 20001
(202) 393-2100
Information for public, private, and government agencies and individuals on parenting and family issues.

FAMILY RESOURCE COALITION OF AMERICA
200 S. Michigan Avenue, Suite 1600
Chicago, IL 60604
(312) 341-0900
E-mail: hn1738@handsnet.org
Network of nationwide family support organizations of various types. Offers numerous services and publications.

FAMILY RESOURCES DATABASE
National Council on Family Relations
3989 Central Avenue NE, Suite 550
Minneapolis, MN 55421
(612) 781-9331
Provides references to literature and information on programs and services offered by other organizations.

FAMILIES AND WORK INSTITUTE
330 7th Avenue, 14th Floor
New York, NY 10001
(212) 465-2044
Research, education, publications, and seminars on balancing work and family responsibilities. Involved in "The Fatherhood Project" to support various options for men in child rearing. Call (212) 268-4846.

FAMILIES ANONYMOUS

P.O. Box 3475
Culver City, CA 90231-3475
(310) 313-5800
Group with many local chapters for people who care about those with drug problems or who deal with drug abuse in the family.

FATHERS FOR EQUAL RIGHTS, INC.

3623 Douglas Avenue
Des Moines, IA 50310-5345
(515) 277-8789
This group publishes a directory of fathers' rights organizations.

FATHERS FOR EQUAL RIGHTS (FER)

P.O. Box 010847, Flagler Station
Miami, FL 33101
(305) 895-6351
Assists parents and grandparents involved in divorce and custody disputes. Various publications and self-help packages.

FATHERS RIGHTS AND EQUALITY EXCHANGE (FREE)

3140 De La Cruz Boulevard, Suite 200
Santa Clara, CA 95054-2444
(415) 853-6877
Advocates in areas related to noncustodial fathers. Educational programs, computer communications.

FIND THE CHILDREN

11811 W. Olympic Boulevard
Los Angeles, CA 90064-1113
(310) 477-6721
Services, education, and assistance to families and law enforcement personnel working to locate missing children. Also provides referrals and publishes a directory of missing children with pictures.

FOUNDATION FOR GRANDPARENTING

P.O. Box 326
Cohasset, MA 02025
Information, reading list, publications, and speakers' bureau dedicated to increasing public awareness of the importance of grandparents in children's lives.

FREEDOM RINGS—JEWELRY FOR THE DIVORCED

P.O. Box 90502
Albuquerque, NM 87199-0502
(505) 898-2386 or 1-800-600-RING

Provides divorce ceremony and custom design of new jewelry from wedding rings; also publishes catalog of gifts, jewelry, and ceremony kits for divorced persons.

GRANDPARENTS ANONYMOUS
1924 Beverly
Sylvan Lake, MI 48320
(810) 682-8384
Assists grandparents who have been denied visitation with grandchildren. Publishes a periodic newsletter.

GRANDPARENTS' RIGHTS ORGANIZATION
555 S. Old Woodward Avenue, Suite 600
Birmingham, MI 48009
(248) 646-7191 or 646-7177
Education and advocacy to assist grandparents who have been denied visition with grandchildren.

INSTITUTE FOR THE STUDY OF MATRIMONIAL LAWS
c/o Sidney Siller
11 Park Place, Suite 1116
New York, NY 10007
(212) 766-4030
Promotes better laws on divorce and related issues, encourages research, and aids communities in programs to help single parents and children. Maintains extensive library.

INSTITUTE OF BUSINESS APPRAISERS
P.O. Box 1447
Boynton Beach, FL 33425
(561) 732-3202
This organization supports education, legislation, and certification of appraisers. Various publications.

INTERNAL REVENUE SERVICE
Employee Plans Technical and Actuarial Division
1111 Constitution Avenue
Washington, DC 20224
(202) 622-6074 or 1-800-829-1040
For information on publications explaining tax laws and consequences in many areas directly or indirectly related to divorce.

INTERNATIONAL ASSOCIATION FOR FINANCIAL PLANNING
5775 Glenridge Drive NE, Suite B-300
Atlanta, GA 30328-5364
(404) 845-0011
Provides names of financial planners and analysts who have met rigorous requirements for membership.

INTERNATIONAL ASSOCIATION FOR MARRIAGE AND FAMILY COUNSELORS
5999 Stevenson Avenue
Alexandria, VA 22304
(703) 347–6647
Various publications.

JOINT CUSTODY ASSOCIATION
10606 Wilkins Avenue
Los Angeles, CA 90024
(310) 475–5352
Provides information on joint custody and the law surrounding it.

JUDEAN SOCIETY
1075 Space Parkway, No.336
Mountain View, CA 94043
(415) 964–8936
This group of divorced Catholic women provides meetings, education, retreats, workshops, publications, and other services for Catholic women and those of other faiths.

KEVIN COLLINS FOUNDATION FOR MISSING CHILDREN
P.O. Box 590473
San Francisco, CA 94159
(415) 771–8477 or 1–800–272–0012
Prevention and education on child abduction. Publishes prevention guide and maintains abduction response team.

KIDS' EXPRESS
P.O. Box 782
Littleton, CO 80160–0782
Publishes a monthly newsletter for children of divorced parents.

LAVENDER FAMILIES RESOURCE NETWORK (LFRN)
P.O. Box 21567
Seattle, WA 98111
(206) 325–2643
Legal, emotional, and financial support for lesbian and gay parents dealing with child custody issues.

MEDICAL NETWORK FOR MISSING CHILDREN
67 Pleasant Ridge Road
Harrison, NY 10528
(914) 967–6854
Educates health care professionals and keeps archive of medical and dental profiles of missing children which are provided to health care professionals to help identify missing children.

MEN/FATHERS HOTLINE
807 Brazos, Suite 315
Austin, TX 78701
(512) 472-3237
Crisis line for men and fathers, refers to other organizations.

MEN INTERNATIONAL
3980 Orchard Hiill Circle
Palm Harbor, FL 34684
(813) 786-6911
Works for men's rights and divorce reform, assists men falsely accused of child abuse or rape.

MISSING CHILDREN ... HELP CENTER
410 Ware Boulevard, Suite 400
Tampa, FL 33619
(813) 623-5437 or 1-800-USA-KIDS
Provides referrals and information to parents and law enforcement. A division of the National Child Safety Council, it promotes community and school programs, conducts seminars, and maintains a toll-free hotline for reporting missing children or reporting the location of a missing child.

MOTHERS WITHOUT CUSTODY
P.O. Box 36
Woodstock, IL 60098
1-800-457-MWOC
Network through which mothers without primary custody of their children can share experiences. Send a self-addressed, business size envelope with two 32 cent stamps for information.

M.S. FOUNDATION FOR WOMEN
120 Wall Street, 33rd Floor
New York, NY 10005
(212) 742-2300
Funds and assists women's self-help organizing efforts. Pursues change in social policy and law to end discrimination.

NATIONAL ACTION FOR FORMER MILITARY WIVES
2090 N. Atlantic Avenue, No.PH2
Cocoa Beach, FL 32931-5010
(407) 783-2101
This group works to promote legislation that supports benefits for former military spouses. Publishes a newsletter.

NATIONAL ASSOCIATION OF ENROLLED AGENTS

200 Orchard Ridge Road, No.302
Gaithersburg, MD 20878
(301) 212-9608
Provides names of accountants qualified to practice before the IRS.

NATIONAL ASSOCATION FOR FAMILY DAY CARE

1361 E. Guadalupe, No.201
Tempe, AZ 85283-3916
Promotes family day care services in private homes, operates an accreditation program for family day care providers, and advocates and promotes high-quality standards for family and other day care providers.

NATIONAL ASSOCIATION OF CHILD CARE

Resource and Referral Agencies
1319 F Street NW, Suite 606
Washington, DC 20004
(202) 393-5501

NATIONAL ASSOCIATION OF FAMILY AND CONSUMER SERVICES

3900 E. Camelback Road, Suite 200
Phoneix, AZ 85018
(602) 912-5386
Conferences, volunteer training, and information for families coping with issues such as child care, nutrition, and budgeting.

NATIONAL ASSOCIATION OF PROFESSIONAL ORGANIZERS

1033 La Posada Drive, Suite 220
Austin, TX 78752-3880
(512) 454-8626
Provides home organization services.

NATIONAL ASSOCIATION OF RETIRED FEDERAL EMPLOYEES

1533 New Hampshire Avenue NW
Washington, DC 20036
(202) 234-0832
Information on pension rights.

NATIONAL CENTER FOR MISSING AND EXPLOITED CHILDREN

2101 Wilson Boulevard, Suite 550
Arlington, VA 22201
(703) 235-3900
Provides assistance and a clearinghouse of information for parents and law enforcement. Merged with The AdamWalsh Child Resource Center to work toward

legislative changes to better protect children, advocate child safety, and conduct prevention and awareness programs. Publications and toll-free hotlines to exchange information on sightings of children: 1-800-843-5678, or, for the hearing impaired, 1-800-826-7653.

NATIONAL CHILD SUPPORT ADVOCACY COALITION
P.O. Box 420
Hendersonville, TN 37077
(615) 264–0151
This group of individuals and organizations advocates improved child support enforcement, changes in relevant laws, and public awareness of the effects of unpaid child support. Produces various publications and operates a referral service.

NATIONAL CHILD SUPPORT ENFORCEMENT ASSOCIATION
Hall of States
444 N. Capital NW, Suite 444
Washington, DC 20001
(202) 624–8180

NATIONAL CLEARINGHOUSE ON CHILD ABUSE AND NEGLECT AND FAMILY VIOLENCE INFORMATION
P.O. Box 1182
Washington, DC 20013–1182
(703) 385–7565 or 1–800–394–3366
Provides information to professionals on family violence prevention. Its computerized services are accessible through Dialogue.

NATIONAL COALITION AGAINST DOMESTIC VIOLENCE
P.O. Box 18749
Denver, CO 80218–0749
(303) 839–1852
Various publications; several categories of membership.

NATIONAL COALITION OF FREE MEN
P.O. Box 129
Manhasset, NY 11030
(516) 482–6378
Advocate for legal rights of men in various legal fields, including custody. Speakers' bureau, library, and publications.

NATIONAL CONGRESS FOR MEN
11705 N. Adrian Highway
Clinton, MI 49236
(202) 328–4377
This coalition includes organizations and individuals promoting the rights of fathers and

divorce reform. It maintains an electronic bulletin board at (602) 840-4752 and produces various publications.

NATIONAL CONGRESS FOR MEN AND CHILDREN
400 Renaissance Center, Suite 1900
Detroit, MI 48243–1508
1–800–773–DADS
Provides advocacy for fathers trying to obtain or modify custody, visitation, or support orders.

NATIONAL COUNCIL FOR CHILDREN'S RIGHTS
aka The Children's Rights Council
220 Eye Street NE, Suite 140
Washington, DC 20002–4362
(202) 547–6227
Advocacy group for child support, joint custody, visitation, and custody reform.

NATIONAL COUNCIL ON CHILD ABUSE
AND FAMILY VIOLENCE
1155 Connecticut Avenue NW, Suite 400
Washington, DC 20036
(202) 429–6695 or 1–800–222–2000
Information, publications. Call toll-free number for referrals to local services.

NATIONAL COUNCIL ON FAMILY RELATIONS
3989 Central Avenue NE, Suite 550
Minneapolis, MN 55421
(612) 781–9331
Maintains an on-line database with a bibliography of marriage and family literature, and publishes a directory.

NATIONAL COURT APPOINTED
SPECIAL ADVOCATES ASSOCIATION
100 W. Harrison Street, No.500
Seattle, WA 98119
(206) 270–0072
This organization, composed of juvenile court judges, attorneys, and advocates support programs that provide court-appointed special advocates for abused or neglected children. Produces various publications.

NATIONAL DISPLACED HOMEMAKERS NETWORK
1411 "K" Street NW, Suite 930
Washington, DC 20005
(202) 467–6346
Information for displaced homemakers on employment and other issues.

NATIONAL DOMESTIC VIOLENCE HOTLINE
1-800-799-7233 (SAFE), 1-800-787-3224 (TDD)
This hotline is staffed 24 hours a day by trained counselors who can provide crisis assistance and information on help available in the callers area.

NATIONAL FOUNDATION FOR CONSUMER CREDIT
8611 Second Avenue, Suite 100
Silver Spring, MD 20910
(301) 589-5600
This coalition of various businesses and services sponsors consumer credit counseling services and distributes various publications. Call 1-800-388-2227 for a directory of offices.

NATIONAL ORGANIZATION TO INSURE
SURVIVAL ECONOMICS (NOISE)
c/o Diana D. DuBroff
12 W. 72nd Street
New York, NY 10023
(212) 787-1070
This organization promotes programs and seeks new ways to deal with support problems for families facing divorce. It supports establishment of "divorce insurance," homemakers' services insurance, and other innovative changes in the insurance industry and dispute resolution.

NATIONAL ORGANIZATION FOR MEN
11 Park Place
New York, NY 10007
(212) 686-MALE (6253)
(212) 766-4030
This organization includes both men and women who work to promote equal rights of men in issues of alimony, child custody, domestic abuse, child abuse, and divorce.

NATIONAL ORGANIZATION FOR WOMEN (NOW)
1000 Sixteenth Street NW, Suite 700
Washington, DC 20036
(202) 331-0066

NOW LEGAL DEFENSE AND EDUCATION FUND
99 Hudson Street, 12th Floor
New York, NY 10013
(212) 925-6635
This organization produces resource kits on divorce and separation, child support, and child custody for $5 per kit.

NATIONAL ORGANIZATION OF SINGLE MOTHERS
P.O. Box 68
Midland, NC 28107–0068
(704) 888–5437

NATIONAL RESOURCE NETWORK
3631 Fairmount
Dallas, TX 75219–4710
(214) 528–9080
This organization is composed of banks, savings and loan companies, and others seeking to help individuals with financial planning. Numerous publications.

NATIONAL WOMEN'S LAW CENTER
11 DuPont Circle NW, Suite 800
Washington, DC 20036
(202) 588–5180
This organization works to advance women's legal rights in areas such as child support enforcement and family law.

NATIONWIDE PATROL
P.O. Box 2629
Wilkes–Barre, PA 18703
(717) 825–9684
This group of volunteers assists parents trying to locate a missing child by distributing fliers, organizing search efforts, and offering fingerprinting and other services. Works to increase public awareness, sponsors programs, and publishes a national directory.

NORTH AMERICAN CONFERENCE OF SEPARATED AND DIVORCED CATHOLICS
P.O. Box 1301
La Grande, OR 97850
(541) 963–8089
Helps develop regional groups of divorced Catholics. Organizes workshops, retreats, and training programs and distributes resource materials.

OLDER WOMEN'S LEAGUE (OWL)
666 11th Street NW, Suite 700
Washington, DC 20001
(202) 783–6686
Provides information to older women facing divorce and related issues, such as health insurance rights.

ORGANIZATION FOR THE ENFORCEMENT OF CHILD SUPPORT
1712 Deer Park Road
Finksburg, MD 21048
(410) 876–1826

This group works with various branches of government to improve the child support enforcement system. Various publications, including a self-help guide.

PARENTS ANONYMOUS
675 W. Foothill Boulevard, Suite 220
Claremont, CA 91711–3416
(909) 621–6184
Works for prevention and treatment of child abuse. Sponsors support groups for parents who have abused or fear they could abuse their children. Local chapters found throughout the nation.

PARENTS SHARING CUSTODY
420 S. Beverly Drive, Suite 100
Beverly Hills, CA 90212–4410
(310) 286–9171
Education, training, and advocacy for professionals and individuals dealing with shared custody and access of children to both parents. Publications and audiocassettes.

PARENTS UNITED INTERNATIONAL, INC.
615 15th Street
Modesto, CA 95354–2510
(209) 572–3446
This organization supports families in which child sexual abuse has occurred, and acts as an umbrella group for related organizations.

PARENTS WITHOUT PARTNERS
401 N. Michigan Avenue, Suite 220
Chicago, IL 60611–4267
(312) 644–6610 or 1–800–637–7974
Support group for single parents and children, with local chapters. Referrals, resource lists, and numerous publications.

PENSION RIGHTS CENTER
918 Sixteenth Street NW, Suite 704
Washington, DC 20006
(202) 296–3776
The purpose of this public interest group is to protect and promote pension rights and work toward solving the nation's retirement income problems. It operates a lawyer referral service and assists with complex pension issues. Produces various publications.

RAINBOWS
1111 Tower Road
Schaumburg, IL 60173–4305
(847) 310–1880
This international organization provides training and curricula for peer support groups aimed at those who have suffered a loss due to a divorce or other reasons. Publications and newsletter.

SECOND SATURDAY—WOMEN'S INSTITUTE FOR FINANCIAL EDUCATION
13569 Tiverton
San Diego, CA 92130
(619) 792-0524
Holds seminars to educate groups on how to prepare for divorce, the legal process, what to expect, mediation, and coping emotionally.

SINGLE PARENT RESOURCE CENTER
31 E. 28th Street, 2nd Floor
New York, NY 10016-7923
(212) 947-0221
National group working to establish a network of regional single parent organizations. Publishes newsletter.

SOCIETY FOR YOUNG VICTIMS, MISSING CHILDREN CENTER
1920 Mineral Spring Avenue, No. 16
North Providence, RI 02904-3742
This organization helps parents whose children have been abducted in connection with child custody disputes. Also works toward abduction prevention and publishes various materials.

STEPFAMILY ASSOCIATION OF AMERICA, INC.
650 J Street, Suite 205
Lincoln, NE 68508
(402) 477-STEP or 1-800-735-0329
Local chapters, numerous publications, and educational resources.

STEPFAMILY FOUNDATION
333 West End Avenue
New York, NY 10023
(212) 877-3244 or 1-800-SKY-STEP
Provides information and counseling for stepfamilies and training for professionals who work with them. Telephone counseling service, many publications.

TRW COMPLIMENTARY REPORT REQUEST
P.O. Box 2350
Chatsworth, CA 91313-2350
1-800-392-1122
Call or write for details on how to obtain your free credit report.

UNITED FATHERS OF AMERICA
595 The City Drive, Suite 202
Orange, CA 92668
(714) 385-1002
This organization seeks equal rights for fathers in child custody, and provides counseling, assistance, and referrals.

U.S. DEPARTMENT OF HEALTH AND HUMAN SERVICES

Administration for Children and Families
Office of Child Support Enforcement
370 L'Enfant Promenade SW, 4th Floor
Washington, DC 20447
(202) 401-9373
This agency helps states develop, operate, and improve child support enforcement programs according to federal regulations. Its services include the Federal Parent Locator Service, which helps locate parents who are not paying child support or those who have kidnapped children.

VOCAL (VICTIMS OF CHILD ABUSE LAWS)

930 G Street
Sacramento, CA 95814
This organization seeks to protect the civil rights of people falsely accused of child abuse or neglect, and to protect children from real abusers.

WOMEN IN TRANSITION

21 S. 12th Street, 6th Floor
Philadelphia, PA 19107
(215) 564-5301
This group provides various services including training for women facing problems such as abuse, unpaid child support, and issues related to divorce. It maintains a 24-hour telephone crisis line for counseling, information, and referrals at (215) 922-7500.

WOMEN IN TRANSITION

Women's Resource Center
Santa Fe Community College
P. O. Box 4187
Santa Fe, NM 87502
(505) 438-1274
Provides workshops for divorced and widowed women and for single mothers to help build self-esteem and prepare to reenter the workforce.

WOMEN'S LAW PROJECT

125 S. 9th Street, Suite 401
Philadelphia, PA 19107
(215) 928-9801
Nonprofit feminist law firm that conducts class-action and test case litigation in family law, among other activities publishes books on child support and custody.

WOMEN'S LEGAL DEFENSE FUND

1875 Connecticut Avenue NW, Suite 710
Washington, DC 20009
(202) 986-2600
This organization, composed of attorneys and others, seeks to secure equal rights for women through litigation, advocacy, legal counseling, and education.

WOMENWORK! THE NATIONAL NETWORK FOR WOMEN'S EMPLOYMENT
1625 K Street NW, Suite 300
Washington, DC 20006
(202) 467–6346
Provides and helps develop programs and services for displaced homemakers. Publishes a directory of programs and provides information and fliers.

State Laws

All states now have some form of no-fault divorce. In addition, many allow a period of separation or various "traditional grounds"—adultery, cruelty, desertion, insanity, addiction, or nonsupport—to be stated as grounds for divorce.

Each state has an agency to enforce child support. These are listed below. Also, state bar associations can provide information, guidance, and referrals. I have noted the special services offered by some; others may also have publications, recorded messages, educational programs, and various services available to the public. These programs change, so it is best to call and inquire about what is available. Local bar associations, law schools, bar foundations, courts, legal aid groups, and other organizations also provide services at the local level in some areas. Contact your state bar for information.

ALABAMA
Statutes: 30-2-1 through 12
30-2-30 to 54
30-3-1 through 99 (child custody)
Grounds: No-fault, separation for 2 years, or traditional grounds
Residency: 6 months by at least one spouse
Alabama Bureau of Child Support: (205) 242-9300, (334) 242-9300, or 1-800-762-8903
Alabama State Bar: (205) 269-1515

ALASKA
Statutes: 24.24, 25.24.050, 25.24.080, 25.24.120, 25.24.120, 25.24.130, 25.24.200, 25.25.101
25.30.010 (child custody)
Grounds: No-fault, if both consent and agree on property, support, and custody rights or by one spouse physically present for 30 days with intent to remain if whereabouts of other are unknown, or traditional grounds
Residency: None as long as one party is bona fide resident of Alaska
Child Support Enforcement Division: (907) 269-6829 or 1-800-478-3300
Alaska State Bar: (907) 272-7469

ARIZONA
Community Property State

Statutes: Uniform Marriage and Divorce Act
   25–311 et seq.
   25–431 et seq.
Grounds: No-fault (conciliation conferences may be required of parents
   with minor child)
Residency: 90 days domicile by one spouse
Arizona Child Support Enforcement Administration: (602) 252–4045
Arizona State Bar: (602) 252–4804 (publishes various brochures and videotapes
   on divorce and related issues)

ARKANSAS

Statutes: 9–12–301 et seq.
   9–13–101 et seq. (child custody)
Grounds: 18 months separation, or traditional grounds
Residency: 60 days by at least one spouse to file;
   resident 3 months before final decree granted
Arkansas Office of Child Support Enforcement: (501) 682–8710
Arkansas Bar Association: (501) 375–4606
E-mail: arkbar@ipa.net

CALIFORNIA
Community Property State

Statutes: Fam. C. 310 et seq.
   Fam. C. 3401 et seq. (child custody)
   Fam. C. 3900 et seq.; see also other sections of the Family
   Code generally
   Community property, Civ. C. 5107 et seq.
   California Rules of Court prescribe specific procedures and forms
   Cal.R.ct. 1–201 et seq.
Grounds: No-fault, or incurable insanity
Residency: 6 months residency by at least one spouse to file;
   3 months in county where filing. Decree is not final until service
   of petition on respondent or respondent's entry of appearance,
   whichever comes first.
California Child Support, Management Bureau: (916) 654–1212 or 1–800–952–5253
State Bar of California: (415) 561–8200
California Divorce Helpline: (408) 464–1114 or 1–800–359–7004

COLORADO

Statutes: 14–10–105, et seq.
   Uniform Marriage and Divorce Act

14-10-123 et seq. (child custody)
See also 19-1-117 et seq.
Grounds: No-fault
Residency: 90 days domicile by at least one spouse
Colorado Division of Child Support Enforcement: (303) 866-5965
Colorado Bar Association: (303) 860-1115 or 1-800-332-6736

CONNECTICUT
Statutes: Title 466
46b-56, 46b-59 (child custody)
Grounds: No-fault, separation, or traditional grounds
Residency: 1 year by at least one spouse, some exceptions
Connecticut Child Support Division: (860) 569-6233
Connecticut Bar Association: (860) 721-0025
Connecticut Self-Help/Mutual Support Network: (203) 789-7645

DELAWARE
Statutes: Title 13-1503 et seq.
13-721 et seq. (child custody)
Grounds: No-fault, separation, or traditional grounds
Residency: 6 months by at least one spouse
Delaware Division of Child Support Enforcement: (302) 577-4804
Delaware State Bar Association: (302) 658-5279

DISTRICT OF COLUMBIA
Statutes: 16-901 et seq.
16-911 et seq., 16-914 (child custody)
Grounds: Mutually voluntary separation for 6 months, separation
for 1 year/separation may be within one home or
traditional grounds
Residency: 6 months by at least one spouse
District of Columbia Bureau of Paternity and Child Support Enforcement: (202) 645-5330
District of Columbia Bar: (202) 737-4700
DC Bar PSAC Pro-SC Plus Divorce Clinic: (202) 737-4700, ext. 295

FLORIDA
Statutes: Chapter 61, in particular, 61.021, 61.031, 61.052, 61.19
61.13 et seq. (child custody)
Grounds: No-fault or insanity
Residency: 6 months by at least one spouse to file
Florida Office of Child Support Enforcement: (904) 922-9564 or 1-800-622-KIDS
Florida Bar: (904) 561-5600; in-state 1-800-342-8060; out of state 1-800-874-0005

GEORGIA
Statutes: 19-5-1 et seq.
　　19-9-1 et seq. (child custody)
　　See also 19-7-1 et seq.
Grounds: No-fault, traditional grounds, and various others
Residency: 6 months by at least one spouse to file
Georgia Office of Child Support Recovery: (404) 657-3784 or 1-800-227-7993
State Bar of Georgia: (404) 527-8755

HAWAII
Statutes: HRS 580
　　571-46 (child custody), 571, 576, 580-47
Grounds: No-fault, separation
Residency: 6 months by at least one spouse to file
Hawaii Child Support Enforcement Agency: (808) 587-3717
Hawaii State Bar Association: (808) 537-1868

IDAHO
Community Property State
Statutes: 32-603, 32-698, 32-610, 32-616, 32-901
　　32-717 et seq. (child custody)
　　32-1008
Grounds: No-fault, separation, traditional grounds
Residency: 6 weeks by at least one spouse to file
Idaho Bureau of Child Support Enforcement: (208) 334-5710
Idaho State Bar: (208) 334-4500

ILLINOIS
Statutes: 750 ILCS 5/401 et seq.
　　750 ILCS 5/601 et seq. (child custody)
Grounds: No-fault, separation, traditional grounds
Residency: 90 days by at least one spouse to file
Illinois Child Support Enforcement Division: (217) 785-1692 or 1-800-447-4278
Illinos State Bar Association: (217) 525-1760

INDIANA
Statutes: IC 31-1-11.5-1 et seq.
　　IC 31-1-11.5-20C et seq. (child custody)
Grounds: No-fault, insanity, impotency, conviction of a felony
Residency: 6 months by at least one spouse to file
Indiana Child Support Enforcement Division: (317) 232-3447

Indiana State Bar Association: (317) 639-5465 or 1-800-266-2581,
E-mail: isbaadmin@inbar.org

IOWA
Statutes: 598.1 et seq.
Grounds: No-fault, separation
Residency: Bona fide residency or 1 year
Iowa Child Support Recovery Unit: (515) 281-5580
Iowa State Bar Association: (515) 243-3179

KANSAS
Statutes: 60-1601 et seq., 38-129
           60-1610 et seq. (child custody)
Grounds: No-fault, failure to perform material marital duty or obligation, insanity
Residency: 60 days by at least one spouse to file
Kansas Child Support Enforcement Program: (913) 296-3237
Kansas State Bar Association: (785) 234-5696
Kansas Self-Help Network: (316) 978-3843 or 1-800-445-0116

KENTUCKY
Statutes: KRS C. 403, 465
Grounds: No-fault (irretrievable breakdown of marriage relationship)
Residency: 180 days by at least one spouse to file
Kentucky Division of Child Support Enforcement: (502) 564- 2285
Kentucky Bar Association: (502) 564-3795

LOUISIANA
Community Property State
Statutes: L.R.S.A. §9:301 et seq.
           § 9:331 et seq. (child custody)
Grounds: No-fault, separation, adultery, conviction of crime
Residency: Domicile by at least one spouse to file
Louisiana Support Enforcement Services: (504) 342-4780, Hotline 1-800-256-4650
Louisiana State Bar Association: (504) 566-1600

MAINE
Statutes: Title 19 Sections 661 through 752
           19 752 (child custody)
           T. 19, §§801-825

Grounds: No-fault, separation, traditional grounds
Residency: 6 months by at least one spouse to file, or residence of defendant, or marriage or cohabitation in state, or cause arose in state
Maine Division of Support Enforcement and Recovery: (207) 287-2886
Maine State Bar Association: (207) 622-7523
E-mail: info@mainebar.org

MARYLAND
Statutes: Family Law Articles 7-103 et seq.
9-102, Fam. 5-203 (child custody). *See also* Maryland Rules 570-577
Grounds: No-fault, separation, traditional grounds
Residency: None unless parties did not marry or cohabit in Maryland, then 6 months by one spouse
Maryland Child Support Enforcement Administration: (410) 767-7682
Maryland State Bar Association, Inc.: (410) 685-7878
E-mail: msba@msba.org

MASSACHUSETTS
Statutes: c.208, 209, 119
208.28 et seq. (child custody)
Mass.R.Don.Rel.P.
Grounds: No-fault, traditional grounds
Residency: Parties cohabited in Massachusetts or 1 year by plaintiff
Massachusetts Child Support Enforcement Unit: (617) 246-0774
Massachusetts Bar Association: (617) 542-3602; various publications, information, advice, and referral services available to public; call for details
Massachusetts Clearinghouse of Mutual Help Groups: (413) 545-2313

MICHIGAN
Statutes: MCLA §552, et seq.; MSA§25.81 et seq. Rules 721 to 731
MCLA§552, MSA§25 et seq. (child custody)
Grounds: No-fault
Residency: At least 180 days by one spouse to file
Michigan Office of Child Support: (517) 373-7570
State Bar of Michigan: (517) 346-6300
Michigan Self-Help Clearinghouse: (517) 484-0827 or 1-800-777-5556

MINNESOTA
Statutes: C. 518 et seq., 257.022
518.17, 518.551 (child custody)
Grounds: No-fault
Residency: 180 days by at least one spouse to file

Minnesota Office of Child Support: (612) 297–5846
Minnesota State Bar Association: (612) 333–1183 or 1–800–882–MSBA
First Call for Help: (612) 224–1133

MISSISSIPPI
Statutes: 93–5–1 et seq., see also 93–11–3; 93–23–1 et seq.
    93–16–1, 93–5–23, 93–5–24 (child custody)
Grounds: No-fault only if uncontested, traditional grounds
Residency: 6 months bona fide residency by at least one spouse to file
Mississippi Division of Child Support Enforcement: (601) 359–4869
Mississippi State Bar: (601) 948–4471
E-mail: msbar@msbar.org

MISSOURI
Statutes: C. 452
    452.375 (child custody)
Grounds: No-fault
Residency: One spouse a resident for at least 90 days
Missouri Division of Child Support Enforcement: (573) 751–4224
Missouri Bar Association: (314) 635–4128, E-mail mobar@mobar.org
Missouri Self-Help Clearinghouse: (314) 773–1399

MONTANA
Statutes: 40–4–101 through 40–4–221
    40–7–101 et seq., 40–4–211 et seq. (child custody)
Grounds: No-fault, separation
Residency: 90 days domicile by at least one spouse to file
Montana Child Support Enforcement Division: 1–800–406–442–7278
State Bar of Montana: (406) 442–7660, Lawyer Referral Service (406) 449–6577

NEBRASKA
Statutes: 42–341 through 42–823
    42–357, 42–364 (child custody)
Grounds: No-fault
Residency: Marriage took place in Nebraska, or one spouse resident for 1 year
Nebraska Child Support Enforcement Office: (402) 471–9160
Nebraska State Bar Association: (402) 475–7091 or 1–800–927–0117
    Pamphlets available
Nebraska Self-Help Information Services: (402) 476–9668

NEVADA
Community Property State
Statutes: 125.010 et seq.
125.134, 125.140 (child custody)
Grounds: No-fault, separation, insanity
Residency: 6 weeks by at least one spouse to file
Nevada Child Support Enforcement Program: (702) 687-4744
State Bar of Nevada: (702) 382-2200

NEW HAMPSHIRE
Statutes: C. 458 et seq.
458.16-20 (child custody)
Grounds: No-fault, separation, traditional grounds
Residency: Both parties domiciled or one domiciled 1 year to file
New Hampshire Office of Child Support Enforcement Services: (603) 271-4428
New Hampshire Bar Association: (603) 224-6942

NEW JERSEY
Statutes: Title 2A, c.34
Title 2A, c.34 §23; Title 9, c.2; Rule 5:8 (child custody)
Grounds: No-fault if both agree and file jointly, separation, traditional
grounds
Residency: One party a bona fide resident for 1 year
New Jersey Child Support and Paternity Programs: (609) 588-2385
New Jersey State Bar Association: (908) 249-5000
New Jersey Self-Help Clearinghouse: (201) 625-9565 or 1-800-367-6274

NEW MEXICO
Community Property State
Statutes: 40-4-1 et seq.
40-4-7 et seq., 40-10-1 et seq. (child custody)
Grounds: No-fault, separation, traditional grounds
Residency: New Mexico domicile and 6 months residence by at least one
spouse to file
New Mexico Child Support Enforcement Bureau: (505) 827-7200
State Bar of New Mexico: (505) 842-6132 or 1-800-867-6228 (lawyer referral
service). Other services and publications: call for details

NEW YORK
Statutes: D.R.L. 170, 200-240
D.R.L. 240 (child custody)
Grounds: Separation, traditional grounds

Residency: Cause occurred in state and both parties residents, or cause occurred in state and are party resident 1 year, or one party resident two years
New York Office of Child Support Enforcement: (518) 474-9081
New York State Bar Association: (518) 463-3200; 1-800-342-3661 (lawyer referral service); other information services, education programs, and publications available
Brooklyn Self-Help Clearinghouse: (718) 875-1420

NORTH CAROLINA
Statutes: c.50
    50-13.1 et seq., 50A-1 et seq., 50-30 to 50-39 (child custody)
Grounds: Separation for 1 year, insanity
Residency: 6 months by at least one spouse to file
North Carolina Child Support Enforcement Office: (919) 571-4114
North Carolina Bar Association: (919) 677-0561 or 1-800-662-7407
Supportworks, Greater Mecklenberg Area: (704) 331-9500

NORTH DAKOTA
Statutes: 14-05-03 et seq., 14-09-05.1, 14-08.1-01
    14-05-22-24 (child custody)
Grounds: No-fault (irreconcilable differences), traditional grounds
Residency: 6 months by at least one spouse to file
North Dakota Child Support Enforcement Agency: (701) 328-3582
State Bar Association of North Dakota: (701) 255-1404

OHIO
Statutes: c.3105R.C. et seq.
    3109 et seq., Ch 3115, (child custody)
Grounds: No-fault, separation, traditional grounds
Residency: 6 months by at least one spouse to file
Ohio Office of Child Support Enforcement: (614) 752-6567
Ohio State Bar Association: (614) 487-2050

OKLAHOMA
Statutes: Title 43-101, et seq.
    43-107 et seq. (child custody)
Grounds: No-fault, traditional grounds
Residency: 6 months by at least one spouse to file
Oklahoma Child Support Enforcement Unit: (405) 522-2550
Oklahoma Bar Association: (405) 524-2365

OREGON

Statutes: c.107
107.105, 107.137, 107.159, 109.121, 109.700 (child custody)
Grounds: No-fault
Residency: 6 months by at least one spouse to file, unless married in Oregon and one still resides in state
Oregon Child Support Enforcement Agency: (503) 986–6015 or (503) 373–7300
Oregon State Bar: (503) 620–0222 or 1–800–452–8260; for lawyer referral service, (503) 684–3763 or 1–800–684–3763. Other information services and pamphlets
Oregon Recovery Services Section: (503) 378–5439
Northwest Regional Self-Help Clearinghouse: (503) 222–5555

PENNSYLVANIA

Statutes: Title 23* 3101 through 23* 3707, Pa. Rules of Civil Procedure 400 et seq. and 1920 et seq.
23* 5301 et seq. (child custody)
Grounds: No-fault, traditional grounds
Residency: 6 months by at least one spouse to file
Pennsylvania Bureau of Child Support Enforcement: (717) 772–4940 or 1–800–932–0211
Pennsylvania Bar Association: (717) 238–6715
Self-Help Network of the Pittsburgh Area: (412) 261–5363
S.H.I.N.E. (Self-Help Information Network Exchange): (717) 961–1234

RHODE ISLAND

Statutes: 15–5–1 through 15–5–28
15–5–16 et seq. (child custody)
Grounds: No-fault, separation, traditional grounds
Residency: 1 year by at least one spouse to file
Rhode Island Bureau of Family Support: (401) 277–2847
Rhode Island Bar Association: (401) 421–5740

SOUTH CAROLINA

Statutes: 20–3–10 through 20–3–440, 20–7–420
20–3–160, 21–21–10 et seq., 20–7–100 (child custody)
Grounds: Separation for 1 year, traditional grounds
Residency: 3 months if both parties resident, 1 year if only one resident
South Carolina Child Support Enforcement Division: (803) 737–5875
South Carolina Bar: (803) 799–6653; 1–800–868–2284 or (803) 799–7100 for lawyer referral service. Other information services available
Midland Area Support Group Network: (803) 791–9227

SOUTH DAKOTA
Statutes: 25-4-2 et seq.
25-4-45, -56 (child custody)
Grounds: No-fault, traditional grounds
Residency: None; plaintiff must be a bona fide resident
South Dakota Office of Child Support Enforcement: (605) 773-3641
State Bar of South Dakota: (605) 224-7554 or 1-800-952-2333

TENNESSEE
Statutes: 36-4-101 et seq.
36-6-101 et seq. (child custody)
Grounds: No-fault (if uncontested), separation, traditional grounds
Residency: No requirement if plaintiff was a resident when grounds arose;
otherwise, 6 months by at least one spouse to file
Tennessee Child Support Services: (615) 313-4880
Tennessee Bar Association: (615) 383-7421 or 1-800-899-6993
Tennessee Self-Help Clearinghouse: (901) 323-0633
Tennessee Support Group Clearinghouse: (615) 584-6736

TEXAS
Community Property State
Statutes: Fam. C. Ch.3
Fam. c.152-157 (child custody)
Grounds: No-fault, separation, traditional grounds
Residency: 6 months domicile by at least one spouse to file, 90 days resident
of county where filed.
Texas Child Support Enforcement Division: (512) 463-2181
State Bar of Texas: (512) 463-1463 or 1-800-204-2222
Dallas Self-Help Clearinghouse: (214) 871-2420
Greater San Antonio Self-Help Clearinghouse: (512) 826-2288
Houston Self-Help Clearinghouse: (713) 523-8963
Tarrant County Self-Help Clearinghouse: (817) 335-5405
Texas Self-Help Clearinghouse: (512) 454-3706

UTAH
Statutes: 30-3-1 et seq., 30-5-2
30-3-10 (child custody)
Grounds: No-fault, separation, traditional grounds
Residency: Bona fide residency in state and county for 3 months by at least
one spouse to file
Utah Office of Recovery Services: (801) 531-9077
Utah State Bar: (801) 531-9077 or 1-800-257-9156

VERMONT
Statutes: Title 15-551, 15-554, 15-562, 15-563, 15-592, 15-631, 15-1101
15-291, 15-296, 15-292, 15-664 (A), 15-656-661 (child custody)
Grounds: 6 months, separation, traditional grounds
Residency: 6 months by at least one spouse to file, 1 year before final hearing
Vermont Office of Child Support Services: (802) 241-2888
Vermont Bar Association: (802) 223-2020

VIRGINIA
Statutes: 20-91 et seq.
20-103, 20-107.2, 20-108, 20-109.1, 20-124.2 (child custody)
Grounds: Separation, traditional grounds
Residency: 6 months by at least one spouse to file
Virginia Division of Support Enforcement Program: (804) 692-1491
Virginia State Bar: (804) 775-0500; lawyer referral service, 1-800-552-7977 or
(804) 648-4041
E-mail: vsb@usb.org Publications and pamphlets
Self-Help Clearinghouse of Greater Washington (northern Virginia): (703) 941-5465

WASHINGTON
Community Property State
Statutes: 26.09.010 et seq.
26.09.050 et seq. (child custody)
Grounds: No-fault
Residency: No time requirement.
Washington Office of Support Enforcement: (306) 586-2125
Washington State Bar Association: (206) 727-8200. Programs and publications

WEST VIRGINIA
Statutes: 48-2 et seq.
48-2-13 et seq. (child custody)
Grounds: No-fault, separation, traditional grounds
Residency: If parties married in state, one must be resident, then no time
limit; otherwise, 1 year, with some exceptions
West Virginia Child Advocate Office: (304) 558-3780
West Virginia Consumer Services Division: (304) 558-3386
West Virginia Bar Association: (304) 342-1474
West Virginia State Bar: (304) 558-2456

WISCONSIN
Community Property State
Statutes: 767.001 et seq.
    767.23, 767.24, 767.325 (child custody)
Grounds: No-fault
Residency: 6 months by at least one spouse to file, 30 days in county
    where filed.
Wisconsin Bureau of Child Support: (608) 267–0924 or 1–800–362–8096 (statewide),
    1–800–728–7788 (nationwide)
State Bar of Wisconsin: (608) 257–3838; , 30 days in county where filed. Lawyer
    referral service, 1–800–362–9082 or (608) 257–4666. Publishes
    pamphlets and videotapes

WYOMING
Statutes: 20–2–101 et seq.
    20–2–13, 20–2–113 et. seq., see also 20–4; 20–6; 20–7. (child custody)
Grounds: No-fault, insanity
Residency: 60 days by at least one spouse to file, unless couple was married
    in Wyoming and resided there from marriage until filing
Wyoming Child Support Enforcement Section: (307) 777–6948
Wyoming State Bar: (307) 632–9061

REGIONAL REPRESENTATIVES OF THE ADMINISTRATION FOR CHILDREN AND FAMILIES/OFFICE OF CHILD SUPPORT ENFORCEMENT

This federal agency, a division of The Department of Health and Human Services, administers The Child Support Enforcement Program. This program is a joint federal/state partnership which assists in securing child support payments. Assists in enforcing child support orders, especially when the parents live in different states or the parent refusing to pay has crossed state lines.

AFC Atlanta Federal Center
61 Forsyth Street SW, Suite 4M60
Atlanta, GA 30303
(404) 562-2900
(*serving Alabama, Florida, Georgia, Kentucky, Mississippi, North Carolina, Tennessee*)

Blanchard Plaza
2201 6th Avenue
Room 610–M/S Rx–70
Seattle, WA 98121
(206) 615-2547
(*serving Alaska, Idaho, Oregon, Washington*)

50 United Nations Plaza
Room 450
San Francisco, CA 94102
(415) 437-8400
(*serving Arizona, California, Hawaii, Nevada*)

1301 Young Street, Suite 914
Dallas, TX 75202
(214) 767-9648
(*serving Arkansas, Louisiana, New Mexico, Oklahoma, Texas*)

Federal Office Building, Room 1185
1961 Stout Street
Denver, CO 80294-3528
(303) 844-2622
(*serving Colorado, Montana, North Dakota, South Dakota, Utah, Wyoming*)

John F. Kennedy Federal Building, Room 2000
Government Center
Boston, MA 02203
(617) 565-1020
(serving Connecticut, Maine, Massachusetts, New Hampshire, Rhode Island, Vermont)

Gateway Building, Room 5450
3535 Market Street
P.O. Box 8436
Philadelphia, PA 19104
(215) 596-0351
(serving Delaware, District of Columbia, Maryland, Virginia, Pennsylvania, West Virginia)

105 W. Adams Street, 20th Floor
Chicago, IL 60603
(312) 353-4237
(serving Illinois, Indiana, Michigan, Minnesota, Ohio, Wisconsin)

Federal Office Building, Room 384
601 E. 12th Street
Kansas City, MO 64106
(816) 426-3981
(serving Iowa, Kansas, Missouri, Nebraska)

Room 4049
26 Federal Plaza
New York, NY 10278
(212) 264-2890
(serving New Jersey and New York)

GUIDES TO STATE LAW

As of this printing, I am aware of books or other publications on the specifics of divorce under the applicable state laws of Alabama, Arizona, California (many books and kits published), Colorado, Connecticut, District of Columbia, Florida, Hawaii, Illinois, Kentucky, Maine, Maryland, Massachusetts (many publications), Michigan, Minnesota, Mississippi, Missouri, New Jersey, New Mexico, New York, North Carolina, Ohio, Oregon, Pennsylvania, Rhode Island, South Dakota, Tennessee, Texas, Virginia, Washington, and Wisconsin. Such publications are becoming more common. Contact a law library, public library, or your state bar association for information.

Index